PENCILS AND PROCESS

Thoughts on Returning to Art, Portraits, and Colored Pencil Painting

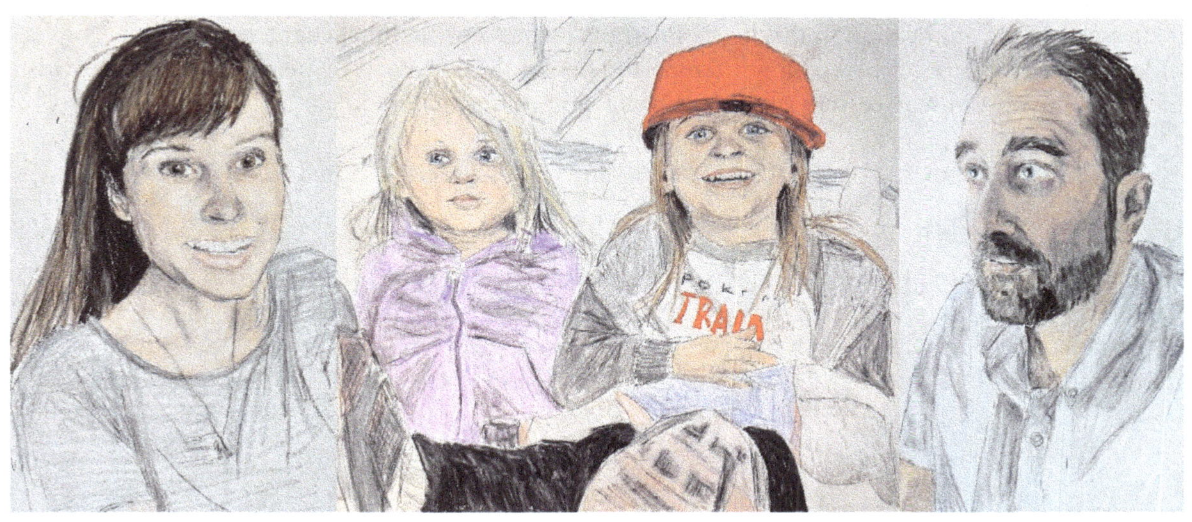

Jon Amdall

Grateful acknowledgment is made for use permissions and licensing granted below:

Artwork inspired by The Dark Tower series is used by permission of Stephen King.
Artwork derived from photograph by Jessica Truscott is used by license from Shutterstock.
Artwork derived from photograph by Jeremy Bishop is used by license from Unsplash.
Artwork derived from photograph by Fizkes is used by license from Shutterstock.
Artwork inspired by Pillars of Eternity is used by permission of Obsidian Entertainment, Inc.

FIRST EDITION

Library of Congress Cataloging-in-Publication Data pending.

ISBN 978-1-7339210-0-8

To Michelle, Alice, and Audrey - the best pizza sharing partners on the planet. I couldn't have done any of this without you. Also, thank you to all the friends and family who have made up the vast majority of my artwork.

And my appreciation to all of the talented and supportive artists in the WordPress community. Thank you for all the kind words and advice.

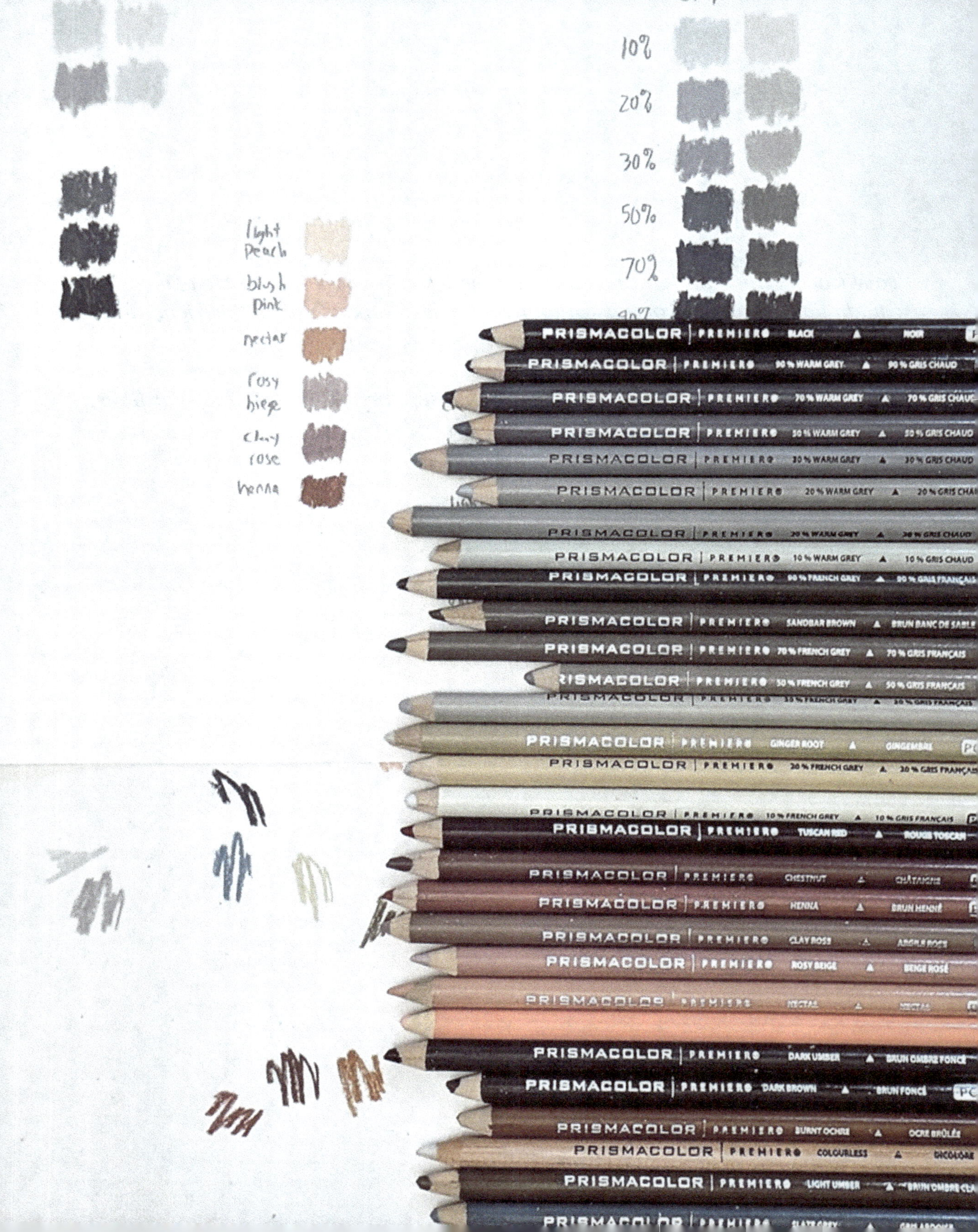
light peach
blush pink
nectar
rosy biege
clay rose
henna
10%
20%
30%
50%
70%
90%
PRISMACOLOR PREMIER BLACK NOIR
PRISMACOLOR PREMIER 90% WARM GREY 90% GRIS CHAUD
PRISMACOLOR PREMIER 70% WARM GREY 70% GRIS CHAUD
PRISMACOLOR PREMIER 50% WARM GREY 50% GRIS CHAUD
PRISMACOLOR PREMIER 30% WARM GREY 30% GRIS CHAUD
PRISMACOLOR PREMIER 20% WARM GREY 20% GRIS CHAUD
PRISMACOLOR PREMIER 20% WARM GREY 30% GRIS CHAUD
PRISMACOLOR PREMIER 10% WARM GREY 10% GRIS CHAUD
PRISMACOLOR PREMIER 90% FRENCH GREY 90% GRIS FRANÇAIS
PRISMACOLOR PREMIER SANDBAR BROWN BRUN BANC DE SABLE
PRISMACOLOR PREMIER 70% FRENCH GREY 70% GRIS FRANÇAIS
PRISMACOLOR PREMIER 50% FRENCH GREY 50% GRIS FRANÇAIS
PRISMACOLOR PREMIER 30% FRENCH GREY 30% GRIS FRANÇAIS
PRISMACOLOR PREMIER GINGER ROOT GINGEMBRE
PRISMACOLOR PREMIER 20% FRENCH GREY 20% GRIS FRANÇAIS
PRISMACOLOR PREMIER 10% FRENCH GREY 10% GRIS FRANÇAIS
PRISMACOLOR PREMIER TUSCAN RED ROUGE TOSCAN
PRISMACOLOR PREMIER CHESTNUT CHÂTAIGNE
PRISMACOLOR PREMIER HENNA BRUN HENNÉ
PRISMACOLOR PREMIER CLAY ROSE ARGILE ROSE
PRISMACOLOR PREMIER ROSY BEIGE BEIGE ROSÉ
PRISMACOLOR PREMIER NECTAR NECTAR
PRISMACOLOR PREMIER DARK UMBER BRUN OMBRE FONCÉ
PRISMACOLOR PREMIER DARK BROWN BRUN FONCÉ PC
PRISMACOLOR PREMIER BURNT OCHRE OCRE BRÛLÉE
PRISMACOLOR PREMIER COLOURLESS DÉCOLORÉ
PRISMACOLOR PREMIER LIGHT UMBER BRUN OMBRE CLAIR
PRISMACOLOR PREMIER SLATE GREY GRIS ARDOISE

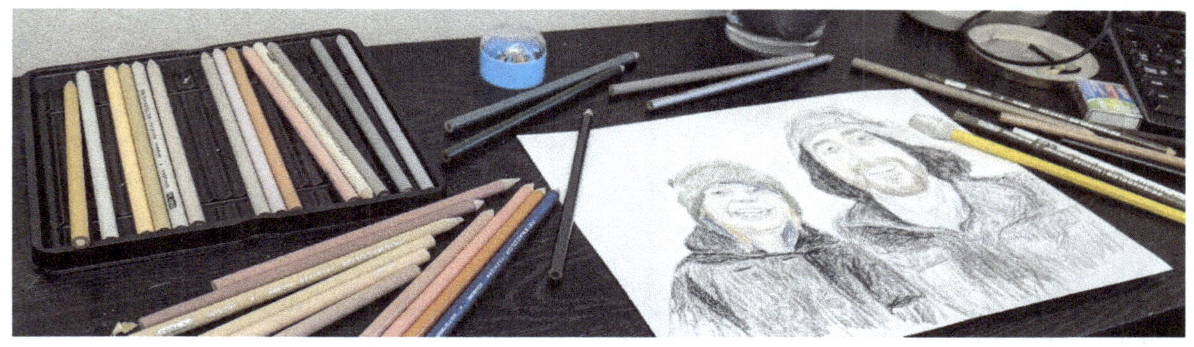

Foreword

As the cover suggests, this is a book about art and process. More specifically, it's the exploration of an amateur artist trying to relearn how to draw after an extended break. Within these pages, I'll discuss in what I hope is an honest and straightforward way the lessons I've taken through a hobbyist's experience. My goal is to make the stories and descriptions accessible to possibly help another on a similar journey. I will cover some basic techniques that I've found useful, such as measuring grids for proportion and colored pencil "painting" to achieve a smooth look using thickly blended layers.

The most important lesson I've learned over the last couple years sounds like a weak cliche', but is absolutely accurate – practice is the best path to improvement as an artist. Creating art over and over again, and just attempting whatever is on your mind, is the most effective path to growth. Beyond practice though, I've found the next best thing is simply reading about the experiences of other artists. It's incredibly helpful to the learning process. Interacting with other artists through blogging communities and reading as they share their challenges and successes has been a surprisingly valuable resource. I honestly don't think I could have made the improvement I have over the last couple of years without it. Therein lies the central purpose of this book. I wanted to share my experiences in the hope that it might provide a small spark for someone else.

For the most part, this book follows a chronological flow; it starts with my early pencil sketching in high school and my mysterious long break from art. Then we get into my experiments with a blog and the subsequent transition into drawing again. Each chapter that follows covers a phase as I learned and refined new techniques. As you might expect, these phases aren't concrete and rigidly defined. Instead, they flow into each other; I just tried to group them for the sake of organization.

First though, I'm going to provide a bit of background on Jon. It's really not my intent to roast myself here. But there are a few personality traits that come together to drive some of my habits related to art, projects, and writing. The first is that I can be sort of lazy when it comes to my recreational time. I tend to operate with periods of driven, motivated workmanship punctuated by valleys of low activity. This might be the case for many people; after a long day at work, sometimes hobbies take a back seat to passive relaxation. There may be a period of a week when I crank out two or three portraits, but then I might crash and do none at all for weeks. Maybe laziness is too harsh. I just know people who ambitiously approach even their off time.

The second personality aspect I want to mention is that there are times when I overestimate myself. During a radio show I used to listen to, the hosts discussed people who are "medium smart" but think they're geniuses. They referenced people who declare they're going to be Orthopedic Surgeons or wealthy entrepreneurs, yet haven't proven themselves or put the work in to really lay claim to those achievements. Big ideas, but lacking in follow through.

Don't get me wrong; I'm not trying to say I haven't accomplished anything. I've earned a couple of degrees, and I've made a career as an analyst in the public and private sectors. I think I'm an attentive father and husband (counterpoint: don't most people think that?). All that being said, I have always just assumed I could do anything I put my mind to. That perhaps I was only an unexplored step or two away from being a Senator Astronaut Football Star Rembrandt.

The third and final aspect, which brings the other two together and drops us into this book, is that I always have a ton of ideas. Most of these ideas don't really go anywhere, to be honest, but I have many half-formed aspirations, plans, and new things I want to try or learn. I actually keep track of them in a note-syncing app, and the list is fairly unwieldy.

Some things on the list I follow through with, like relearning art, starting a website, and teaching myself some basic coding. But many ideas fizzle out…here are a few of my grand plans that didn't go far:

- ✕ Learn another language
- ✕ Create a smartphone app
- ✕ Make a video game
- ✕ Go to medical school
- ✕ Master creating digital art
- ✕ Buy Bitcoin in 2010 (that would have certainly given me more time for artwork)

Another of these ambitious goals has been to write a book. I read a lot of books, and have always thought it would be fun to try. One day, I realized that through writing about art processes on my website, I already had a lot of content ideas. Of course, much of it had to be pretty thoroughly re-written to make sense in book form. But the more I thought about it, the more I believed it might make an interesting read.

Perhaps this book can provide some insight and process ideas that may help someone else along the way. So here it is, and here you are…I hope you enjoy.

Jon Amdall

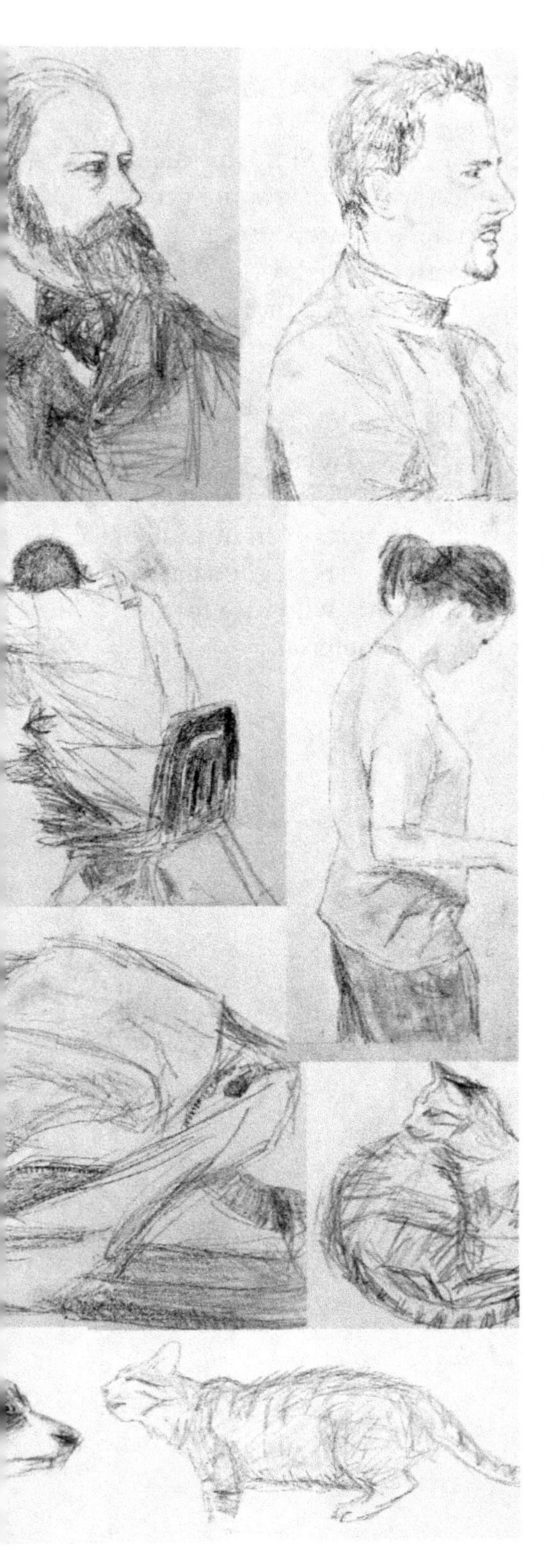

Old Art &

Rediscovering the Hobby

When I was a kid, I used to draw quite often. Not to sound like a Grandpa Simpson yelling at a cloud, but back then the Internet didn't exist, so it was a good way to pass some time on a lazy Sunday. As I became a teenager and entered high school, I still drew pretty frequently. Then, about a year or two after high school ended, I just stopped. I can't remember any clear reason or explicit decision to quit; I think I just became more interested in other things. Eventually, enough time passed that I became out of practice and didn't have any supplies, so the hobby faded into the background.

A few years ago, I had a random inspirational spark (the "grand plans" I mentioned in the foreword) and became interested in learning to build a website. My career is centered around data and analysis, and I also happen to be interested in these topics even outside of work. Initially, I posted about various pieces of data; things like U.S. sports league salaries, airline leg room, and home price increases. At some point, I had another wild idea for the site's direction. Before I get ahead of myself, let's talk about the older materials.

CHILDHOOD ART

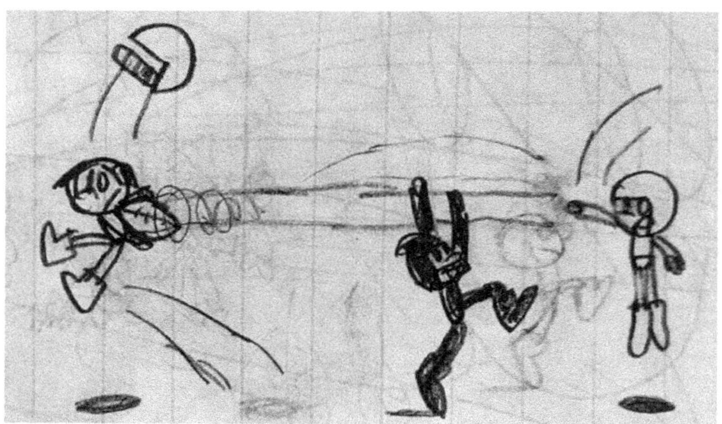

According to seven-year-old me, these guys are supposed to be football players. They look more like astronauts, I think.

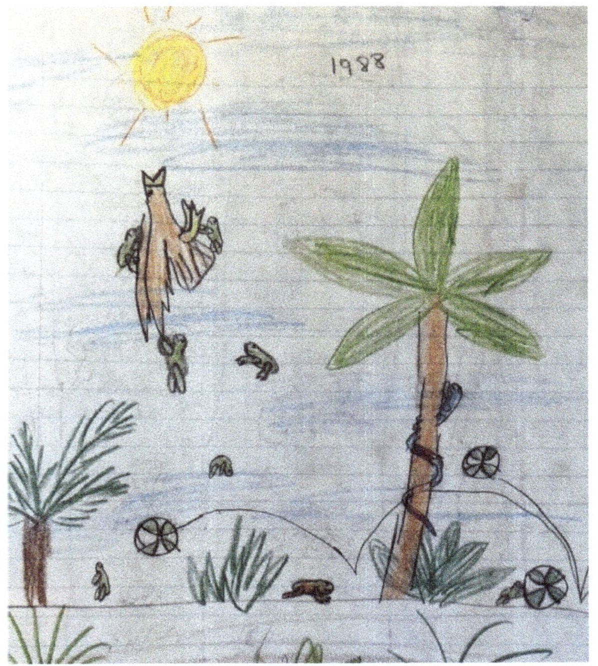

Some highly aggressive frogs attacking a hawk, drawn around age seven.

When I was a young kid, probably from around the age of seven or eight until junior high school, I used to draw in lined/ruled notebooks. You know the type - just the plain, cheap books with three punched holes. From what I remembered, I usually doodled characters and action scenes based on my daydreams. Since we're talking about a child in the late 80s and early 90s, these scenes most often involved Mario from Super Mario Bros., Ninja Turtles, and Link from the Legend of Zelda. I wasn't necessarily a "good" artist, but I was a kid and this was an enjoyable outlet for my imagination.

As I grew older, I ran into a significant roadblock. I vividly remember being frustrated by my inability to accurately depict what was in my head. I knew how I wanted something to look, but couldn't make the pencil obey my brain. I continued to draw because it was fun, but felt like there was this barrier to doing exactly what I wanted. Looking back, I think this is the root of my deep interest in realism, and my deeply held admiration for artists with the talent to capture subjects with high fidelity.

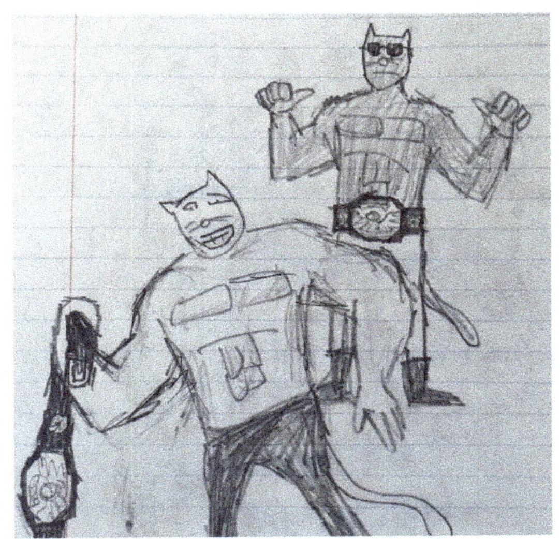

Our family cats, who were apparently also professional wrestlers. Probably done between age 11-13.

HIGH SCHOOL ART

It seems like a sudden change, but by high school, my sketching ability made a noticeable leap. It may have been practice that helped or the fact that starting Freshman year I was enrolled in art classes throughout high school. Or it may just be that my developing brain was getting better and hand-to-eye coordination. We should probably also credit video games for helping me in that respect! Regardless of the reason, sometimes I was able to sketch a person who was recognizable and resulted in a satisfying end product. Certainly not every time (I had quite a few throw-aways and abandoned ideas), but "sometimes" is better than "never."

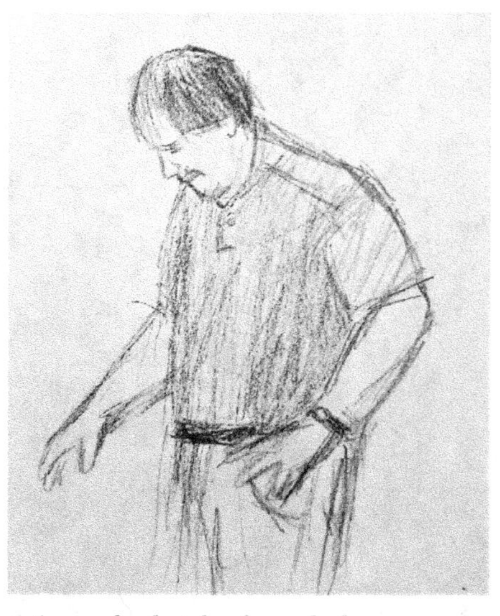

A rough sketch of my dad.

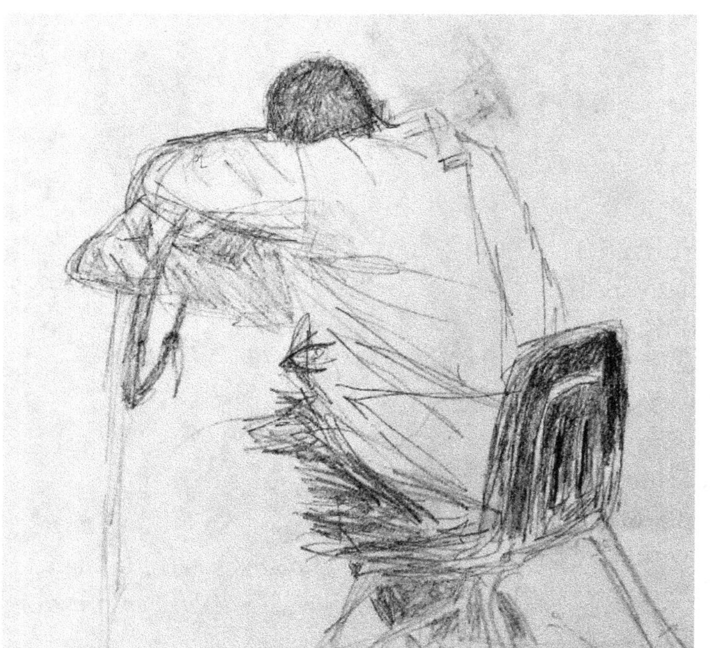

A fellow art student meditating, drawn age 14-16.

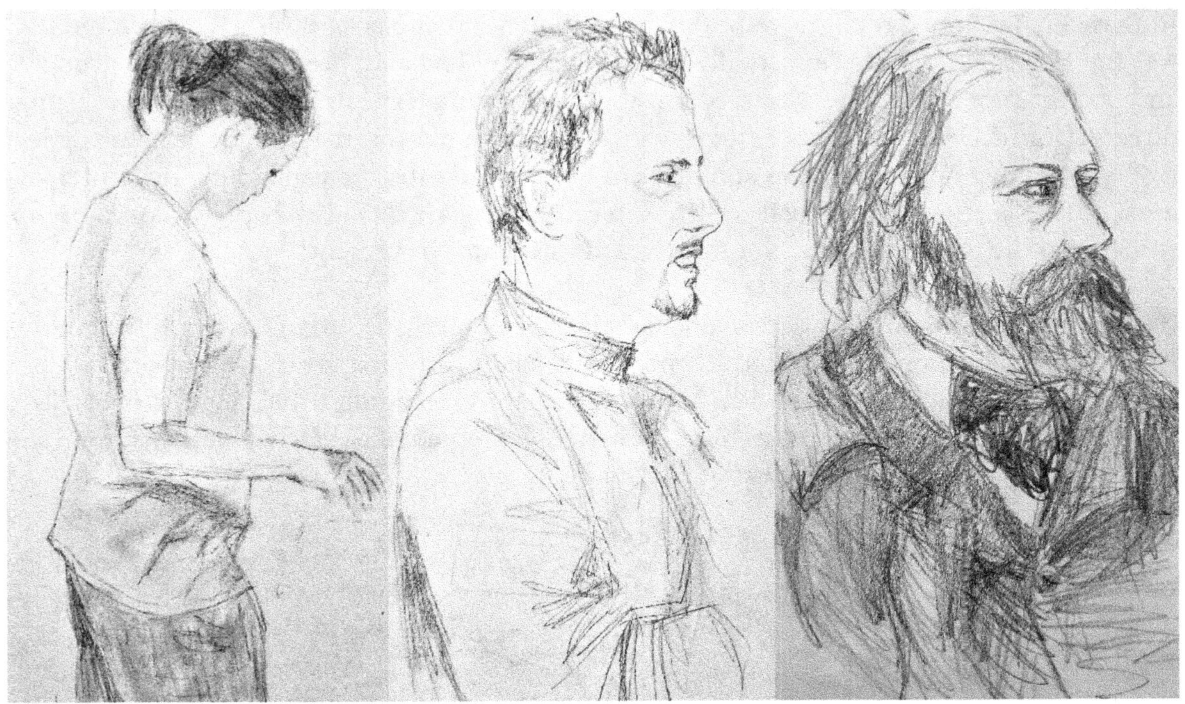

Various art class sketches, age 14-17 (from left to right); another student posing/pretending to throw something away, a high school senior self-portrait, and an old bearded man who I think is supposed to be Alfred Lord Tennyson.

After I started drawing again in 2017, I spent some time going through the older artwork I saved. Unfortunately, I don't have all of the notepads, pages, and books anymore. But I saved a few sketchbooks. Going through them, particularly the set from high school, was actually a challenge; it was difficult to sort exactly when they were done. Because I had the same art teacher all four years of high school and many sketches were assignments, the years blend together a bit. And of course, I wasn't organized enough to write dates on them. I have to go from my memory, and some of this stuff may go back 20 years at this point.

In these high school days, I moved to slightly different art subjects; I was a teenager and it was the 1990s. Hard rock was actually still popular, so I had a lot of influence from grunge and post-grunge music. In fact, I recognize some of the material in my sketchbook as being directly from CD sleeve inserts. Others were either from photos, magazines, or newspapers; it's hard to imagine, but this was still prior to widespread internet availability. Beyond that, most of the sketches were actually of live subjects during art class. It was pretty common for students in the class to draw each other, which was quite convenient.

It's pretty surprising to consider in hindsight because I rarely use an in-person subject now. Although I do believe I am technically more skilled currently, it appears I was more adventurous with my portraits when I was a teenager. As an adult, my sketches are focused on specific, real subject groupings. But, back then, it seemed like sketches were just random groups of images and weird stuff.

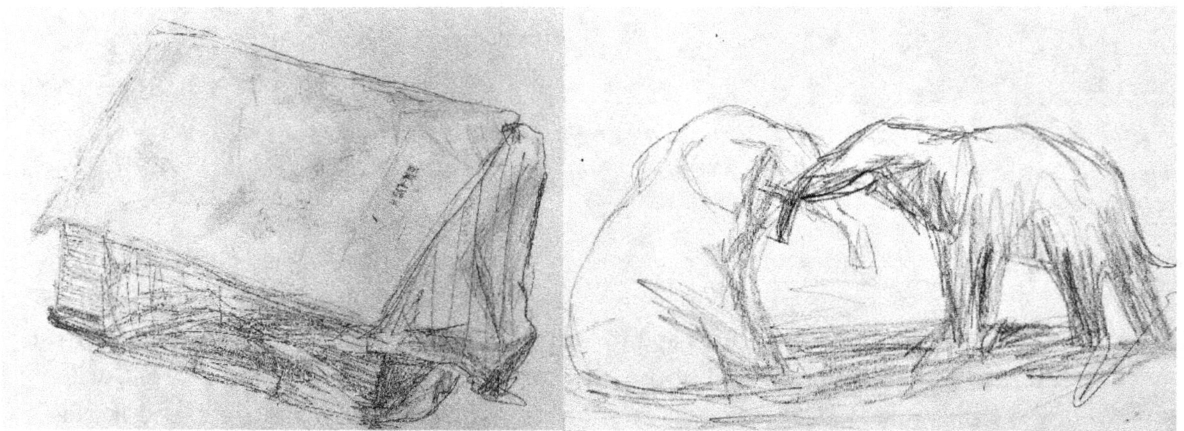

My favorite filing system in high school; paper jammed in a book. Plus some elephants.

POST HIGH SCHOOL/PRE-UNIVERSITY

Although we're nearing my "long break from art" stopping point, I didn't drop the hobby completely as I was handed my high school diploma. I kept drawing for a couple of years, but around age 20 or 21, life started giving me more stuff to do and seemingly less time to do it in. I got serious about college (relatively speaking) and became more involved in the usual extracurricular activities of 20-somethings. Eventually, other things like relationships, graduate school, and career concerns kept me rolling along. Suddenly, I found myself in 2017 having not drawn in 15 years! I guess that's how time passes when you look back on it; blink and a decade or two might slip behind you.

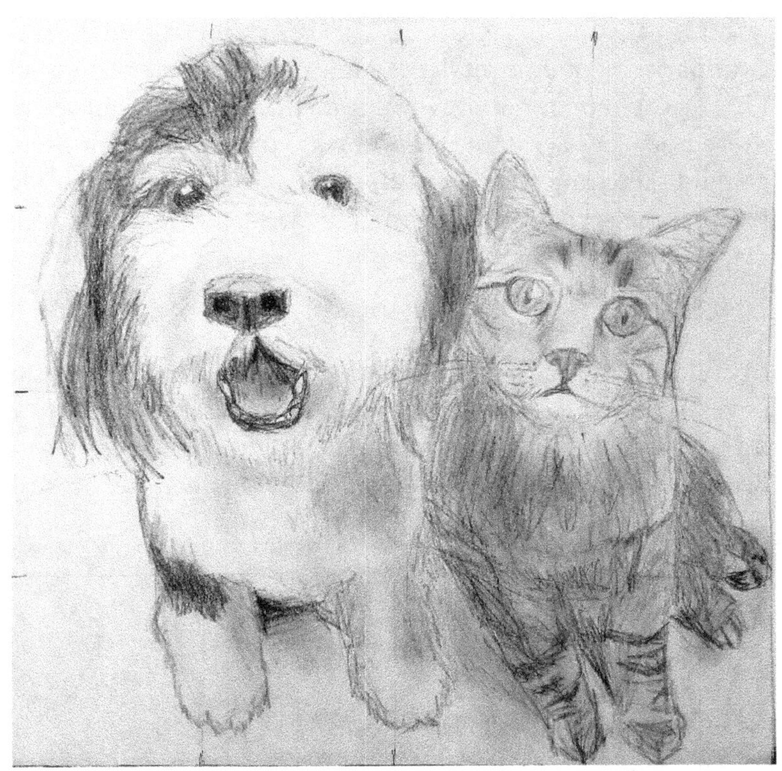

A post-high school drawing, age 18-20. You can see the remnants of the grid/measuring lines I used at that point.

I think these sketches from early adulthood were of better quality overall than my high school collection. It was during this time that I started using a grid/measurement system, and the realism improved a bit. Using measuring lines was a great learning tool to help me get accustomed to proportions and perspective.

I still informally doodled occasionally during this post-high school phase, and the sketches looked pretty similar to the art class portfolio. But I definitely got better at handling detail when I really put the effort in. This is a skill I'm glad didn't completely fade away. Comparisons of current art to high school and post high school are quite similar; although I have gotten better at drawing realistic subjects, I can see how my "grown-up" self is a bit more boring as an artist. When I was younger, I was more apt to use my imagination and go wild sketching whatever I thought was fun. Although I love drawing my kids, and hope I'm making something they might value later, I am just trying to achieve near-realism.

COLLEGE AND GRADUATE SCHOOL STUDY AIDS

In college and graduate school, my creative art side had effectively gone into hibernation. I never sketched for fun at that point in my life. It's unfortunate because I sometimes wonder if I would have continued to improve, and what sort of artist I might be now if I had. Leaving "what ifs" aside, I did still occasionally draw for utility; I created study materials for the more difficult classes.

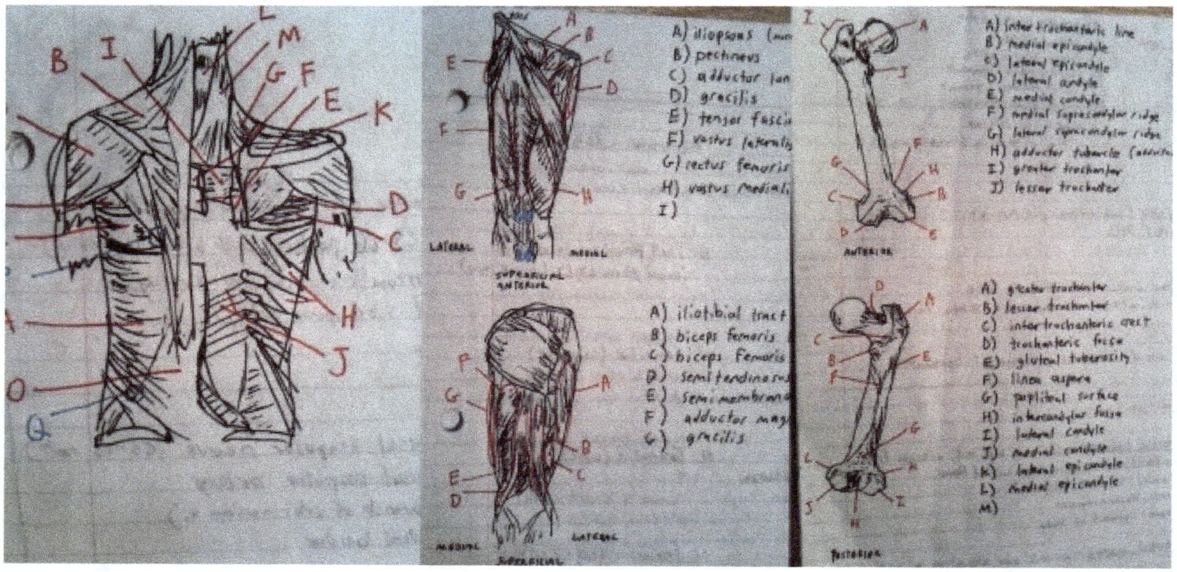

Anatomy and Physiology study/self-quiz sketches, from either college or graduate school.

I was a Biology major as an undergraduate, and my Master's was in Biomedical Science. I took a bunch of classes in each program related to anatomy and physiology, and I am (probably unsurprisingly) a visual learner. A natural tool to help me learn was to sketch out what I was trying to commit to memory. This was even valuable beyond the natural fit of A&P; drawing structures in Organic Chemistry, and visualizing cell processes in Biochemistry and Cell Biology saved me from having to change majors.

The main goal of the drawing to study exercise was two-fold for me. The first was to commit the memory of writing a shape to my brain in a way that just looking couldn't satisfy. The second was to sketch figures so that I could quiz myself. My textbooks usually directly labeled anatomy diagrams, but I wanted something that would allow me to cover the answers with a sheet of paper and repeatedly pound the information into my brain. I've never been great at rote memorization, so I had to come up with something to help me along. I was able to find my old Anatomy and Physiology notebooks, but unfortunately, the cell biology and biochemistry sketchbooks seem to have grown legs and wandered off.

MY FIRST WEBSITE

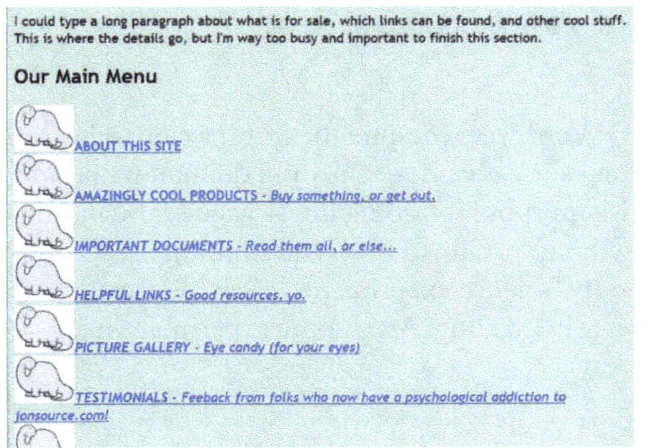

Jonsource.com, an MS Notepad constructed nonsense website from the early 2000s.

At some point in my 15-year art purgatory, probably in the very early 2000s, I got an itch to learn about web design. I was working in software development at the time, so it seemed like something I could use someday (spoiler alert: I never used it). I tried to teach myself how to create a website using HTML and even purchased an "HTML for Dummies" book. I was able to whip up an amazingly terrible site called jonsource.com. I coded the thing in Notepad, paid some company to host it, and was wildly successful with at least 100 hits!

I actually did share some of my high school artwork on jonsource.com. So, even though it was also surrounded by strangeness, in many ways this was the precursor to my current site *Amdall Gallery*.

THE SECOND SITE

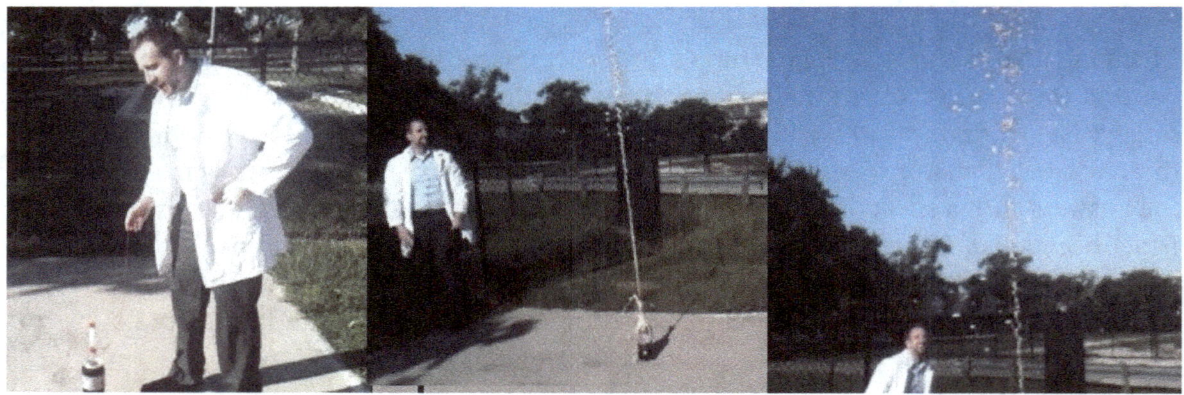

One of the first posts to the early (and quickly abandoned) WordPress site. The Classic Diet Coke and Mentos experiment; we later tried a quick Mentos/Diet Coke drop, seal, and slam (the bottle cap-side first on the concrete). That one was pretty entertaining but did result in an injury.

Fast forward to 2011, and I finally discovered WordPress (despite the fact that it had been around for at least six years already). I had long since abandoned my old domain name and site, so I went with a completely fresh start. My purpose for doing it was vague though, so it never really went anywhere. I didn't have anything specific to host, and nothing I really wanted to blog about. I posted a couple of goofy "science experiments" I did after work with some co-workers, but nothing particularly interesting. After some experimenting, I basically abandoned the site for around six years.

In August 2017, I came back to the site. Although I kept the same URL (jonamdall.com), I rebranded it as *Amdall Gallery* and experimented with some theme and design overhauls. My original intent was to share mostly share some data analysis I'd done for fun, my old artwork, and a few other random things. But to name it explicitly as a gallery, I must have had some subconscious creative impulses lurking. A month and some change after restarting the site, a switch flipped and back to art I went.

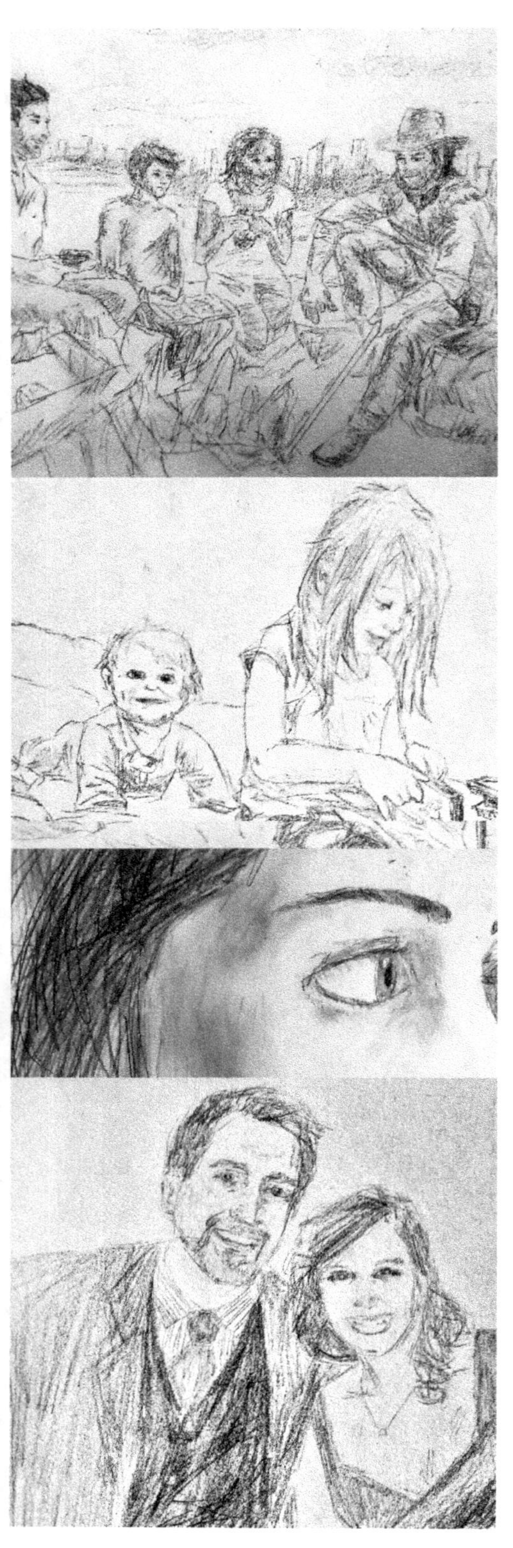

Phase 1 – Getting Back into Art

SEPTEMBER 2017

How would someone who has been away from a hobby for many years get back into it again? If I tried to imagine a scenario, it would probably involve some deliberation, preparation, and maybe some planning. Over the years, a small urge to draw had occasionally surfaced, but there were always excuses not to. Excuses like not knowing where my supplies were, if I had paper, or available desk space always overpowered my relatively weak impulse to try. Also, what would I draw? Enough barriers to give me a pass from trying.

This time though, it was a surprisingly quick decision that involved very little internal monologue. I thought, "I'll run out of old art to share pretty quickly...If I'm going to spend time on this website, why not create something new?" That thought popped into my head, and the vague urge transformed into an actual thing my body was putting into motion. In hindsight, I really don't understand what was different this time as compared to the many others. But it was indeed different, and I found myself doing something that felt both excitingly fresh yet still comfortable.

FIRST PORTRAIT

Those artificial roadblocks I created in the past turned out to be quite easy to navigate. I found my old art supplies without much difficulty and had no issues clearing out some desk space. And determining what to draw was surprisingly easy too. In the distant past, I had sketched friends, family, self-portraits, and even one of my wife before we were married. But since they arrived in the world long after I took my extended vacation from art, I'd never drawn my two little ones. And now that the kids are getting a little older (relatively speaking), it's getting a little easier to do things other than just laying around. Both kiddos seem to enjoy hanging out with me at the computer desk, and once I started drawing, the oldest sat down and sketched with me. Her subject seemed to be a tornado or something, but I decided to draw our girls.

I started with my old measured grid system. I was a bit worried that I wouldn't be able to make it work; I knew I could measure and draw the grid. But I wasn't sure if I could actually put the portrait together, or if I could apply the correct pencil pressure right away. Even though it had been years, it really was like riding a bike. Marking the grids, then starting the outline felt just like it did when I was younger; a slow buildup of preparation culminating in a flurry of relatively decent pencil shading and technique. I put some music on, and just got to it.

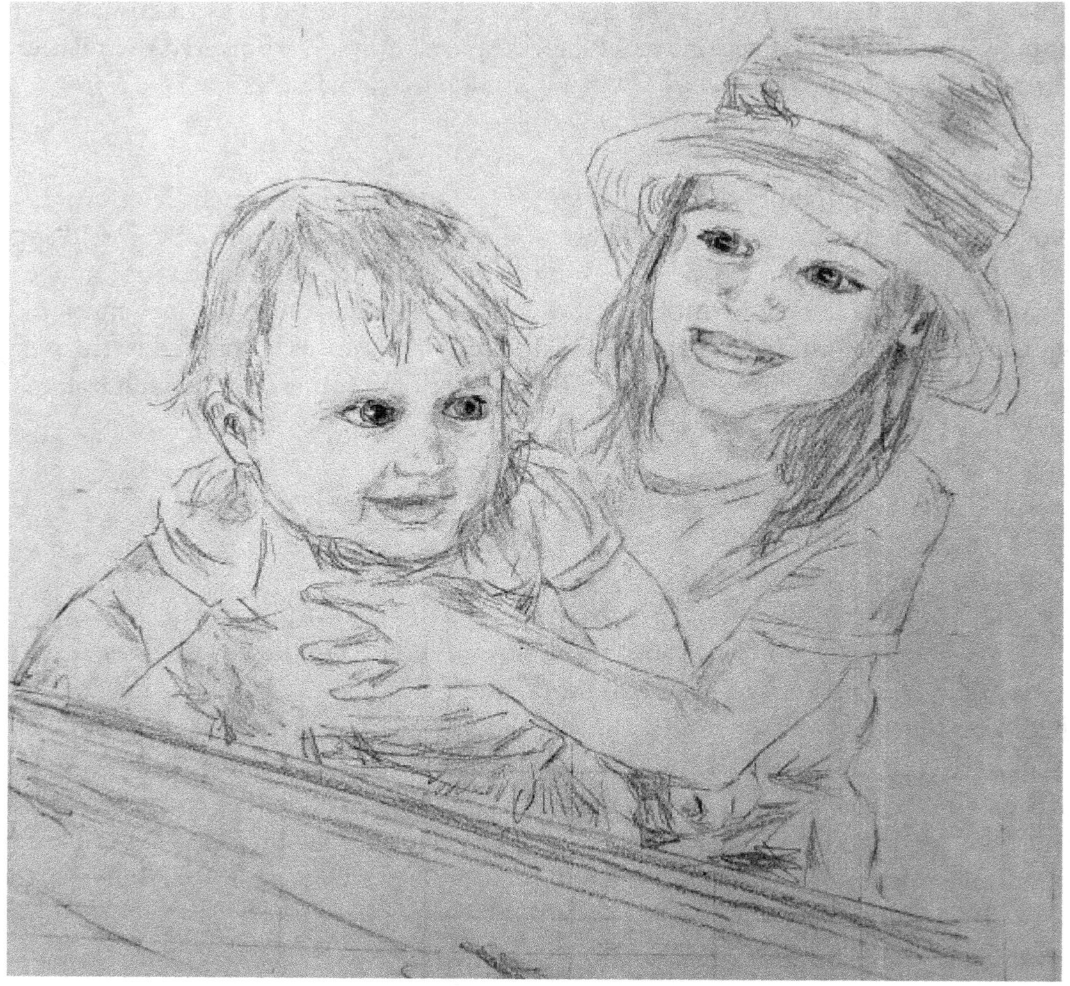

First portrait from my return to art, September 2017. My oldest and youngest daughters.

On the adjacent page is the finished drawing of the kids. It's definitely not perfect, but I was glad that I could at least recognize them. There were a few areas that I was very cautious about, like the noses and mouths. I really couldn't remember how dark to shade or whether to create solid lines versus blended depth. Lack of recent experience really showed in that respect. I almost want to go back to their noses over a year later and scribble some real definition!

Ultimately though, I was really pleased with how it turned out. Another challenge I didn't consider is that I don't think I'd ever drawn a child before. My sketches in high school were always either other teenager or adults, and the people I drew as a kid were of indistinguishable age. My oldest daughter wasn't too hard, but drawing very young kids like my youngest is quite a challenge. Infants and very young toddlers tend to look pretty similar; it seems like it's the minute, subtle difference that parents know just from being with them all the time. That makes babies really tricky to draw for me.

MEASURED GRIDS

Before going further on this journey, I should write a little more on these measured grids. I've mentioned them several times, but haven't really detailed the process. These grids are simply a method to help capture accurate proportions. I used them a lot in that brief time after high school that I still sketched. Coming back to art after so long, I definitely needed grids to help me along as I got my bearing again.

Basic gridlines on paper.

My approach is pretty simple. First, you have to decide on a scale to use, which comes directly from the size of your reference and the size of your paper. Starting with your reference, which could be a printed photograph or some other paper-printed resource, measure its dimensions. Once it's measured, you'll want to decide how to divide it up, making sure to give yourself at least four intervals up and across. For example, if it's a 4" x 6" photograph, one inch would be a perfectly fine grid interval.

Heading over to your paper, you have to decide how big the sketch will be. If you want your artwork to be twice as large, simply double your reference interval. So, if we're still working with a 4" x 6" photograph, you would mark the paper in two-inch intervals with a total size of 8" x 12". Next, using a ruler (I prefer transparent), make hash marks starting from the top left in whichever interval selected. To ensure straight lines, my habit was to mark hashes on both sides of the paper – this helps to line up the ruler.

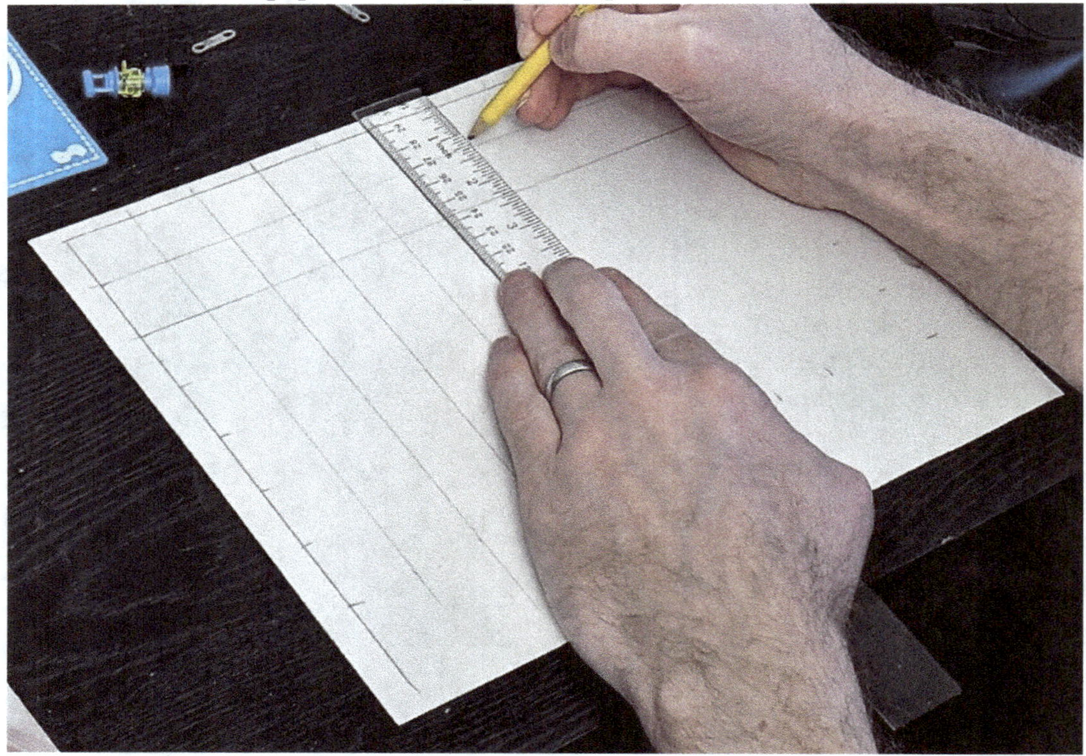

An overhead view of me building a grid on paper.

If you've used consistent intervals, you can focus on the drawing square by square. Within a square, estimate where lines exit the square and positions of shapes inside. As you complete squares, the overall drawing will start to come together. Typically, once I had the basic outline, I then erased as much of the grid as possible and then started the finer details. As you get used to the shapes of your subjects (people in my case), help with proportion becomes less important. In fact, after getting back into drawing, I only did four or five sketches with grids before I started trying to work without them. It was certainly a useful learning tool though, and I'd recommend it to anyone struggling with proportion.

CONTEST DRAWING – TINY ART SHOW

By random coincidence, shortly after I finished this first sketch, a co-worker told me about an interesting art show. A local art center was hosting a "tiny art" 5" X 5" X 5" exhibit. I had mentioned to him I was going to try getting back into my old art hobby, and he said this show was open to amateurs. He makes custom fishing lures and entered some in last year's show. Even though I've never in my life entered anything into an art show, I decided I might as well give it a shot. The worst they could do is just not accept what I submitted.

The first thing I did was conduct some research on River Oaks Art Center, rules for the contest, and how they would handle submissions. It seemed this was the second year of what they were making an annual event. The rules were fairly simple to; original works only, all media, and images couldn't be larger than 25 square inches. They also had some framing rules and the stipulation that the piece must be ready to hang.

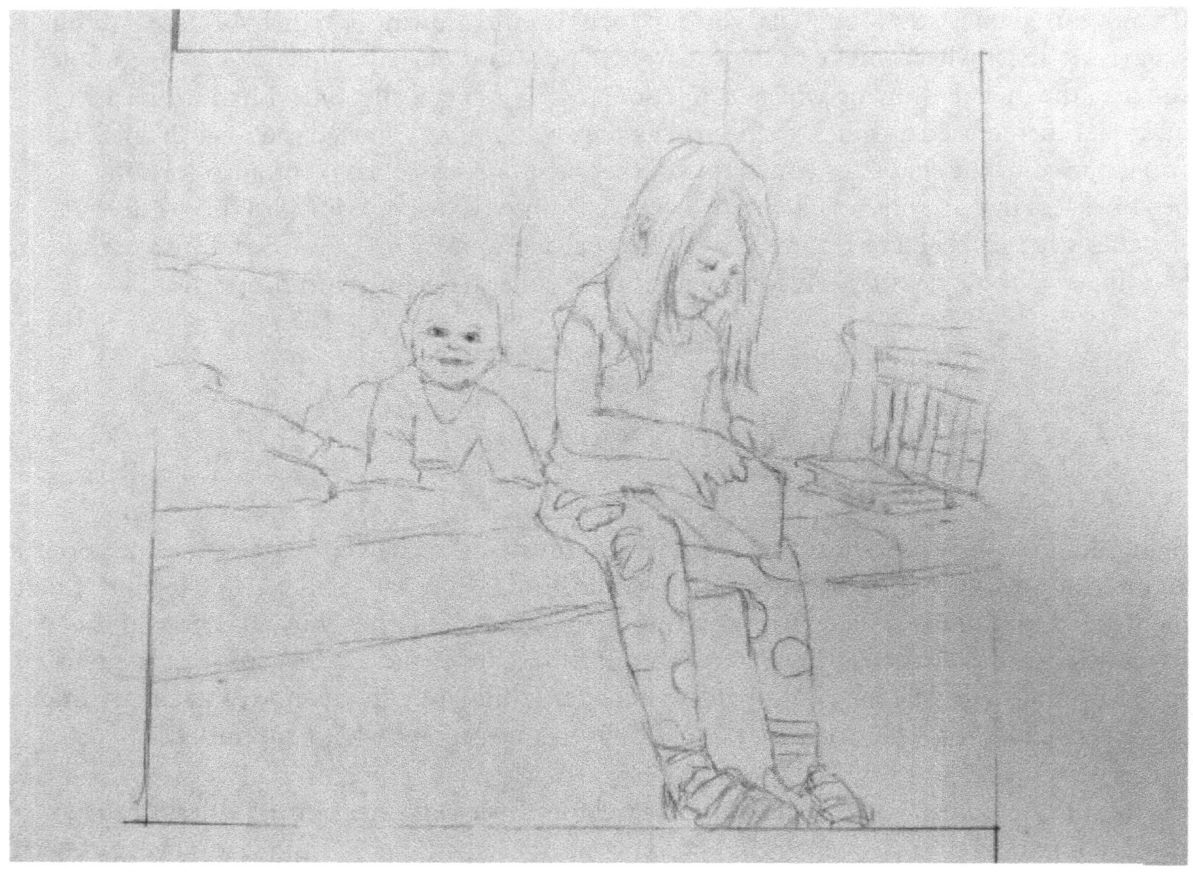

Initial grid and outline for the Tiny Art exhibit. The girls playing on our bed.

As with my last drawing, I decided to go with my little ones as subjects. The challenge here was, of course, the size. Once I started, I realized 5 inches by 5 inches is *really* small and made it hard to add detail. And without detail on distinguishing features, it really takes away from drawings when the goal is realism. Measuring for my usual grid was easy at least – after all, they gave me the measurements.

The final product ended up looking okay. At the time, I was honestly not sure that this was "art show" quality. I still feel the same way, particularly after attending the opening night of the exhibit and seeing how good the other pieces were. I think it does look like the girls for the most part, but it just wasn't big enough to get into finer shading and light lines.

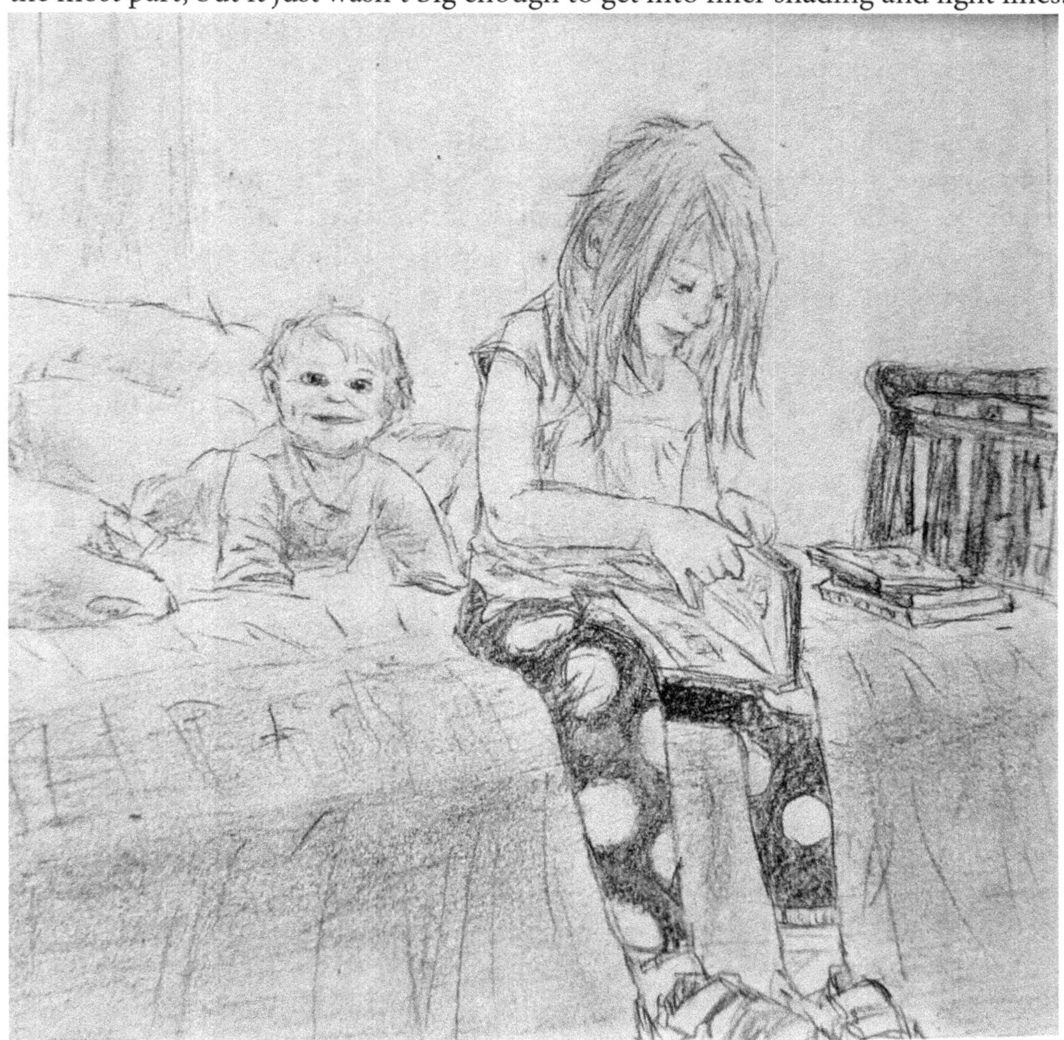

Final sketch for the 5x5x5 art show, September 2017.

After finishing the sketch, then came the submission process. Fortunately, it was quite easy to do via a website called "Call for Entry" (www.callforentry.org). I just created an account, uploaded images to my portfolio, then applied directly in their portal. You can even search for participating galleries' art shows to find others you might be interested in. I was glad I could take care of the administrative aspects online. I hadn't even considered assigning a price, but you can do that too from the portal.

The thought of selling it hadn't even crossed my mind, which really gives you an idea of how much of an amateur I am. I was doing this for fun, and I guess the entire point of an art show slipped my mind; these galleries are in it to sell art and make commissions from them (30% in this case). I didn't put a serious price on my uploads, assuming that would ensure I got the drawing back afterward.

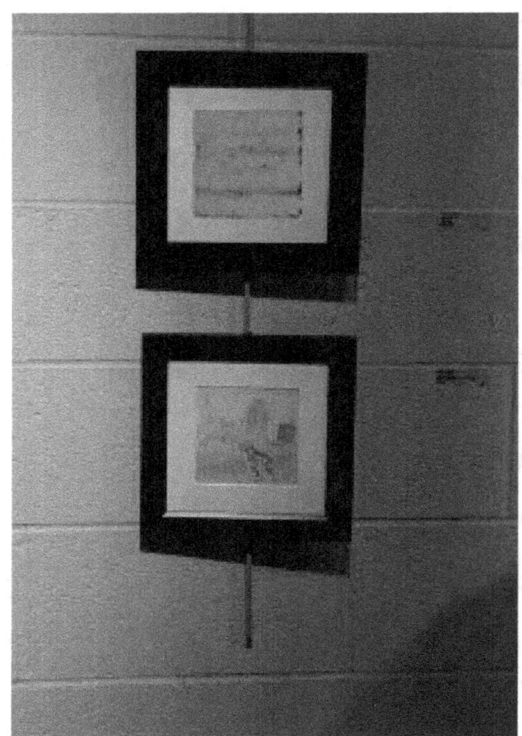

Art show display.

The show was a couple of months after the submission deadline. It was pretty fun; I took the family, and they had snacks which always grabs my interest. According to a sign inside, they had 275 total pieces entered and accepted 113 for the show. Given that acceptance rate, I was actually quite surprised they let mine in. My drawing was fairly close to the entrance.

Overall, I enjoyed the experience and would probably enter art into a show again if I come across another opportunity. I'm not sure that tiny art is my best skill though because I felt like many of the entries were noticeably higher quality than mine. Some of the other pieces were really amazing; there was one, in particular, that was a 1" x 1" painting of candy bars in a vending machine that was incredibly good. There were a few paintings that had such fine detail, I have no clue how they even did it from a mechanical standpoint.

A DARK TOWER DRAWING

Around the time I started getting back into art, I also began reading the Dark Tower series by Stephen King. I've always been a big Stephen King fan, and I enjoy fantasy novels, so it's actually really strange that it took me so long to start the series. After finishing my second drawing of the artwork comeback, I started considering what I should try next. This would become a common theme for me over the next year and a half; draw my family repeatedly, then decide I need to try some variety. As I was right in the middle of the Dark Tower series, I thought that would make a fun thing to try.

The scene I first attempted was one that stuck in my mind from the third book. It featured Roland, Eddie, Susannah, Jake, and Oy all sitting by a campfire in the vast plains ahead of the City of Lud. The challenge here still speaks a bit to my limitations as an artist, if I'm frank about it. I am decent at drawing things I see; live subjects, from photos, and so on. Drawing completely from imagination is much more difficult for me. This was true when I was younger, and it's still true today; I struggle mightily without references.

Because I really needed some reference point, particularly for facial features, I imagined some actors they might resemble. I think a lot of Dark Tower readers have associated Roland the Gunslinger with a young Clint Eastwood, so that felt like a good starting point for him. As for the rest of the crew, I always imagined Eddie Dean as sort of a wiry Rufus Sewell type. I pictured Susannah Dean as a vague mash-up of the original Aunt Vivian from the Fresh Prince of Bel Air and Zoe Saldana. Jake seemed like a generic, possibly book-ish brunette kid, and I wanted to model Oy as a longer version of a raccoon.

I started on the drawing, but once I really got into it, I realized that my paper real estate was probably too small. I discussed a few pages ago in the measuring grids section the importance of determining a good scaling interval; in this case, I seemed to have guess poorly. I should have scaled the reference-to-paper conversion a bit higher, and possibly even used larger paper than the 9" x 12" I used. Because the sketch area was too small, I didn't really have room to add enough detail in the characters' faces. I was able to show some distinguishing features but would have been much more comfortable with more room to maneuver.

This piece turned out just okay; not awful, but definitely with some flaws. As I was sketching the group, Eddie (the guy on the left) and Susannah (woman in the middle) did not really turn out how I always imagined them. But the pencil went where it wanted to go, and I didn't force anything because I was considered that could wreck the drawing. Roland and Jake are mostly how I imagined them though. You may notice some remnants on the right side; I tried to include Oy the Billybumbler, but I was unsatisfied with how he turned out. My representation didn't seem right; it looked basically like a regular dog, and I wanted to lean more towards a raccoon or weasel.

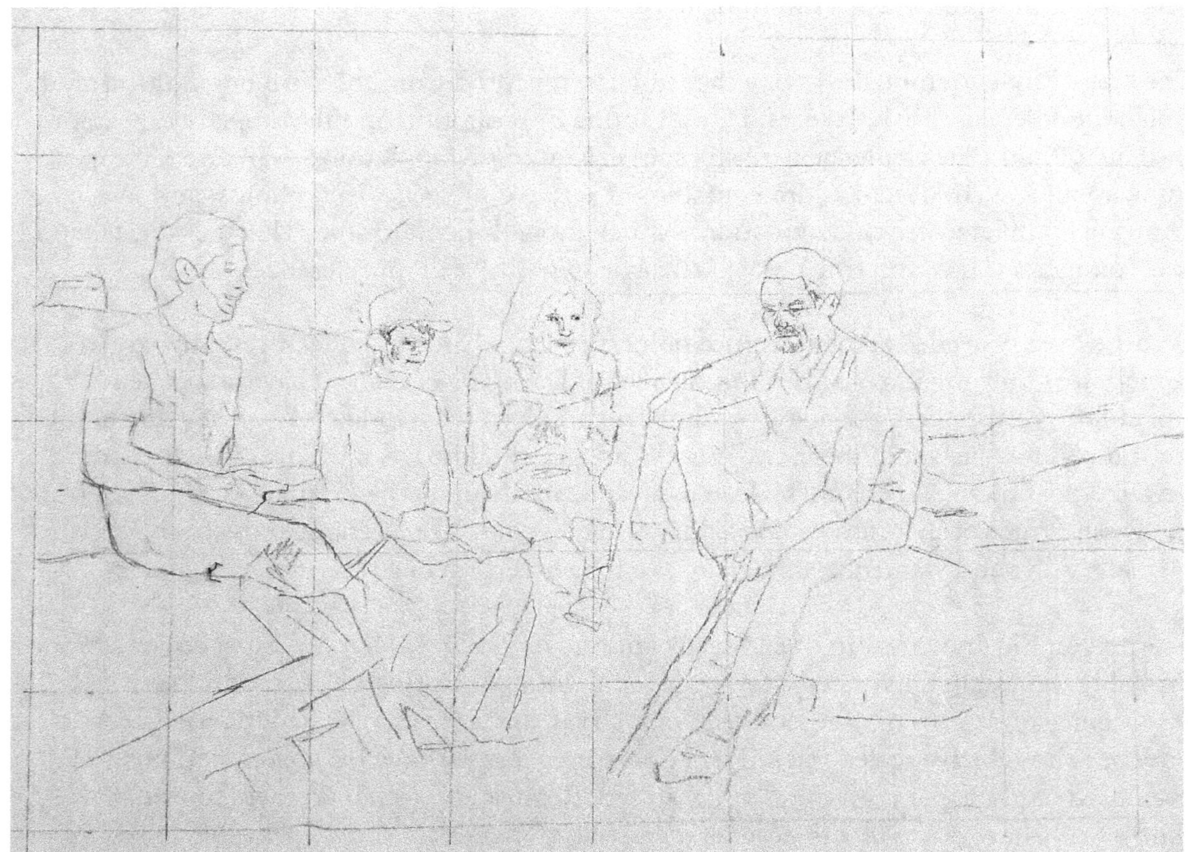

Early grid and outline for the Dark Tower campfire sketch.

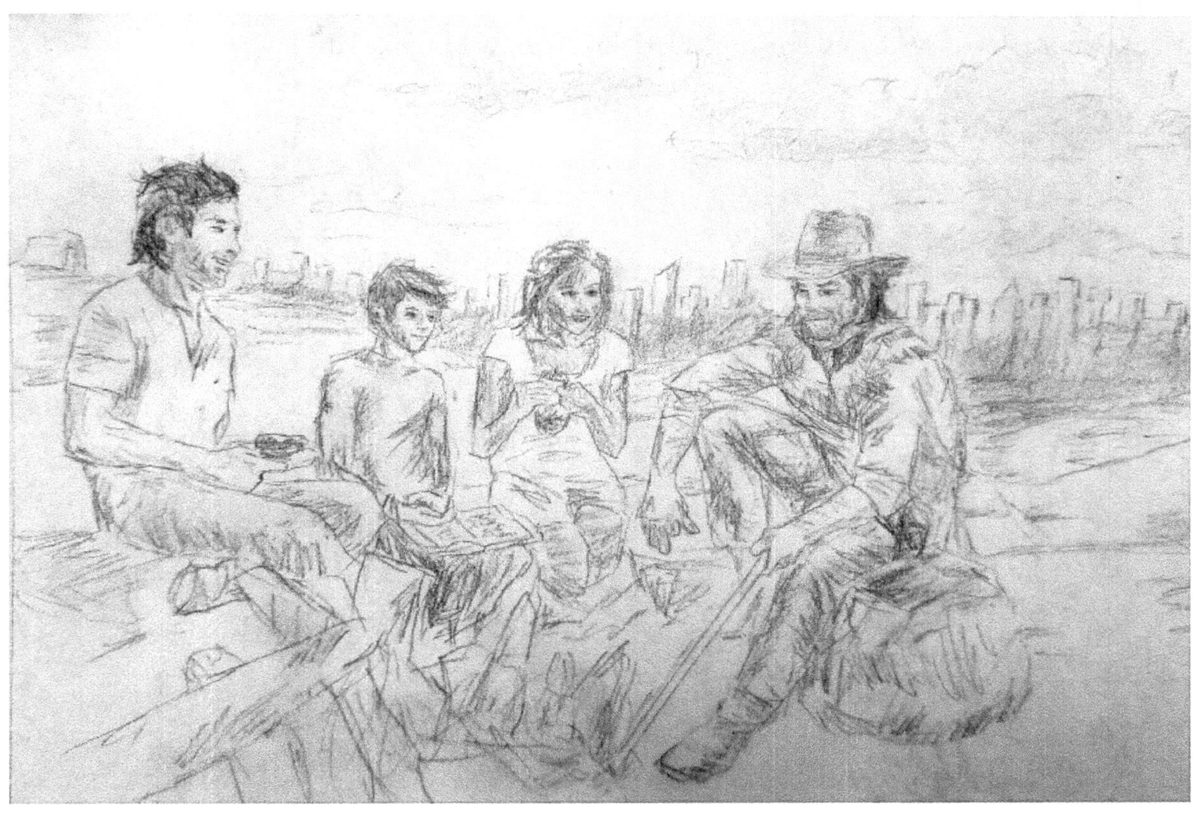

Finished Dark Tower scene, Campfire at the City of Lud.

I had a few details I wanted to make sure I included, and I did remember to add them, fortunately. Susannah is missing her legs below the knee, and Roland's lobstrocity-mangled hand is there. Jake has their all-important joke book (check out the series if you want to hear more about that) in his lap, and Eddie and Susannah are eating Gunslinger Burritos. I was able to get the ruined city in the background, and I think the size/perspective ratio is on point…the implementation isn't great though. But hey – it's scenery, not my best skill.

This would not be my last Dark Tower artwork, and wouldn't even be the last black and white sketch. I also returned to this fantasy world early in my exploration of color, and again to completely re-do a scene much later to see how I improved.

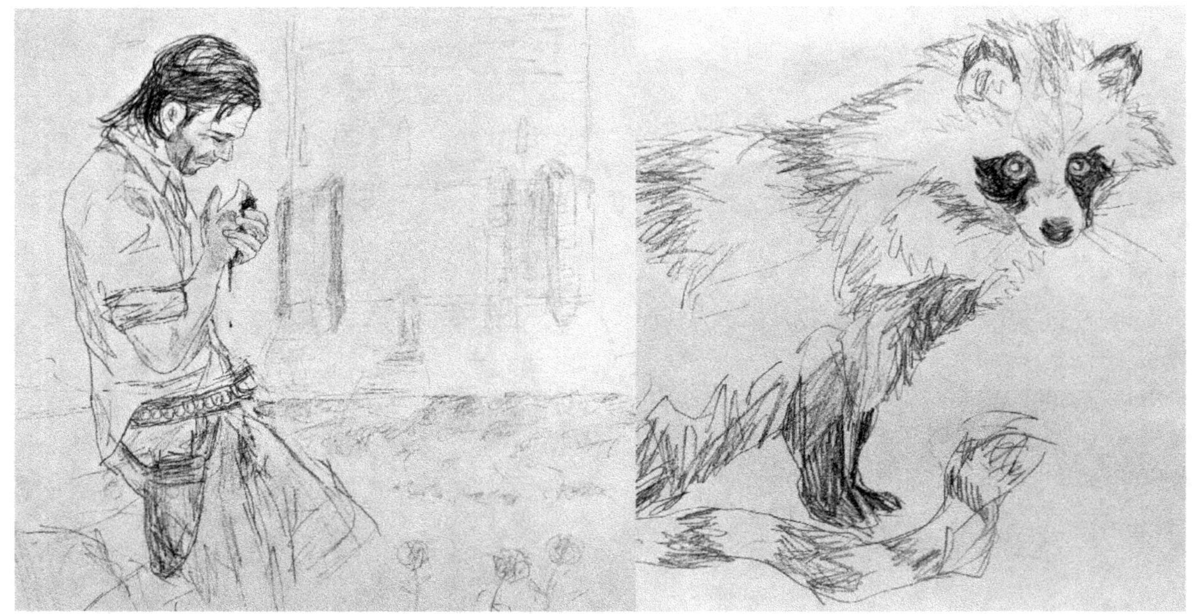

Portions of early attempts at drawing Roland and Oy.

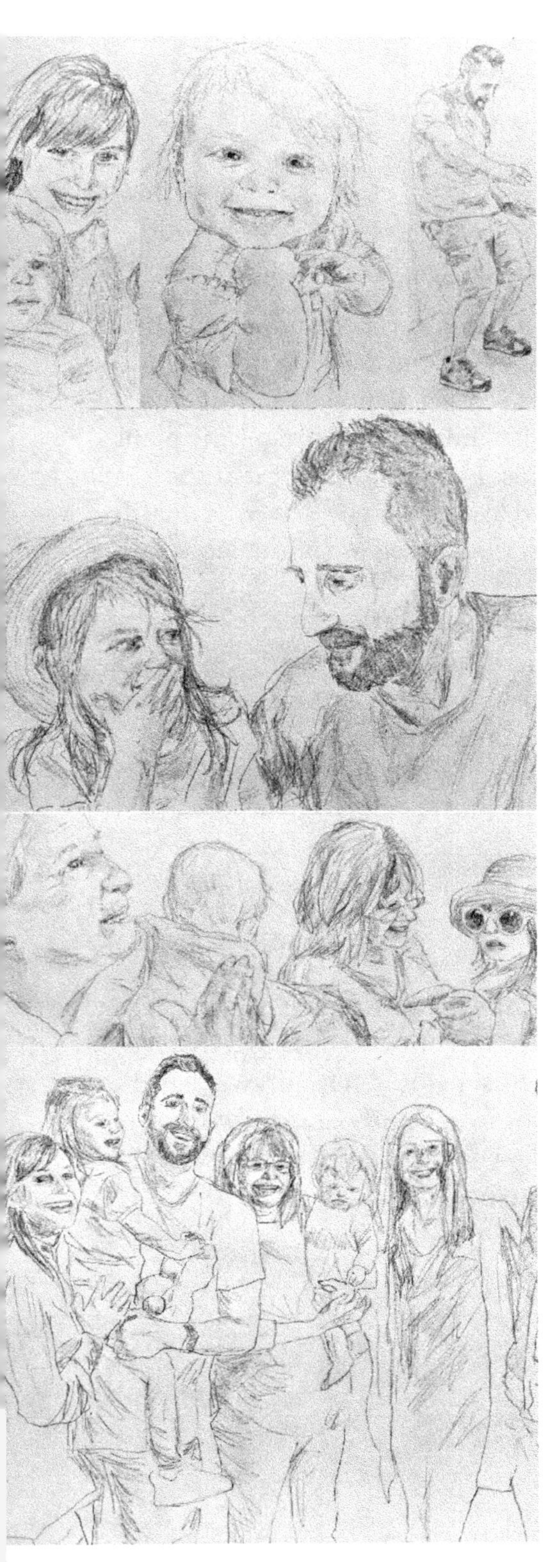

Phase 2 – Drawing Without a Grid

NOVEMBER 2017

When I jumped back into this drawing hobby, I went into it with no expectations and no specific plans. I didn't have plans to work on a second sketch after the drawing of the kids. It just so happened I felt like doing another, so I did. And that's basically how I continued; I was having fun, so I kept going. Along those same lines, I also didn't have any specific plans or preconceived notions to move away from measuring grids. I wasn't aware of it at the time, but this would become a common theme with me and artwork; to be driven primarily by impulse. This is funny because I would certainly not describe myself as spontaneous in any other aspect of my personality.

In this chapter, I'll share a few of the first sketches I attempted without using grids. Many of them are sort of rough and have definite flaws in terms of proportion and positioning. I expected as much though without having grids as a crutch. As I mentioned above, the decision to try this wasn't difficult really. And it wasn't dictated by any thought that I was "ready" to try. I just had an urge to give it a shot.

FAMILY SKETCH, NO PLANNING

Late one evening, after putting the kids to bed, from out of nowhere I was hit with an urge to try to draw my family. I had never drawn myself, my wife, and our two girls together, so it seemed like a natural choice. Usually, for something like this, I would have drawn a grid to help with proportions, but this time I wanted to dive right in. The preparation work to draw gridlines and figure out the right scale would have taken a fair amount of time, and I wasn't in the mood to spend so much time not actually drawing.

As I started, I thought about all the great advice I had received from other more experienced artists in the WordPress community through comments on my prior posts. Some of the most memorable had been the recommendations to "keep it loose" and "gestural." I think it's generally true that the quality of my sketches worsens when I tighten up and worry too much about getting it right. When I can just let it flow, let the pencil go where it wants, I think the portraits are better. So, for this late-night family sketch, as I outlined the figures I didn't obsess about the basic lines.

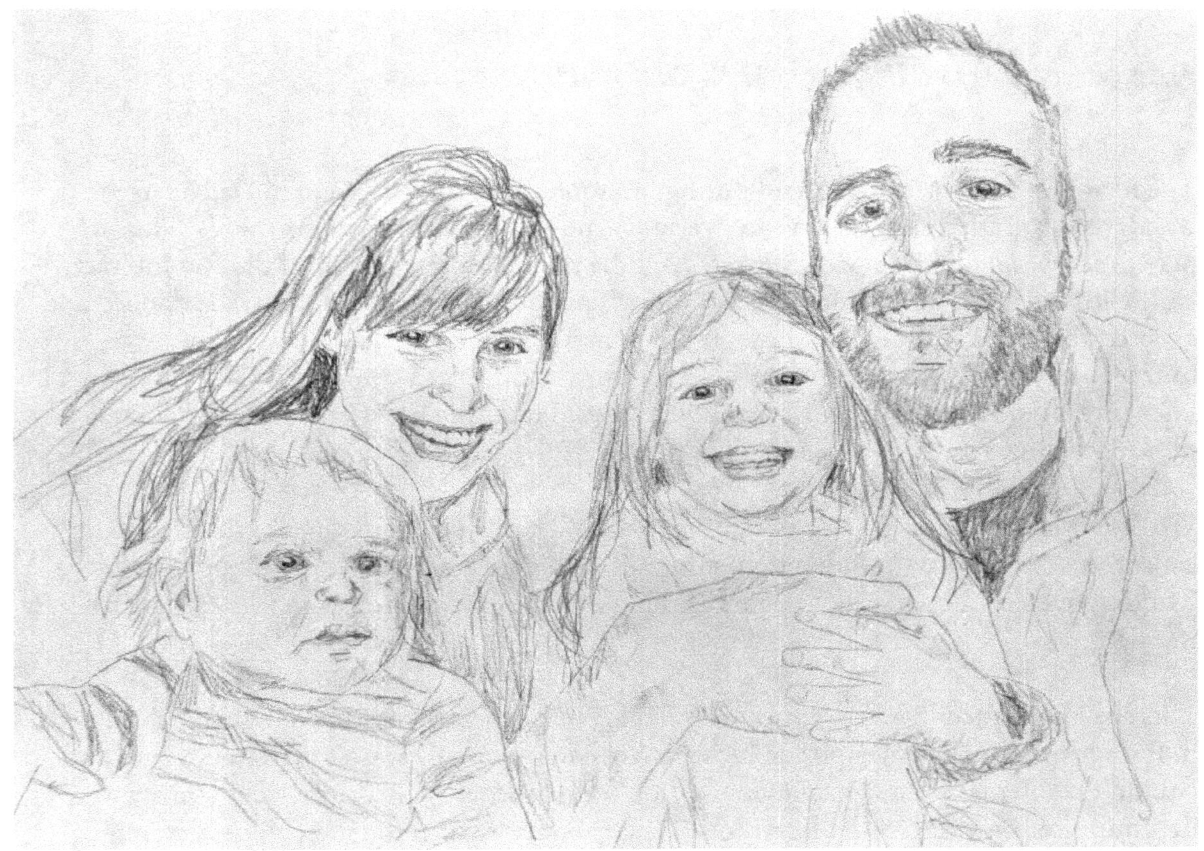

Family portrait done without a grid or measuring with a ruler.

I was a bit surprised with the result; it turned out decently overall. The lines were noticeably squigglier than previous recent sketches, which speaks to the uncertainty I experienced trying to draw without a grid. The proportions seemed somewhat accurate, but the placement and perspective of some features were pretty far off. A good example of an awkward perspective is seen in the position of my eyes; it made sense at the time but looks very strange when viewing now. And our youngest daughter's head position seems a little unnatural. But I did accomplish my goal - we are all recognizable as ourselves.

DANCING DAD – DRAWING FROM A VIDEO

The next sketch is from a weekend outing, we took to North Park Mall in Dallas. As we wandered around, we came across a live song-and-dance performance for kids. The performer was named "David Chicken," and he played guitar, sang, and did fun interactive stuff with the kids in the audience. Our oldest daughter absolutely loved it; she danced and cheered throughout the entire show (if only I had as much energy). Now, I'm an outrageously bad dancer, but when he called for volunteers to come dance during a song, I knew she would love it, so up we went. She danced her little heart out, and I...well, basically moved my limbs randomly while music played.

We didn't get any great photos of it, but we did get some hilarious video. I decided to try to capture a sketch from the video to memorialize the dance party. It was a bit of a challenge working from a video, trying to pause and play short segments to get an idea of how to draw it.

This sketch resulted in a very cartoonish final result, especially for my daughter's face. Even in the age of amazing smartphone cameras, the video actually wasn't extremely clear, and I couldn't really make out satisfying definition for her nose. So, her nose lacks realistic definition to some degree. The cartoon-like appearance aside, the sketch does actually convey movement well, I think. She was literally jumping up and down at that point, and it seems that way from the drawing. I was flailing my arms around with my feet planted, which looks essentially like the situation on paper too.

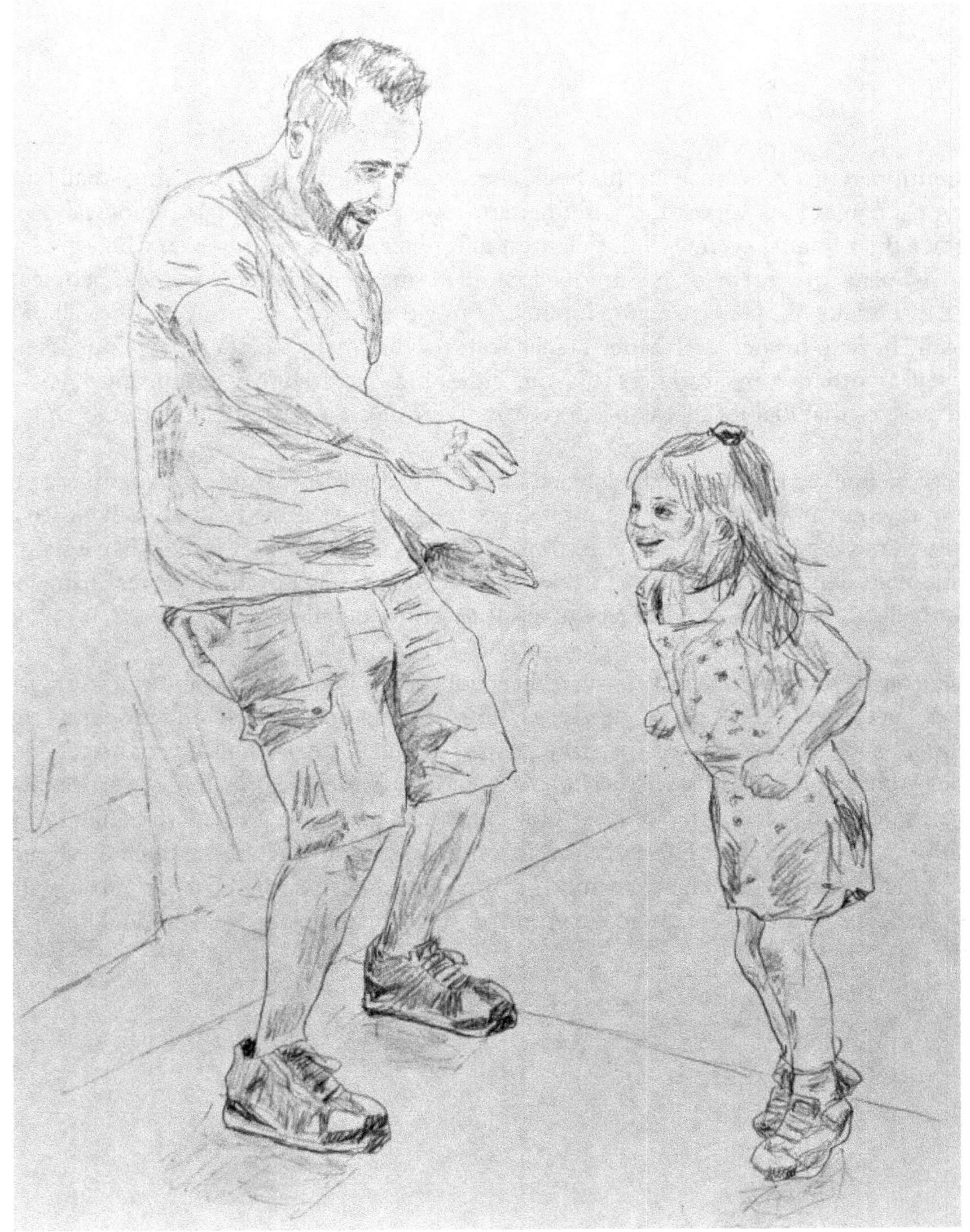

Scene drawn from a video of me and my daughter dancing.

SERIOUS BABY CRACKING A SMILE

I've mentioned this previously in this book already – I have difficulty drawing small babies. I think most babies look very similar, but parents have some sort of innate biological drive to recognize their infants even with the slightest differences. As a parent, even when my kids were newborns, they seemed very unique looking to me. But, probably to most people, they looked essentially like generic crying infants. Trying to draw an infant overcomes all of that; you really have to master the nuanced facial features that make a certain baby look like him or herself. In other words, toddlers (like our oldest kid) have more distinguishing characteristics than babies that you can rely on to create a recognizable portrait.

Along these lines, it has been a challenge to accurately draw our youngest daughter. At this point in my return to art, I had attempted to sketch her three times, and I felt like with all three I was not especially successful. In those drawings, she definitely looked like a baby but didn't look exactly like OUR baby. I decided I needed to try again, this time featuring just her, and a larger sized view of her face to allow for more detail.

I finally completed a sketch that captured her look! If I'm being honest about it though, that may have been because at that point she was approaching one year old and growing out of that "small baby" phase. I based this drawing on one of my favorite photos of her. At this age, our youngest was a fairly serious kid. Although she's much is much more expressive now, from around six months to a year old, she looked at me most of the time like I just told the world's worst joke. This pose was in a moment of pure silliness, which was a nice preview of the funny character she would become after her first birthday. The pose, with her cheesy grin, and those two teeth, make it one of my favorites of the black and white sketches.

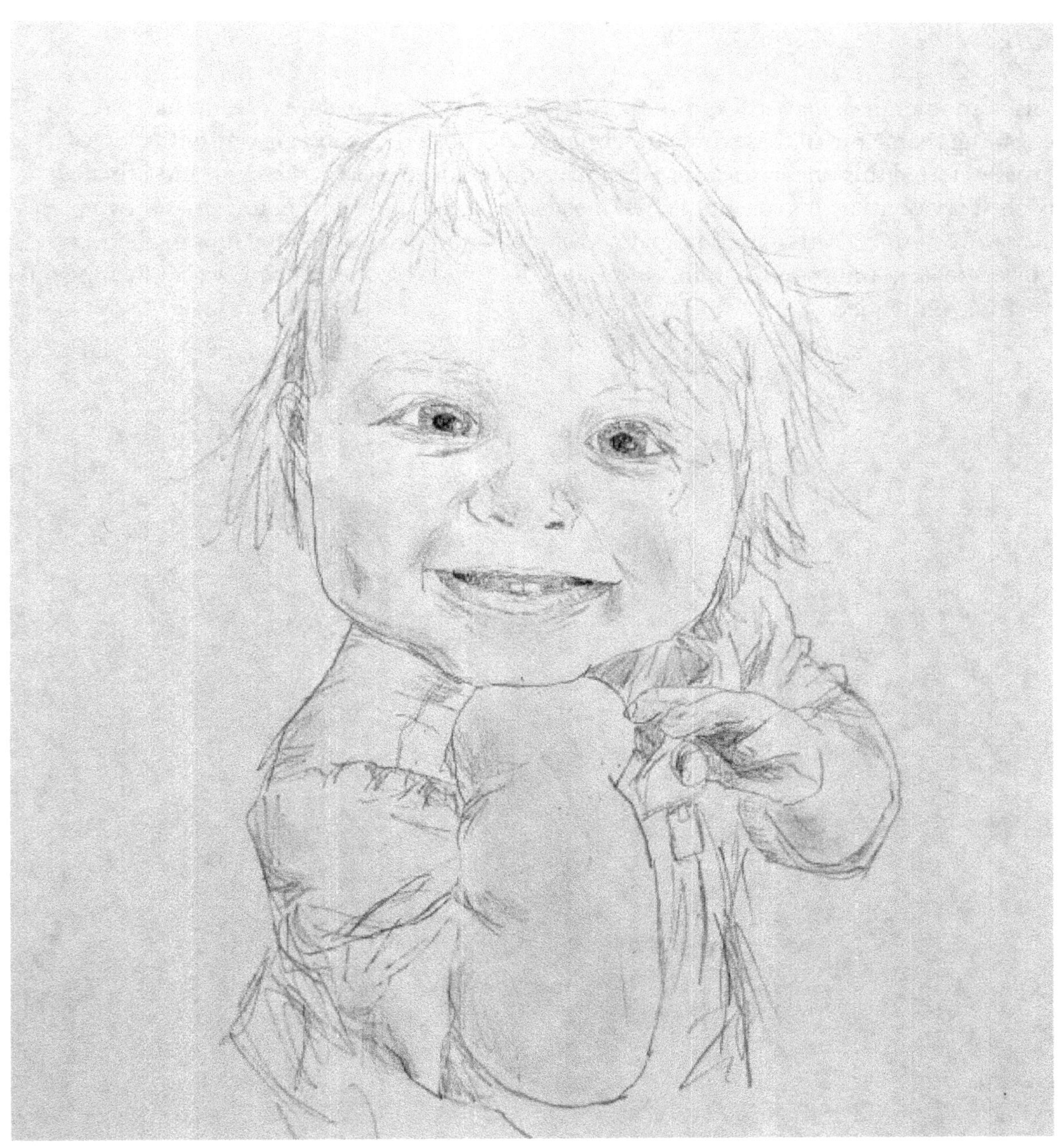

My youngest daughter hamming it up, posing like it's a Mall Photo Studio session.

TIRED DAD, LAUGHING KID

This is another of my favorites from this period of sketches. I'm sure it seems like the prevailing theme for all these drawings, but it's another a did featuring one of the kids. I actually started this one in the same session as one of the previous sketches, and I finally finished it yesterday. It's one of the first instances I recall of me trying to work on two pieces of artwork at once. Although I do that occasionally now because I enjoy flipping between subjects to keep things fresh, in this instance I did it because the drawing wasn't turning out exactly as I intended.

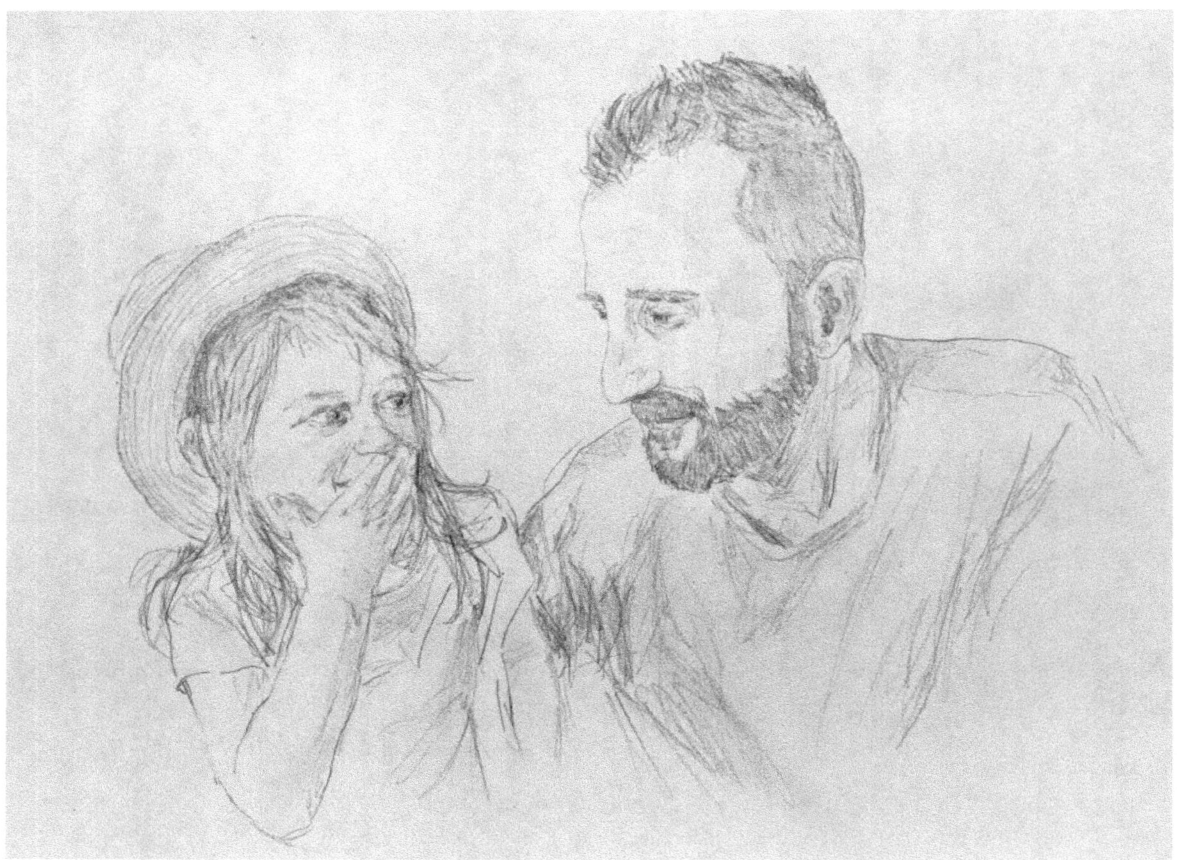

My oldest daughter taking me very seriously.

The look I was aiming for with this drawing was my oldest daughter stifling a laugh, while I was supposed to have a sort of a "dad smirk." Dad smirk being sort of a parental version of covering your mouth as she was, trying not to crack up. But I think the "me" in this portrait just looks tired rather than a fatherly brand of whimsical. "Look at this exhausted middle-aged man! His daughter appears to be laughing because he's about to fall asleep."

This was probably the first of many lessons to come, teaching me that artwork doesn't always turn out exactly as you planned, and that is actually okay. Deviation from your expectations and intentions is not something to be overly concerned about. Although I was frustrated at the time, I really like this sketch looking at it now. It's a drawing that makes me smile as I look at it from my position here ahead in time. I was actually often pretty tired back then, so it all makes sense. I can just re-title this one from "Laughing Kid, Smirking Dad" to "Extremely Tired Looking Man and the Daughter Who Laughed at Him."

THANKSGIVING SCENE

For the next drawing, I wanted to try something new by expanding the subjects significantly. I set out to draw a scene from a Thanksgiving dinner out with my mom, sister, brother-in-law, wife, and our two little ones. This one seemed simple enough since I had been doing so many family sketches. Unfortunately, not all art is going to satisfy the artist...as Billy Bob Thorton's character in Bad Santa said about candy corn, "Well they can't all be winners."

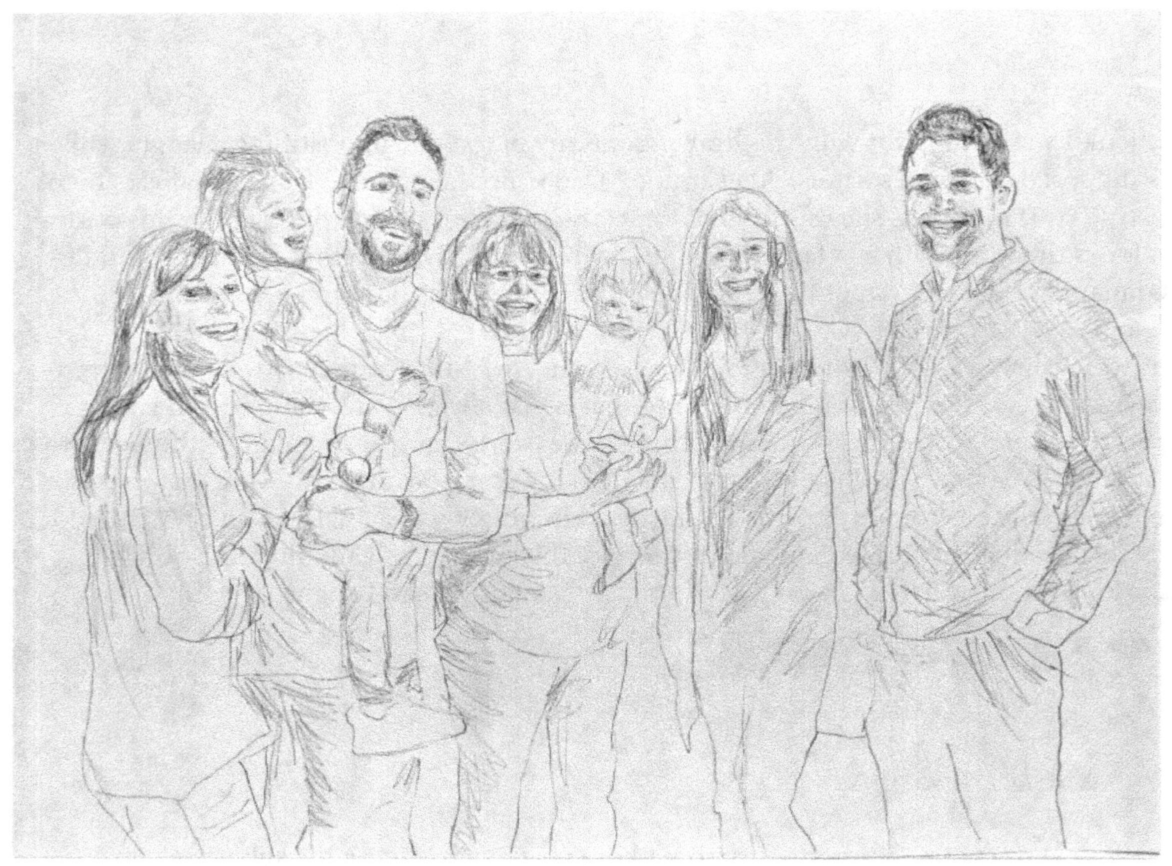

Thanksgiving Day pose with me, my wife, the kids, my mom, sister, and brother-in-law.

I started confidently enough, drawing very rough basic outlines from what I viewed as prominent shadows or similar color. It was still going fine as I went from left to right, filling in detail on my wife, oldest daughter (a bit more difficult this time), and myself. Once I got to my mom though, it started unraveling. I realized it didn't look much like her, so I moved on…then I realized the next figure didn't look too much like my sister. So, I jumped to my brother-in-law and totally botched him.

I think I managed to slightly salvage my sister and my mom to some extent. I mean, they look like decent sketches of people, but how much do they look like my actual mom and sister? Only somewhat of a resemblance, I think. My brother-in-law is closer than he was at first, but I still don't think you could really guess who it is without prompting.

Ultimately, I decided to take this one as a loss and move on.
You can probably tell that I gave up by the "outline" quality, particularly from the waist down on everyone. In this case, it was a challenge to include so many people. I think it could have helped to work from larger paper because it becomes difficult for me to define features with limited room. But sometimes there's only so much erasing you can do before the paper starts to betray you and everything looks like gray smudges. So, I decided to move forward!

GROUP GENERATIONAL SCENE

At this point in the art journey, I was really racking up the sketches. They weren't all great, but I was learning and possibly improving. The previous family group scene that didn't turn out as I'd hoped made me want to try again. I'd wanted to get a few more family members to paper, so this was a good opportunity to try again. With the next one, I thought it might be fun to try something with a few generations of my family tree.

I am much happier with how this one turned out. Granny looks pretty true to life. I struggled a bit accurately portraying my Mom's face, probably because the angle in the photo I referenced was a tricky oblique view. It does mostly look like her, at this point I realized I probably needed to try a straight-on view. Likewise, my sister was obscured by my oldest daughter and her giant "cowboy hat" (as she called it). The main subject of this one was really Granny since I placed her right in the foreground, so I decided it was alright for now. The wheels were already turning though for how to capture my mom and sister in more true-to-life portraits.

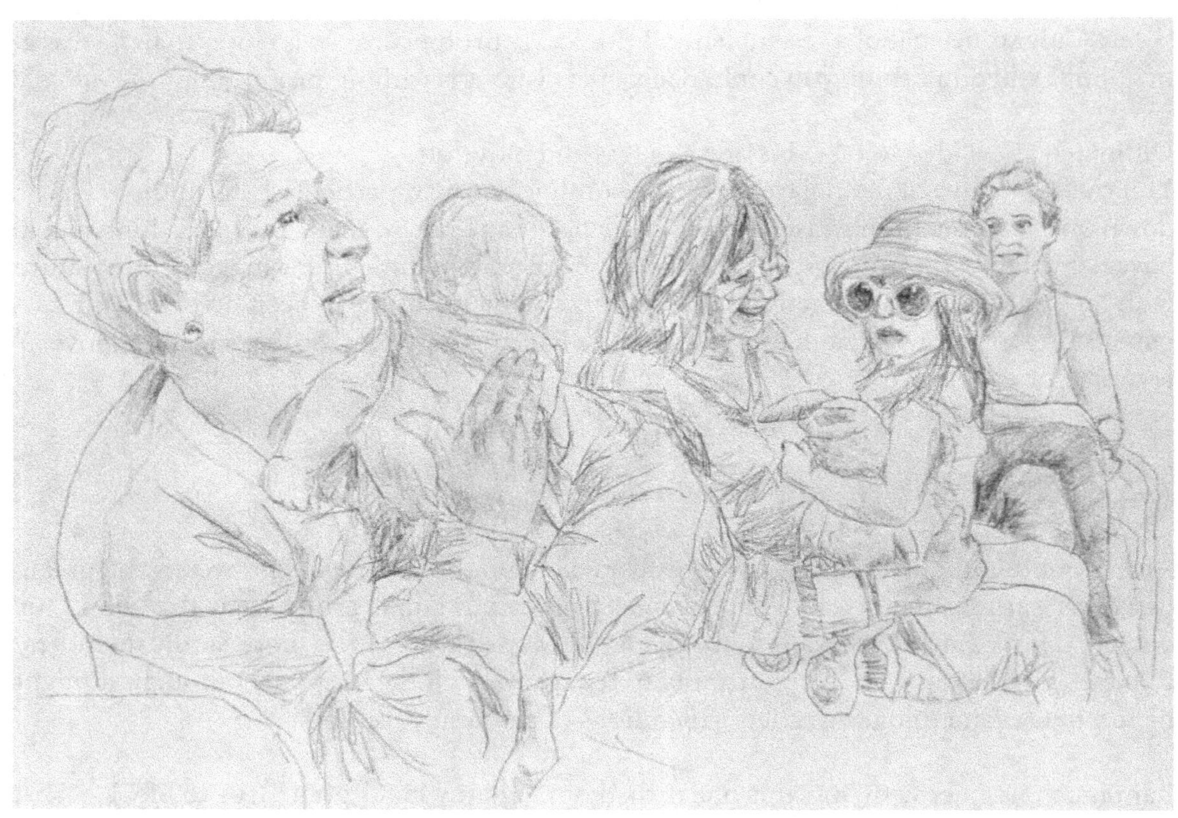

A group sketch featuring my kids, granny, mom, and sister.

If you're wondering what was going on in this scene, it was sort of chaotic. We had just brought the girls over to my mom's place, and my sister and Granny were already there. Our youngest was wiggling and grumbling about something (probably telling us off in baby talk for making her sit in her car seat), and Granny was trying to soothe her. While Granny patted her on the back, our oldest was trying to tell Nana (my mom) about something (probably about Mr. Bunny who she's holding) but was surprised by her sister's yelling. My mom watched all this in amusement, especially the oldest's reaction. Meanwhile, my sister is watching the show, possibly thinking, *"this baby is crazy, why is she yelling at us*?!"

WEDDING PRESENT

My last black and white sketch was done right around Christmas-time. We were fortunate to get to attend an additional event beyond the usual holiday get-togethers. My wife's close friend was getting married, and my wife and our oldest daughter got to be in the wedding. My wife and her friend met in high school, and they've been like family since. I decided to do a sketch of my wife's friend, son, and her husband and give to them as part of our wedding present. I say "part" because I honestly wasn't sure if it was good enough to stand alone, so I figured this could just be a little bonus add-on.

I never know how these sketches are going to go, and the most recent had been a mixed bag. There had been a few that turned out well, and then some that were decent sketches of people, but didn't have high fidelity to their real-life subjects. This one actually turned out pretty well, I think. To make it happen, I actually had to do a little social media creeping to find a picture. I don't think there is any other way I could have pulled off a surprise drawing otherwise. Fortunately, there were some good recent photos to choose from. The "recent" part I think was key, since kids grow and change so quickly.

When it came time to leave the gift, I realized I didn't have any experience giving away sketches, or really even showing them to anyone outside of my wife and via the website. I ended up being sort of nervous about the entire artwork situation. This was the beginning of another trend for me – a lack of confidence in my artistic abilities, and nervousness about sharing art. I'll discuss more about this later on, but I took several different approaches to try to address these feelings.

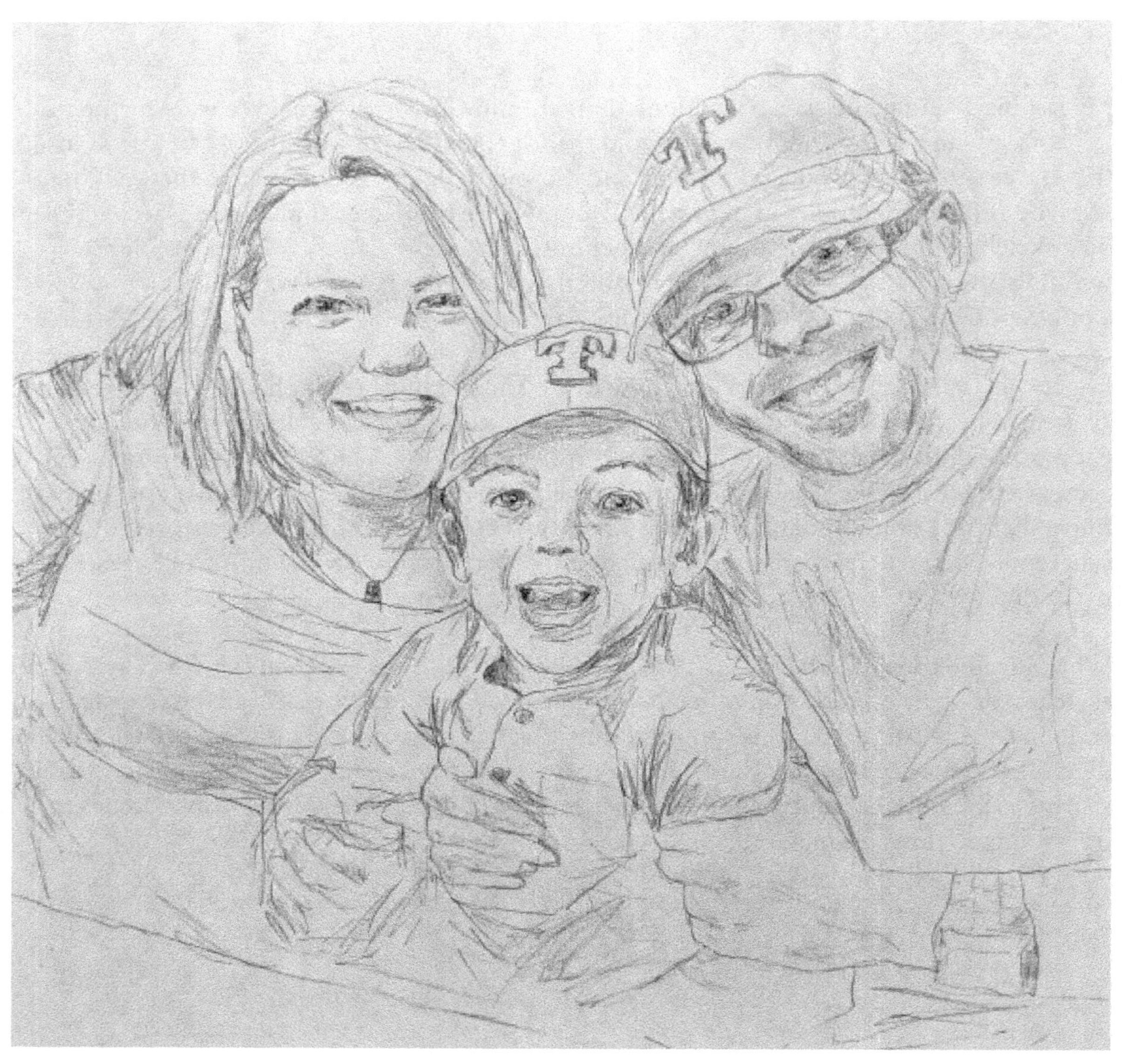

Wedding present for some friends.

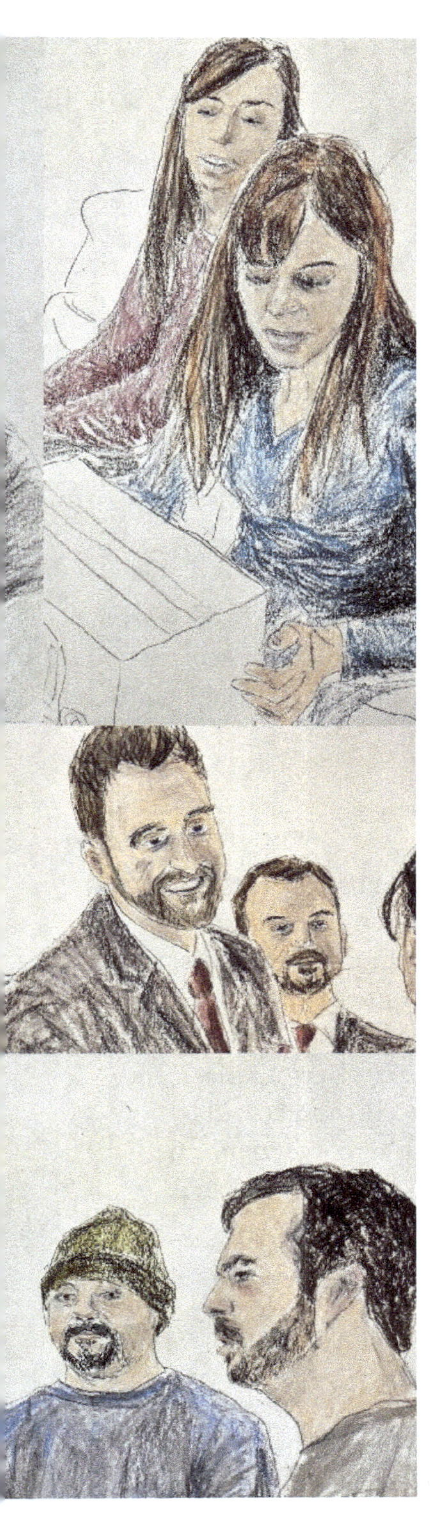

Phase 3 – Learning to Use Color

JANUARY 2018

In this chapter, I'm going to discuss a significant and surprising step taken at the beginning of 2018. After about four months of relatively consistent pencil drawing, I made the decision to try using color. I didn't know if I could even figure out how to do at all, let alone incorporate with any degree of skill. I'm not an adventurous artist, so in hindsight, I am actually sort of impressed I gave it a shot and stuck with it through the rough beginnings.

Colored pencils introduced some entirely new concepts that I had to learn, such as blending and color matching. I may have some degree of blue/green color blindness (undiagnosed). Or to be a bit less dramatic, I could at least say I'm just bad at distinguishing slight color differences. I still think I often get true-to-life color matching completely wrong, but I worry less about that now. More important is to use colors that work together and make sense in the overall scheme of a portrait – and that was another new thing to learn.

FIRST ATTEMPT AT ART WITH COLOR

Prior to 2018, I could almost count on one hand how many times I had used color in artwork. I have a couple of childhood doodles incorporating colored pens, pencils, or crayons. And I did one painting in high school which was probably required for a class. But certainly, as an adult, I hadn't branched out at all from my basic graphite pencil. Exploring other artists' websites through WordPress really opened my mind to it though. I saw amazing artists sharing paintings, sketches, and other mediums that exist beyond black and white; I wanted to create deeper and more vibrant art too. I was especially impressed by painters, especially some of the watercolor artists I'd seen. But having zero experience with paint, that seemed like a huge (and possibly messy) step. I decided to try colored pencils since that was, in theory, closer to what I already did.

As with deciding to start drawing again, this was another random idea followed by a quick decision. I found myself a little envious of the amazing color creations other artists create, realized I might be getting stagnant already, then made the move to purchase materials. I don't remember how long these thoughts rattled around in my brain, but it was probably all one session at the computer desk.

I did some research online, and it seemed like the biggest concern for colored pencils would be how easily they blend. Various sources recommended Prismacolor Premiers as a good balance between cost and quality, so that seemed like a good way to start. After some price shopping, I found what looked like a pretty decent deal on Amazon for 132 pack of Prismacolor pencils for $53. According to the box, these Prismacolor Premiers were *"artist quality"* with *"soft, thick cores to create a smooth, rich color laydown."* I've seen these things for a couple of bucks at retail stores, so that seemed like a bargain for so many.

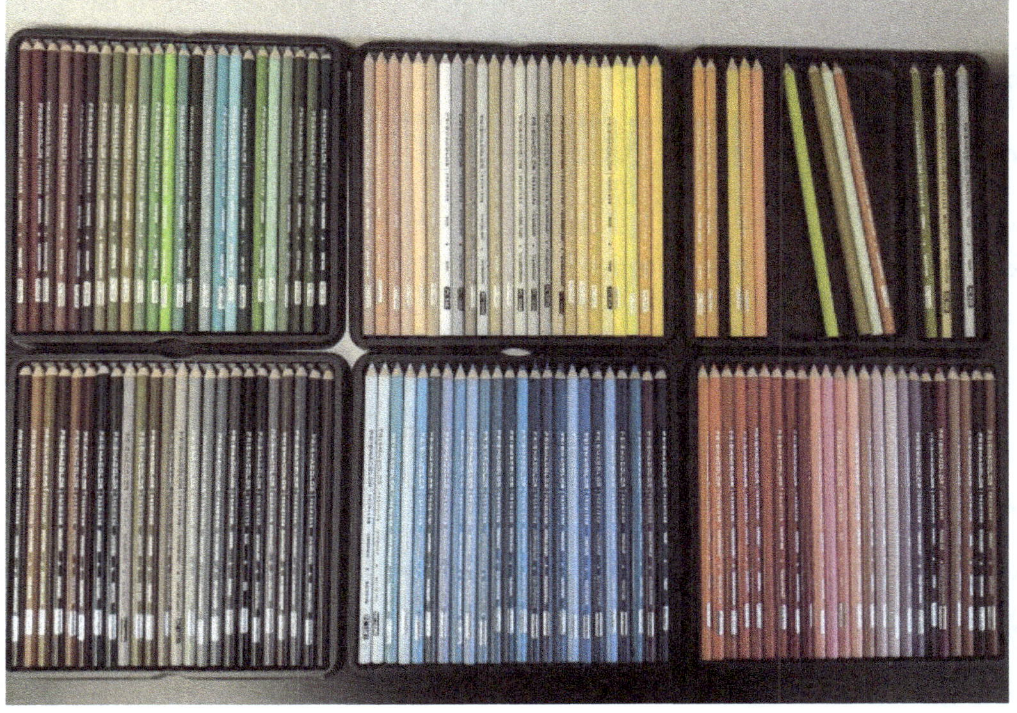

The first Prismacolor Premier set I purchased, which included an intimidatingly large variation of colors. Most of them actually never get used, but I'm glad to have the choices available.

The pencils came several days later in a really nice tin, and…well…there were SO MANY PENCILS. It was actually pretty overwhelming to open the tin and see so many options. After I started working with them, I wondered more than once if perhaps I should have gotten a smaller set. Eventually, I came to really appreciate having so many options. Most of the colors I received in this set actually never get used. But every so often, I'll need a very specific shade of something, and find myself glad I don't have to create it through blending other colors.

Now that I possessed this vast array of colored pencils, I had to decide what to use them on. The thought occurred to me that I could fill in color on some of my previous artwork. This was not actually a good idea, but I had no clue what I was doing. First, I went back to a scene featuring me, my wife, and our two little ones. Before jumping in, I watched a few online videos to get a feel for how others utilize colored pencils. I came across artists creating incredibly lifelike portraits using the same pencils I purchased; not to say could reach those heights any time soon, but I was inspired nonetheless. I picked up a few great tips from these videos, the most important of which was how to blend colors using white. It would ultimately take me months to figure out how to effectively use white to burnish (blend colors smoothly), but it was certainly an important first step to learn the technique exists!

I had a few takeaways from this experiment. The first is that working with color is very difficult. It's basically an entirely new ball game, and would possibly be an even bigger adjustment than I initially thought. It's also more time-consuming than simple graphite, requiring extra patience to lay down the right color combinations. For a relatively basic graphite sketch, I was used to knocking it out in an hour or two. But in the beginning, applying color required much more focus.

I tried to fill in three older sketches with color. I'll be frank; they were really terrible. For the first time dealing with color blending and matching, it might be the best I could have hoped for. I struggled to select the right colors, and I think I botched the coloring around everyone's mouths. Also, some skin coloring around the eyes ended up making us look really tired. I also took for granted that people have many different colors represented in their skin.

But inexperience wasn't the only problem; trying to replace graphite shading with colors just doesn't work. The color plays poorly with graphite. In fact, I completely ruined one of the sketches I tried this with; the black and white definition was eliminated, and the paper became completely saturated with colored pencil wax. I learned over time that colored pencils can work with a very light and basic graphite outline, but any more than that will cause issues.

Another lesson I learned was that I should have used scrap paper to test colors. In the videos I watched of expert pencil artists, they each used a piece of paper as a color palette similar to a painter. Artists scribble a little color to get a feel for the right tones, comparing some side-by-side as needed. I did not do that for these first attempts, which was a mistake. There were several instances in which I applied the color right away and immediately regretted my choice. I'm not sure why I didn't use a scrap paper-based color palette to begin with because every video I saw showed artists using one.

ROUND TWO WITH COLOR

Now that I had a couple of poor trials under my belt, I decided to start fresh. It was time to do a completely new drawing with color. Taking some of the lessons learned from earlier attempts, I focused on keeping the graphite pencil portion very basic. The plan was to keep it to no more than the most basic outline, and the depth and shading would come exclusively from the colored pencils.

For this sketch, I thought it would be fun to try one with my youngest and me. I hadn't done one with just the two of us yet, so I thought that would be a fun one. The challenge with her at that age was that she rarely smiled for photos, which can be difficult to implement when you're still learning and accustomed to drawing smiles. She smiles much more now, but around the age of 12 months, once she saw a camera pointed at her she always got really serious.

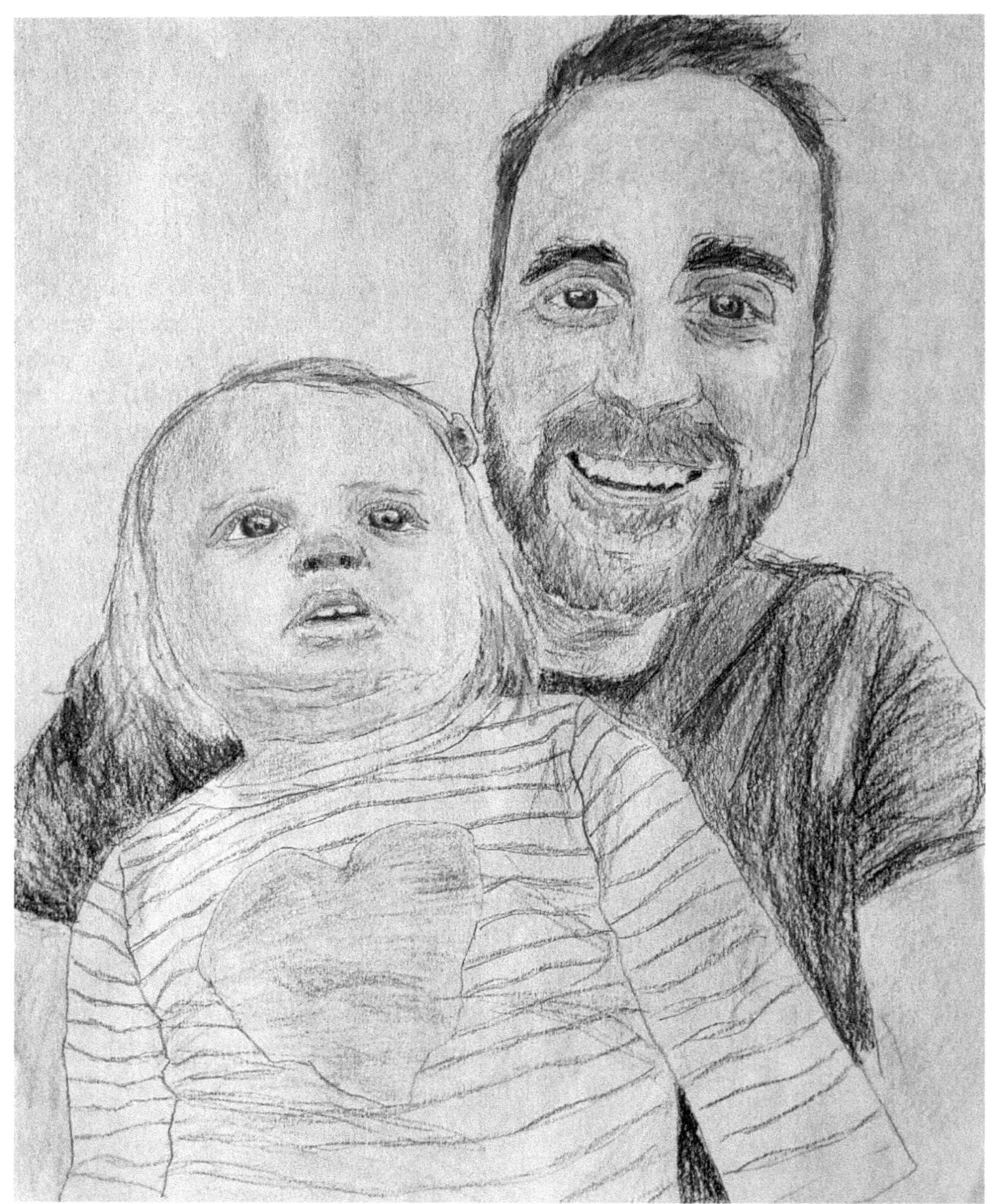

The first fresh color portrait I attempted. Me with my dramatically posed youngest daughter.

This was a much better result than the first attempts. Although it still needs work, I could already see some improvement in my color selection and blending. And it definitely worked better without all of that extra graphite interfering with the wax material from the colored pencils. Overall, these skin tones could have certainly used additional pink and possibly peach variants. Also, the outline probably wasn't perfect; although I do have a long face, I may have distorted it a bit too far here. In hindsight, the biggest issue was clearly my very passive and reluctant blending. I would eventually learn to layer colors and burnish much more heavily, but I would have to put some work in to figure that out. For now, though, this was an encouraging improvement.

SNOW DAY IN LOUISIANA

To my amazement, we actually had a real snow event in Louisiana at the beginning of 2018. We had about 2-3 inches of actual snow, and it was even cold enough that it didn't melt immediately. Although my wife would disagree, it was a nice change of pace from the winters we had seen in our first couple of years in the state. We had previously lived in Northern Virginia for a few years and got to experience true seasons, including winters with actual winter weather. Although it can be inconvenient, I thought the mid-Atlantic region's snow levels were just about where I liked it; some periodic events, but not too many that it becomes a drag. Anyway, it was fun to see our neighborhood covered in snow.

Fortunately, our oldest was also finally old enough to go outside and experience this oddity. She and I wandered around close to the house, and the look on her face was absolutely priceless. It was amazement and extreme joy written all over her face, and it was great to be able to watch her reactions. She had a huge grin plastered to her face the entire time we were outside. I wish our youngest could have joined us, especially considering it didn't snow at all the next year, but she was still too little for 20-degree weather. Such a unique event seemed like a perfect opportunity to draw something.

I initially considered trying to draw the snowflakes flying through the air and on our coats/hats. Eventually, I came back to reality, and realized at that point I lacked the skill and precise hand to depict snow. I figured, "maybe someday, with practice, but definitely not with my current skill set." The main objective was to capture my daughter's pure joy, and I think I was able to do that for the most part.

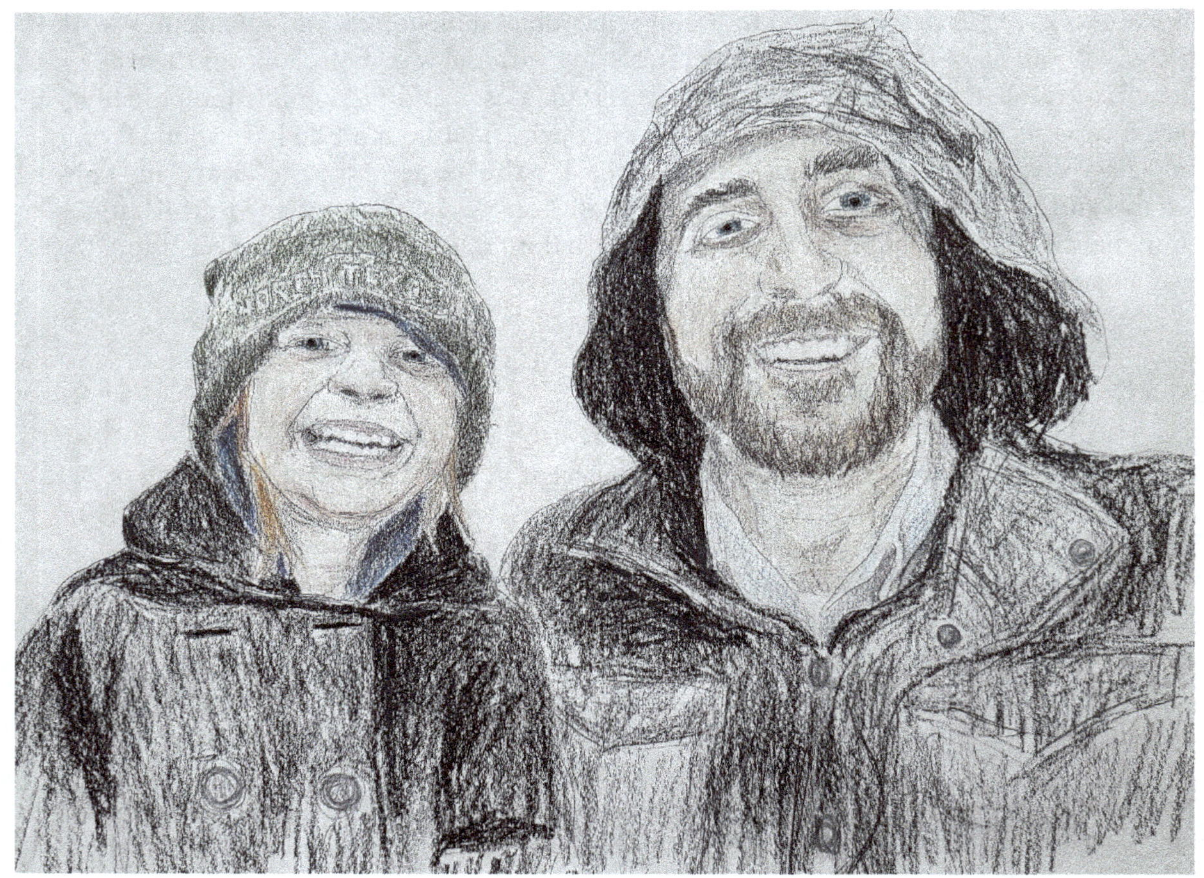

The second color portrait I tried. A snow scene with me and my oldest daughter.

A couple of failures on this one though; my mouth ended up being extremely crooked and out of place. It's sort of crooked in real life, but this was probably too far. It didn't seem like it was when I was drawing, but looking at the end result, it sort of looks hilarious. I think if I had used a grid on this it might have been better. This drawing also provided more evidence of my need to be more aggressive with pressure on these pencils. At the time, I thought it was just related to using black and dark gray colored pencils. I knew that I'd seen other artists achieve a very smooth coloring and that I wanted to emulate the effect, but I couldn't figure out how to get there yet.

I actually prefer the phase of this drawing prior to filling in the darker portions of our clothes. I think because black is naturally more noticeable, the poor job of burnishing I did may have been less noticeable with just the faces colored. Immediately after finishing, I considered whether it might have looked better if I had bypassed the black, and instead just minimally colored the clothing with a lighter color. Of course, I was missing the point entirely of what I needed to address.

As an added bonus, I wanted to include another fun progression of this sketch. For my own entertainment, sometimes as I'm filling in color around the eye, I'll just fill in the pupil. It conveys a zombie-like look to the subjects and makes me laugh every time. This was the first time I'd ever done this but definitely wasn't the last. In this case, the zombie effect also transformed the smiles a bit, from what looked like genuine happiness in the final version into a sort of wicked villain's laugh.

MORE REALISM IN FAMILY PORTRAITS

At this point in my return to drawing, I had done four total sketches of my wife. At that point, I really don't think I had quite captured her accurately. Years ago, I did one of me and her together while we were dating. I also did a sketch of her I used for my marriage proposal; it was basically my wife holding out her hand with a ring on it. I surprised her with the drawing, then while she was trying to figure out what I was up to, I went to one knee with the real ring. Both of these sketches were decent and looked like her, but neither was exactly a Rembrandt in terms of realism. My next goal was to push towards more realistic portrayals of people, particularly my wife.

It's sort of an interesting phenomenon; I've found that it's deceptively challenging to sketch the ones you love the most. I'm not sure why that's the case. Could it be self-imposed pressure? When I'm drawing my wife or our kids, I sometimes find myself thinking, "easy does it, don't mess up this line." It's like when the subject is more important, I get too focused on doing it right, and it doesn't come together. I've learned many times over when it comes to drawing; loose and easy are good. The sketches I just jump into and let flow usually seem to work out the best. Being rigid and hyper-vigilant seems to always negatively impact things for me.

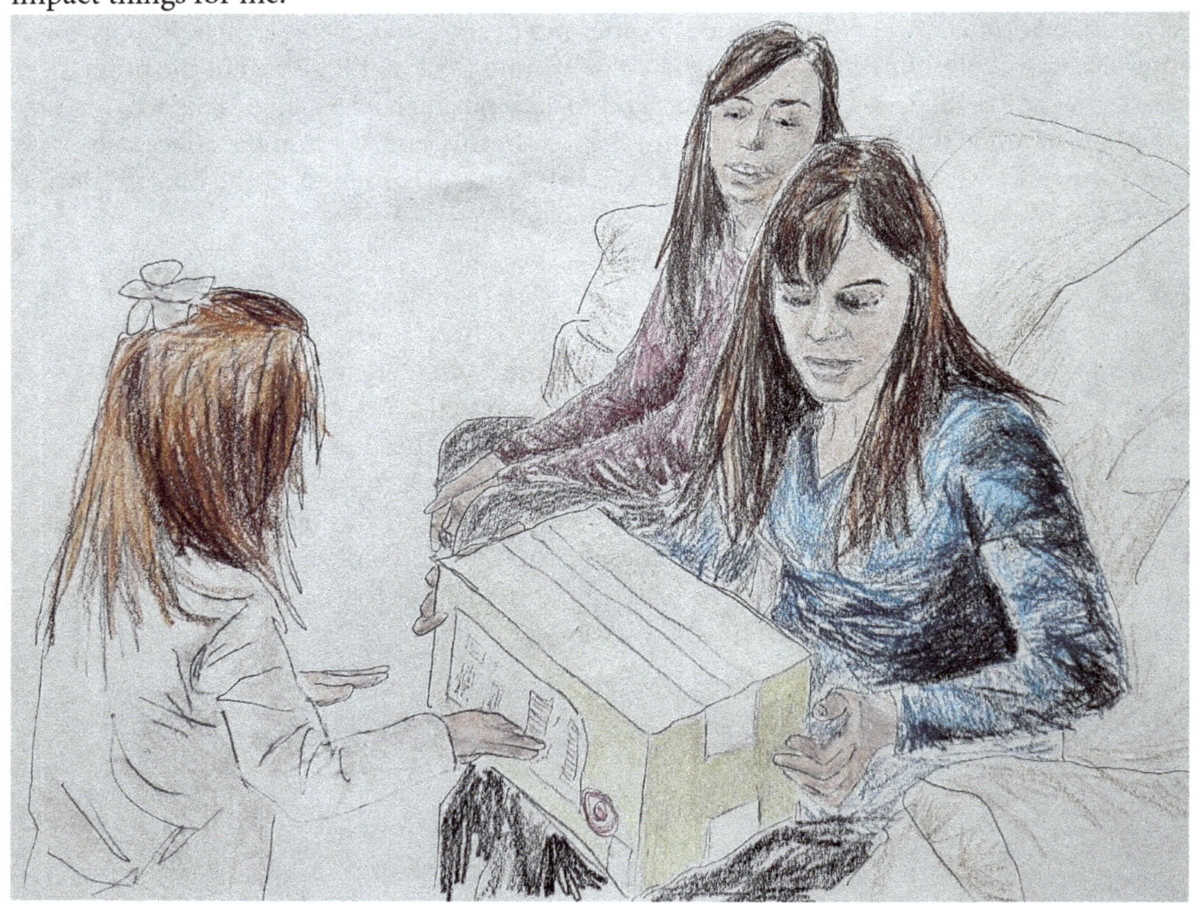

My wife opening a package for our oldest daughter, with my sister-in-law in the background.

For the next couple of sketches, I did some brainstorming and came up with two scenes to work on featuring my wife. The first of these involves my wife, her sister, and our oldest kid. In this one, my wife is helping her open a package, while her sister watches. I tried to stay loose, and part of that was compelling myself to move faster. I think you can see byproducts of going possibly too fast in how the box looks; the lines are not even close to straight. Interestingly enough though, the overall piece works well despite some sloppiness.

My wife and her sister both look fairly true to life. In some ways, this sketch of my wife was a cop-out, because she's not even looking up. So, it was a small step towards better realism, because it was the easiest possible facial position. In terms of color use though, this drawing represents important progression because it's the first time I see noticeably aggressive blending in the subjects' faces. I went for a heavy burnish for skin color, and I think it turned out well. I was still hesitant about blending the clothes, but it still represents noticeable progress from where I started with color.

If the last step was a small one for realism, the next drawing I hoped would be a bigger one. In this one, I went for a close-up drawing of my wife and our two kids. Basically, this was an attempt at a closed-in view with all faces mostly forward. In other words, no hiding behind downturned faces as with the previous one. I wasn't explicitly focused on it, but I also continued forward with my efforts to blend more heavily. This time, I applied thicker layers to more than just skin; I can see progress in the hair and clothes to some extent.

It turned into a pretty funny scene, but that was actually unintentional. When I started out, I was really going for my wife and our oldest smiling, with our youngest being her serious self as usual. As I progressed, my wife's expression changed to a kind of wry humor at our oldest's reaction. And the oldest kid went from a normal smile to either a forced smile, a toddler's discomfort with being bothered, or a mischievous look. As the expressions shifted, I didn't fight it at all because I thought it was an interesting direction.

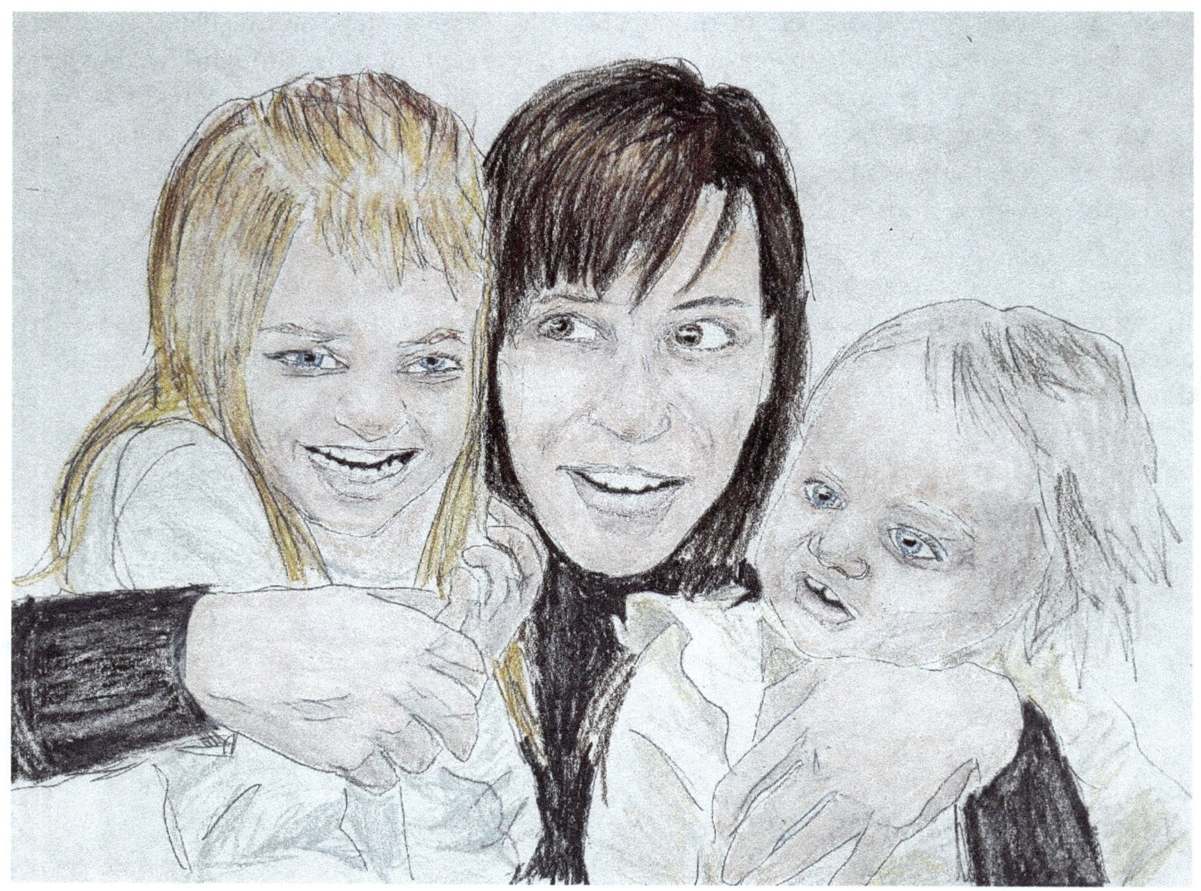

An attempt at some facial expression variety with my wife and two daughters.

HOMETOWN SERIES

I grew up in North Texas, and have been away from home for quite a while. I've elsewhere for almost a decade, which is sort of jolting to think about. That area will always be home to me, and I miss living there. Part of that is just the sense of familiarity that comes with being there, but most of that feeling is because of the people; the family and friends that I spent so much time with. At some point, when I was feeling especially nostalgic, I got into my head that it would be fun to work on a few scenes featuring people from the hometown. I had already drawn many family members and would do so again soon, but I thought it might be fun to use some friends as subjects.

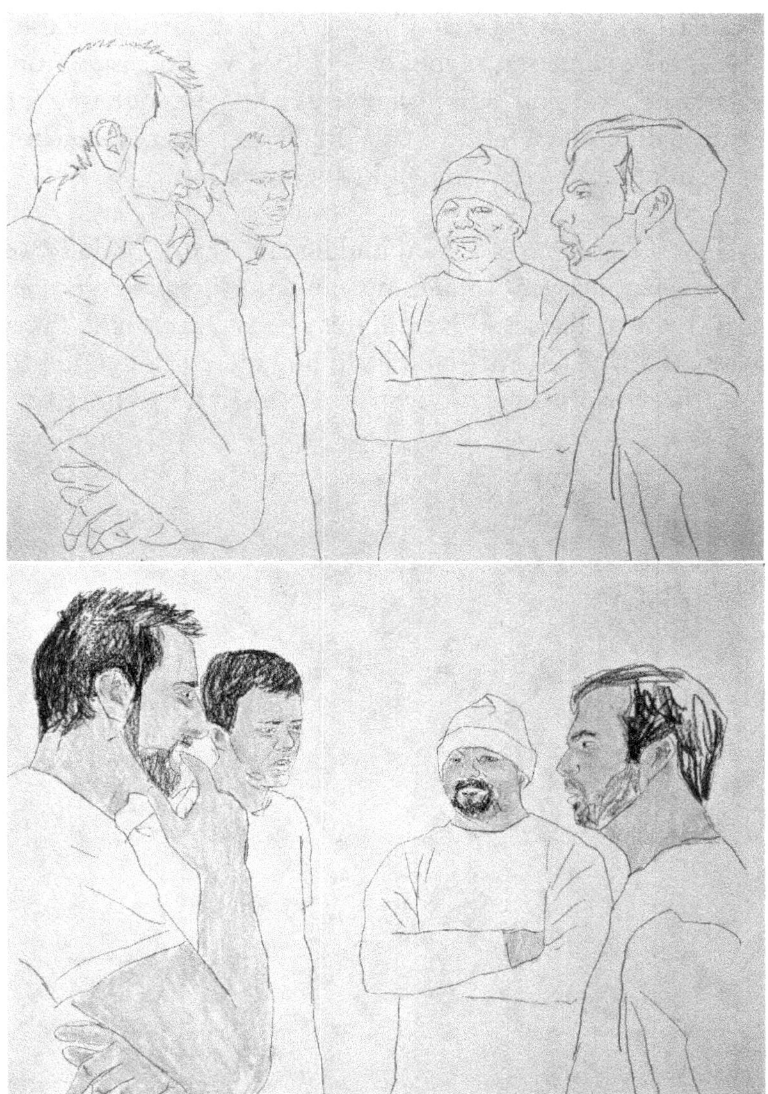

Early progressions of some hometown friends. This was one of our highly strategic football huddles. It was probably less to set up a play and more to catch our breath so we didn't pass out.

I spent a good chunk of my early adulthood hanging out with a great group of people. I had a blast with this crew, and have great memories of all the typical "hey we're finally adults let's have some fun"-types of activities we did. Aside from playing pool, going to our favorite local pub, and just generally hanging out, one fun thing was that we used to play football on the weekends. We didn't do it every weekend, but when we had enough people, we often tried to get something going.

Here's a drawing of a team huddle during one of these weekend games. I imagine the conversation went something along the lines of, "okay, everyone run around like crazy until everyone collapses." Overall, this one is pretty solid. Everyone depicted in the scene looks essentially like themselves, including me. Although in hindsight I think it turned out well, during the process I did feel like I messed it up about halfway through.

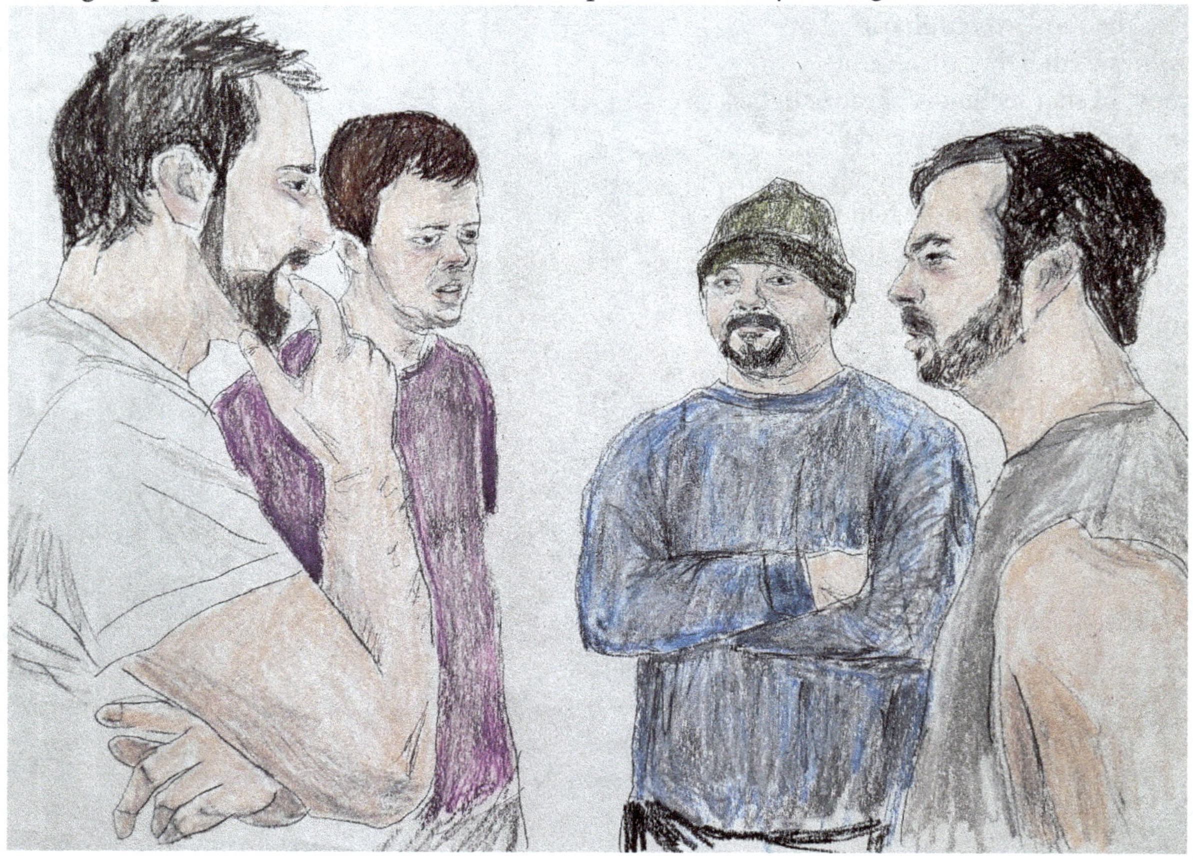

I decided to make this into a full series, with each sketch featuring a few different people (with some overlap). I considered trying one consolidated scene, but it seemed like a fairly daunting task and one that might ultimately be less interesting than multiple portraits. Eventually, this turned into four separate drawings that all worked out well to varying degrees. The continued effort to blend more completely showed dividends throughout, and I saw further improvement as I progressed with the series.

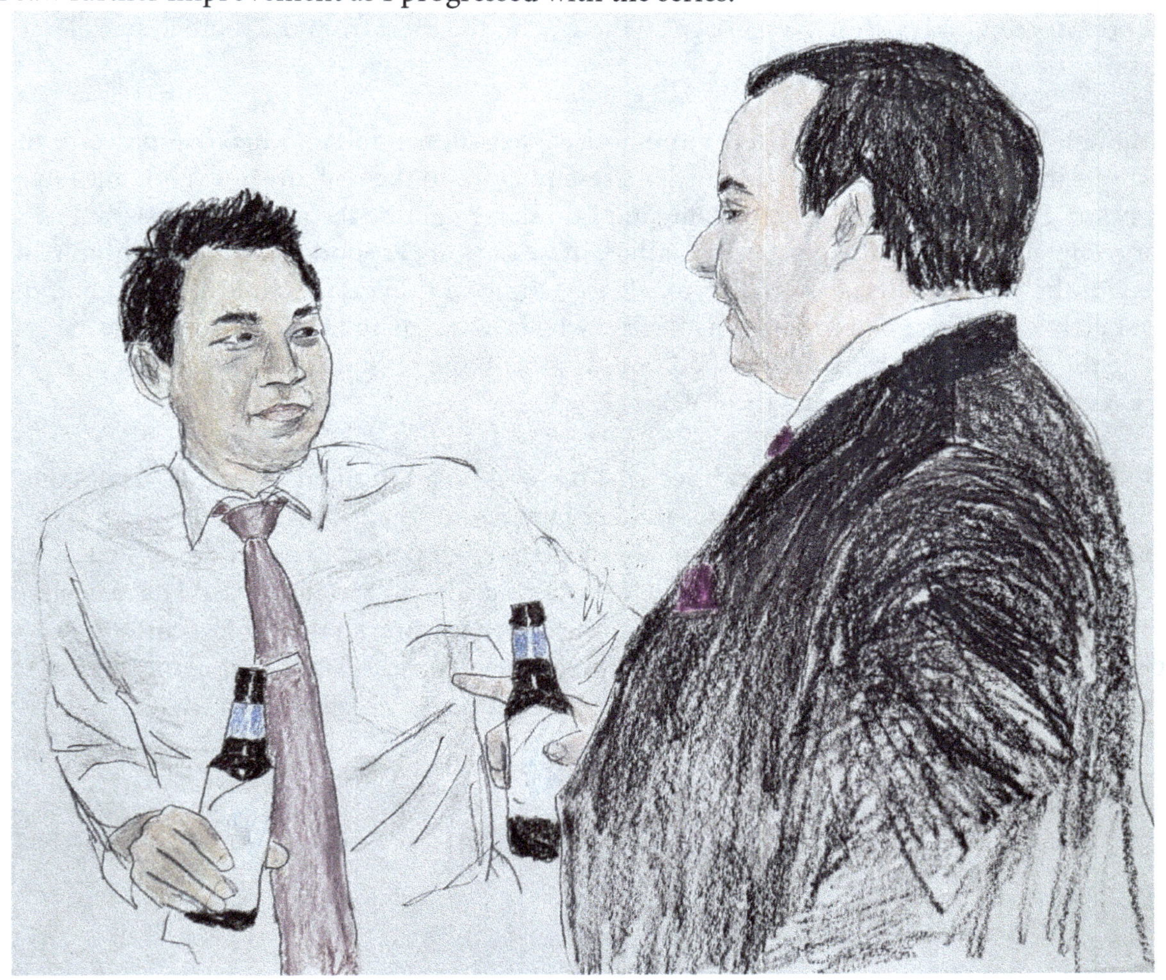

Some distinguished gentlemen chatting, probably about country clubs or the Stock Market.

All of these scenes feel like they weren't very long ago, but we're getting close to measuring that time period in terms of decades instead of just years. Part two features a couple of the guys chatting about something sophisticated if their clothes are any indication. As with the other sketches, I won't include actual names, but the guy on the left also lives elsewhere in the country nowadays. You may recognize the guy on the right from the football huddle sketch.

Although I like this one, it has a few more noticeable issues and flaws when compared to the first one in this series. Left-side buddy has a resemblance to the real guy but is not entirely on point. Something is not exactly right, and I think it might be the mouth/chin area. I'm not completely sold on the perspective either; these guys are around the same height in real life, but the viewing angle I was going for skewed things. I think it's technically sound on the perspective, but first glance makes me think, "why is he so much taller?" Also, I believe I made the suit coat too big or too puffed out the guy on the right. I was going for an open jacket effect, but it doesn't pass the eye test.

For the next sketch, I decided to try a scene at my wedding. I thought I could do a cool one that features my groomsmen, my wife, and her father, with me taking her hand. Unfortunately, this is possibly one of the worst-planned drawings I've ever done. This clearly would have been a great candidate for using a grid, and certainly would have been worth trying on larger paper. I didn't even come close to fitting all the subjects into the space. My wife is barely in it, and her dad is out of the picture, as is the best man. I'm not really sure what I was doing here, but the scene is completely different than what I imagined.

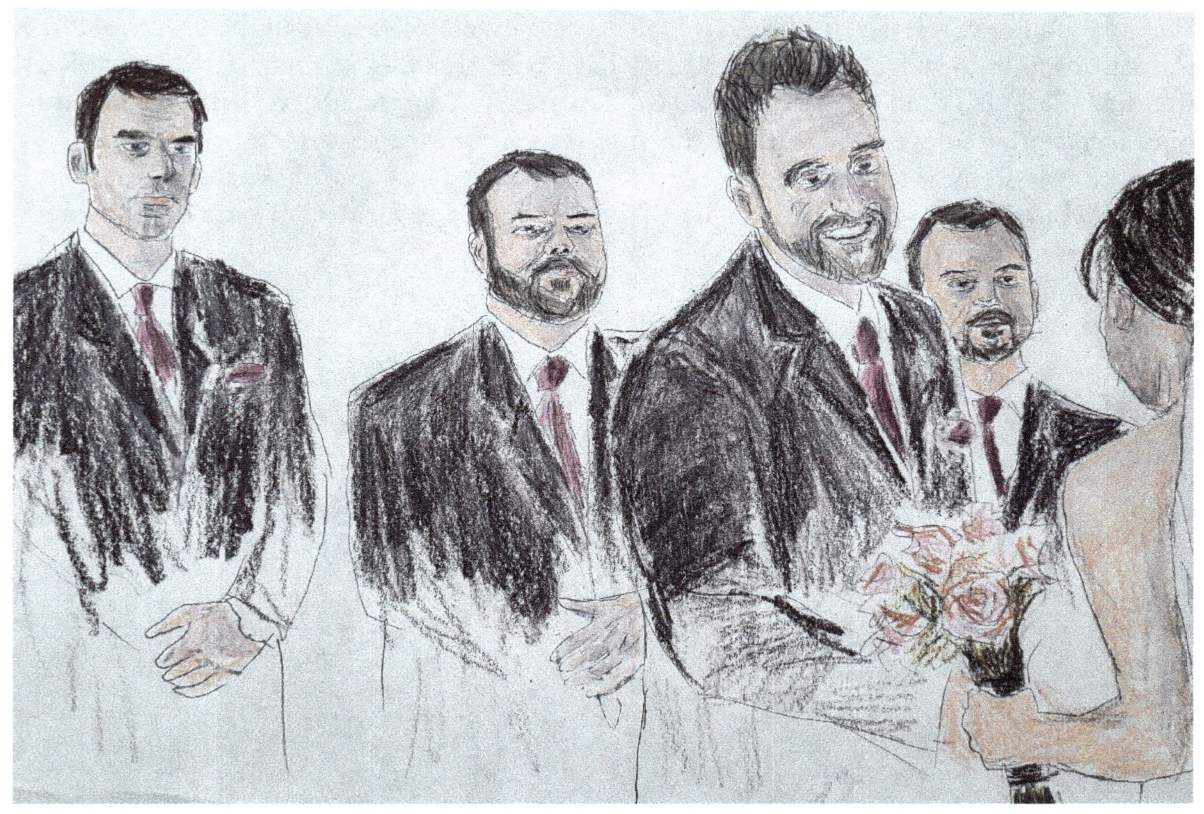

Groomsmen from my wedding. I'm not sure why I didn't finish it. I think I was frustrated because I planned so poorly; my wife and one groomsman are cut off.

Interestingly enough though, the sketch itself isn't too bad. I didn't really finish it though, because I was frustrated with my poor planning. Not what I had in mind, but still decent enough for an unfinished collection of floating heads in disappearing suits. The guys' faces are somewhat well represented at least. In a way, this sketch served as a good reminder of how much I still had to learn, and how far off I was from some of the professional-level portrait artists I've seen.

The final hometown series drawing is one that I actually started earlier in the process, and for reasons unknown, tabled for a bit. It may have been because I wanted to do the previous wedding piece that didn't work out…once that flamed out spectacularly, I went back to this one. That's often how drawings go for me; my art attention span is sometimes short, so sometimes fresh ideas leapfrog current projects. Basically, I just go with whatever I'm compelled to do, and sometimes rough outlines get moved to forward or backward in line for now particular reason than a random whim.

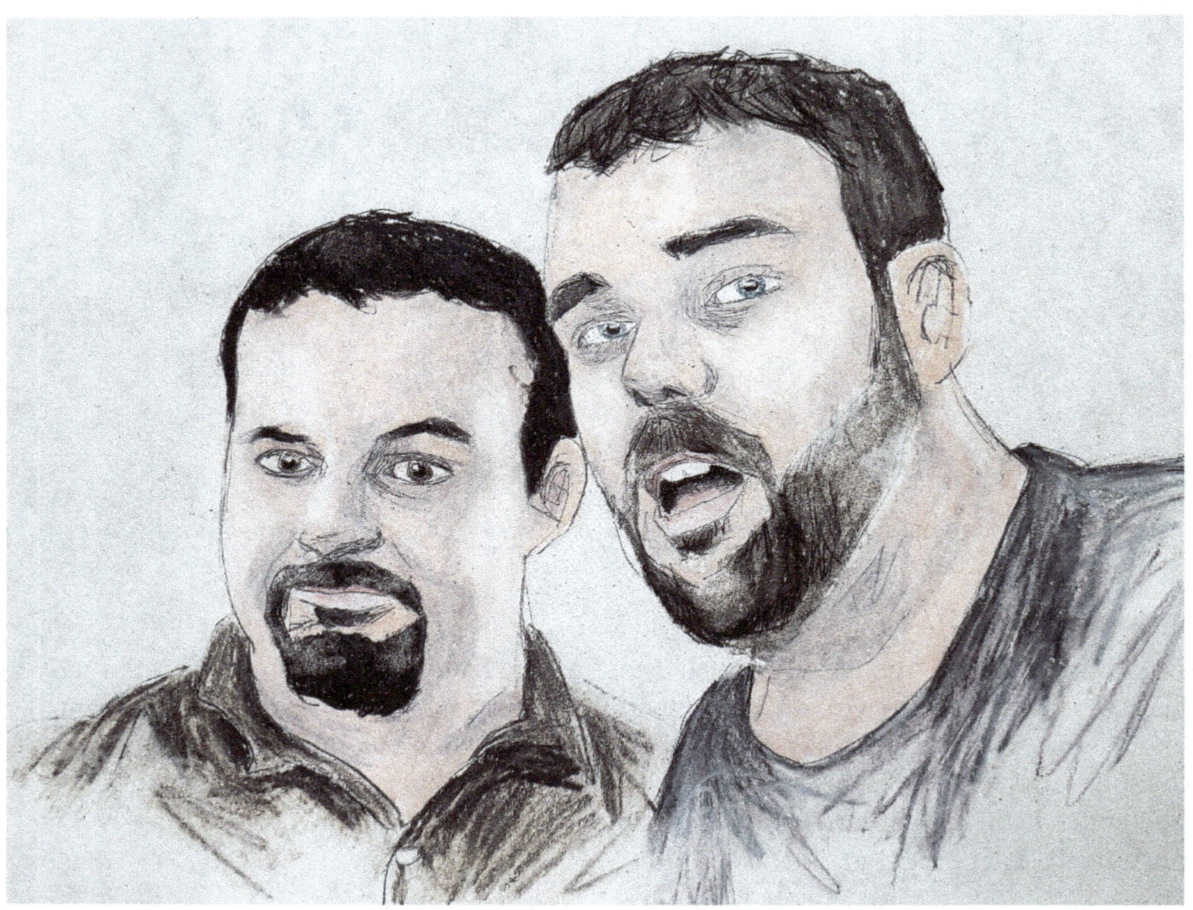

A couple of fellows with black and brown themes going.

The finale turned out pretty well overall. It does look like both of these guys. And I like the theme I went with; black hair/brown shirt, brown hair/black shirt. The only major mistake I made came from a new technique I attempted. There was some bright indoor light, and it was very skin-reflective. I wanted to depict that light, so I tried some light erasing after everything was finished, then re-burnished using white. It worked…but a little too well, and was brighter than I intended. This is a technique that I would continue to use and refine, so it's a good step in the process.

This also marks my best effort of blending to date and what is an important transition into something we'll talk about in depth in the next chapter. It's a colored pencil burnishing and layering method sometimes referred to as "pencil painting." I've read and heard the term fairly often in my research on colored pencil artwork, so it must be a somewhat common technique. Unfortunately, I have little formal training as an artist, so if it's a commonly taught concept in art schools, I wouldn't have a clue.

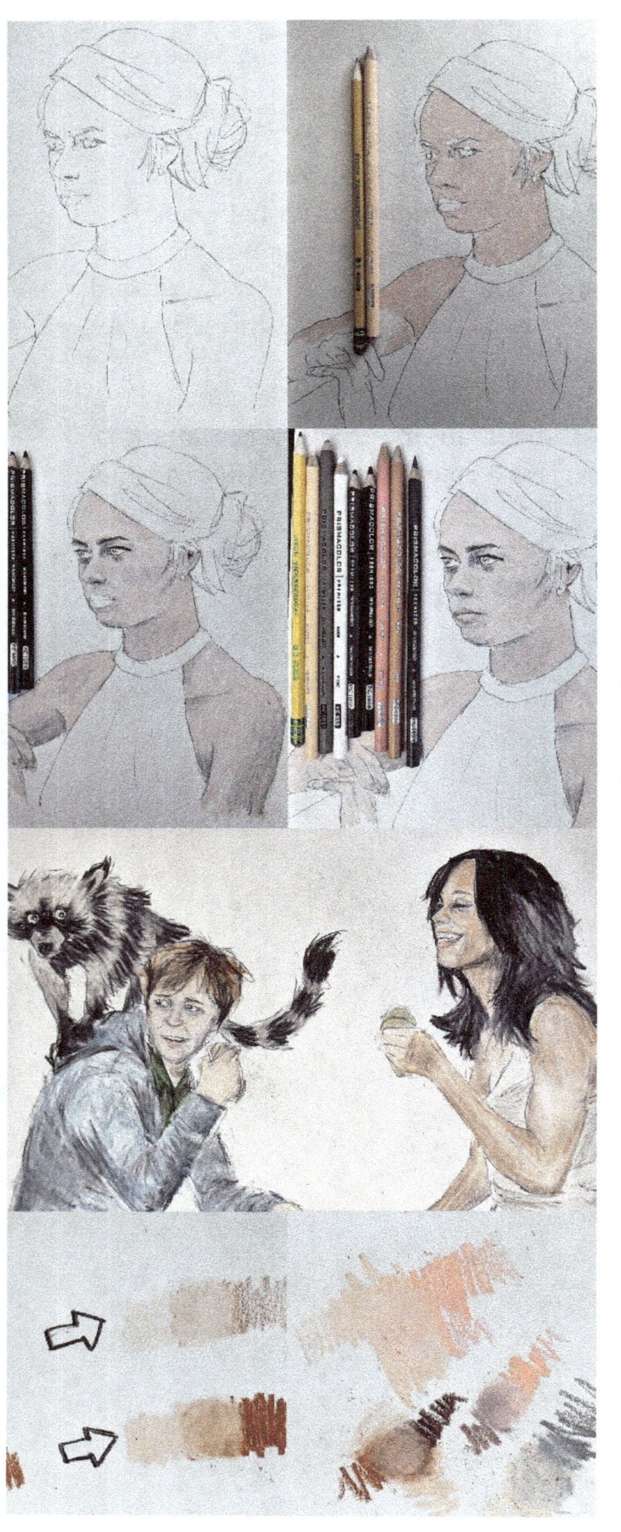

Process Notes –
Pencil Painting

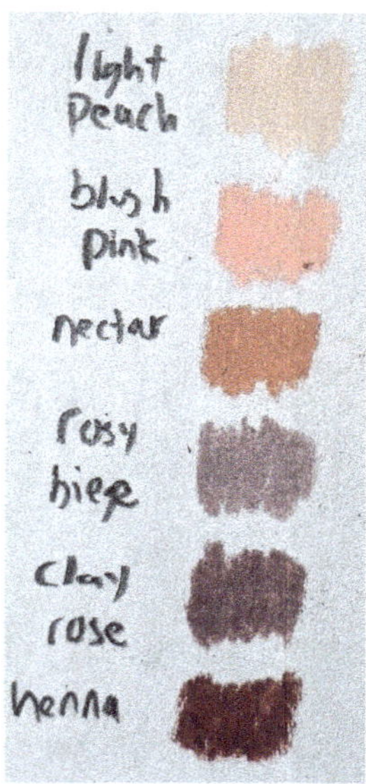

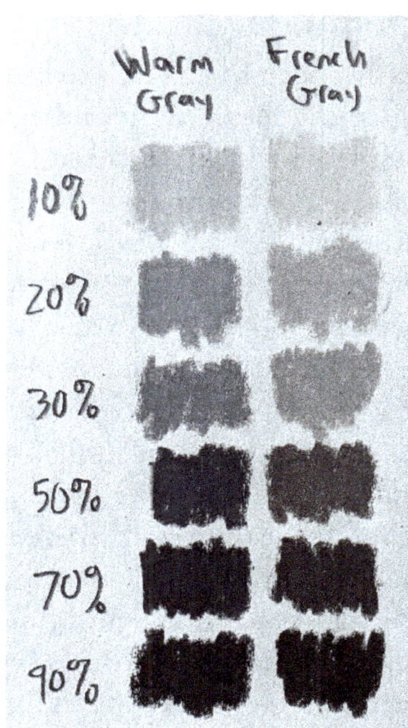

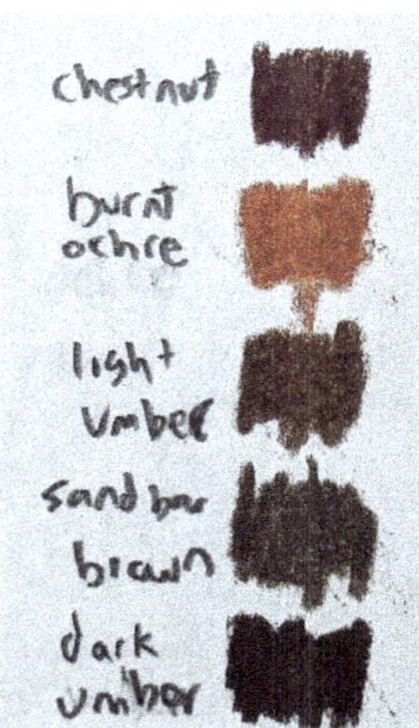

As I became more comfortable working with colored pencils, I started experimenting with more aggressive blending. One of the selling points Prismacolor Premier sets was how smoothly they can blend, and my lighter almost hesitant coloring wasn't bringing that out. It seemed clear that my drawings looked incomplete and like the work of a novice, and I suspected more confident layering might help. I also continued researching how other artists use colored pencils, learning quite a bit from artist sites on WordPress and YouTube channels.

Eventually, this experimentation, practice, and studying trifecta led me to something we'll refer to in this book as "colored pencil painting." Before I go further in this description, I should caveat: As I've said already in this book, I am not an expert when it comes to art. I try my best to accurately describe techniques and aspects of drawing, but it's possible I may not use the best technical term at some point. Hopefully, that doesn't happen at all in this book...but it could. So, my apologies if my language is not as precise as a trained artist's would be.

A selection of my most used colors. Gray variants are on the right, pink and brown hues on the left.

Now, back to this colored pencil painting idea. I'm not talking about using paints with colored pencils or putting paint on a pencil, or anything like that. For my purposes, this refers to layering colored pencil very thickly until the tooth (surface texture) of the paper is gone. Another word I've heard used is for this type of layered blending is "burnishing." Burnishing until the paper's tooth is gone essentially means that in the final state, there is no surface left for additional color to grip onto the paper. The end result of this type of colored pencil painting is that the artwork looks very much like a painting, rather than the sketchy, brushed look pencil otherwise leaves.

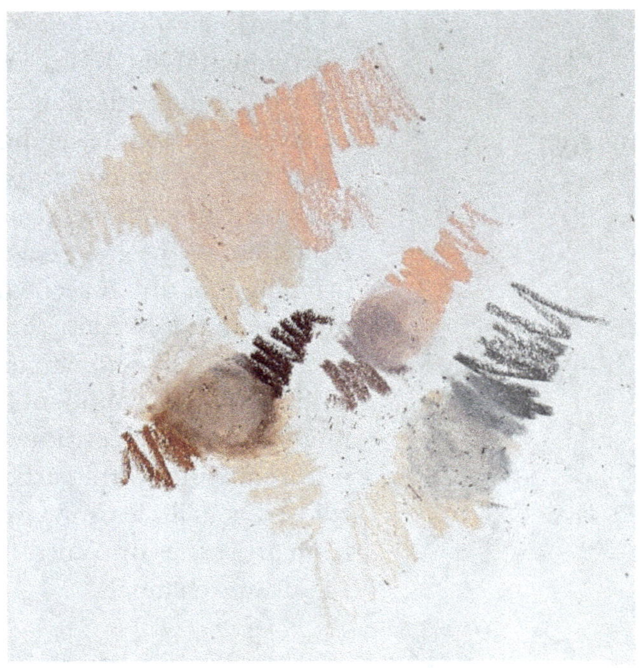

A few rough burnishing examples using white to blend various color combinations.

In this chapter, I am going to take a detour from the progression-based discussion. I want to provide an outline of the overall process I use for colored pencil painting. Although I believe the quality of my artwork has improved between early 2018 and now, the basic process has actually remained fairly consistent.

First, let's talk supplies. I've tried a few different brands of pencils on the economical end of the scale, but my favorite right now Prismacolor Premier. I like the soft cores that allow for smoother blending than some others I've tried. It seems like the higher quality pencils achieve a better paint-like effect from burnishing and blend more effortlessly, but I don't have enough experience with top-end products to say that definitively. Prismacolor Premiers have the right combination of price and functionality for my use. A few artists have recommended trying Caran d'Ache Luminance, but unfortunately, they are out of my price range at this point. Anecdotally, it seems like artists I've come across who create extremely life-like skin textures from pencils often mention using Luminance.

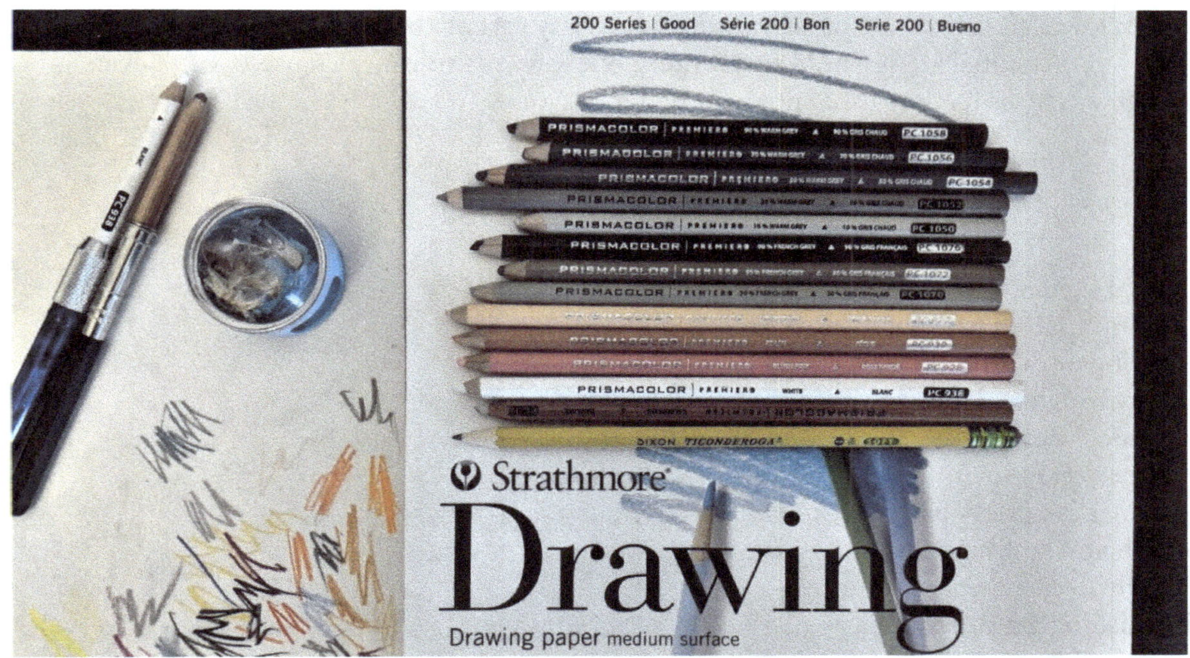

My go-to kit of art supplies. Relatively inexpensive, but the quality is solid: Strathmore medium surface paper, Dixon Ticonderoga soft lead pencil, sharpener, generic pencil extenders, scratch paper for color testing, and Prismacolor Premier colored pencils (Colorless, White, Light Peach, Peach, Blush Pink, Warm Gray Set (30%, 50%, 70%, 90%), French Gray Set (10%, 30%, 50%, 90%). I also pretty frequently use Chestnut, Burnt Ochre, Light Umber, Henna, and Clay Rose.

For quite a while, I carried on drawing, coloring, and learning; my usual process was to work on a portrait, take photographs a few times to show how the work progressed, then share the experience on my website. I didn't give much thought to discussing technical aspects like the type of pencil, exact color name/number, and so forth. Finally, in May 2018 I wrote about that flow after some comments from curious folks wanting to hear a bit more detail. I did a portrait specifically to show the materials I used as I went along.

I am a creature of habit, so while I've tweaked and adapted to some extent, I still use the same flow. I'm definitely not advocating this as any sort of "best practice" or anything; in fact, a professional artist would surely point out ways my routine is flawed I can't even imagine. This is just my usual flow, for better or worse.

First, I sketch just the bare minimum lines without any shading or definition. This is a very rough and basic outline. I don't worry if it's not perfect (sometimes my outlines are pretty bad). The depth and realism will come together once the layers and burnishing getting rolling. This outline actually serves a similar function to what the measured grids once did; essentially to keep the art train on the tracks. I should probably lean on this crutch less actually because some outlined features don't exist as clean lines in real life (shadows and form of the nose, lip transition, etc.)

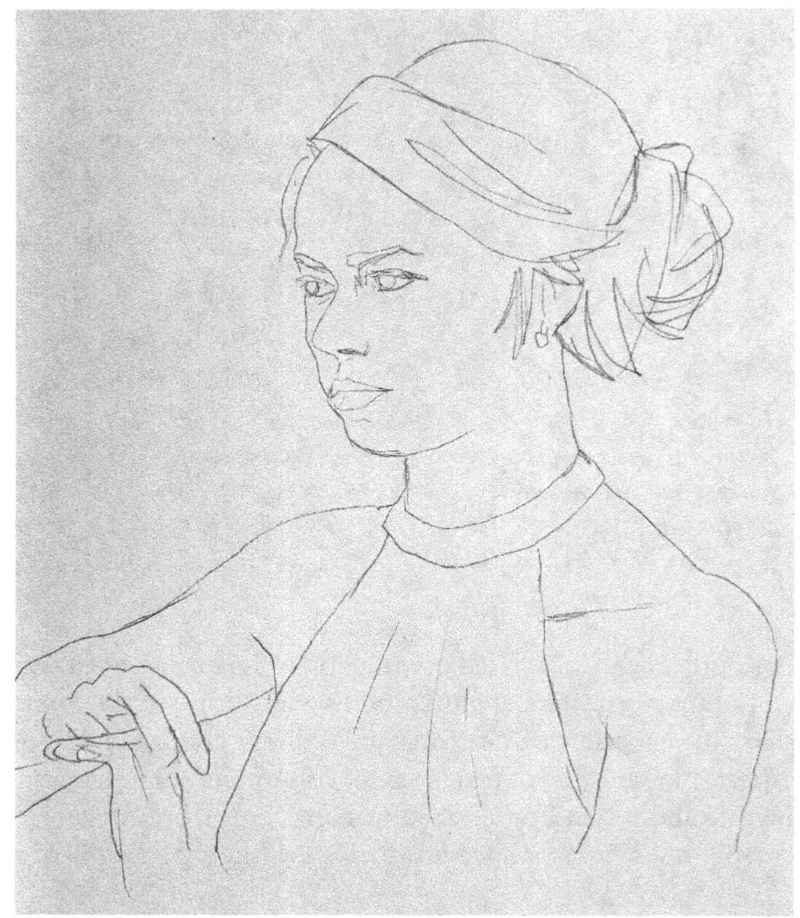

Step 1 is to draw an outline using a graphite pencil.

The second step is an indicator of my amateur status and is probably where I start to significantly diverge from actual professionals. I think the most important decision in colored pencil painting is when to burnish; once you start the heavy layering and blending, you will soon lose the paper's tooth. If there is no more paper material to grip the colored pencil wax, you are pretty much done adding new color. Most experts that I've read or watched online seem to burnish very late in the game. They lightly apply layers of various colors they need to blend, then the final move is to heavily blend

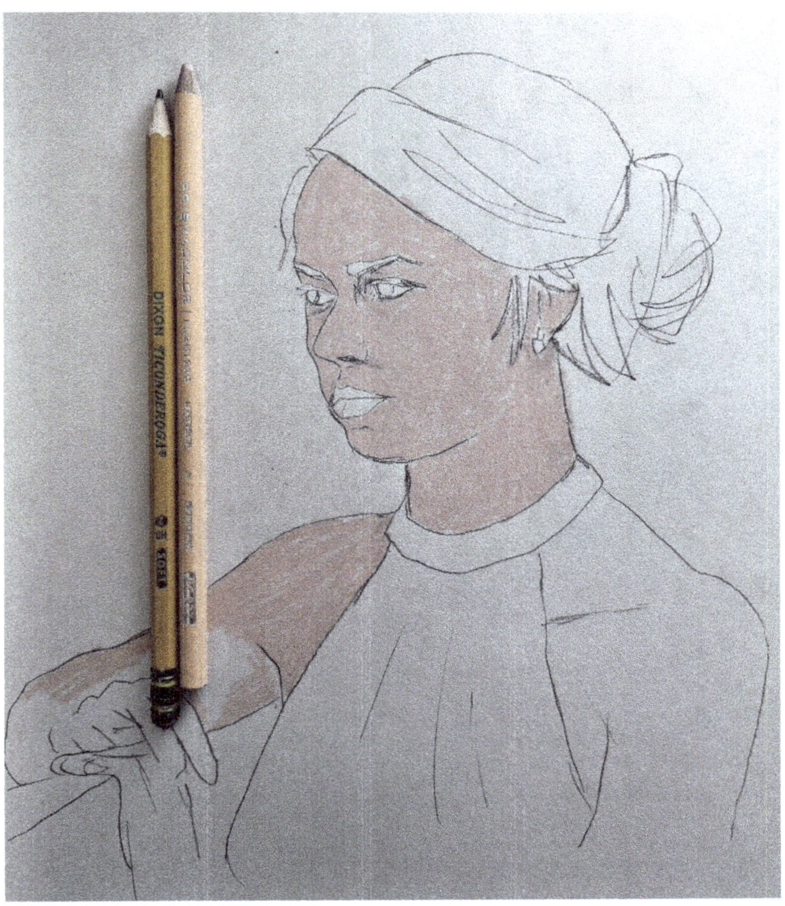

Step 2 create a heavy/thick base layer.

My usual method is sort of different than most experts I've seen. I tend to obliterate much of my available paper tooth right away, and then it's a game of how much fine-tuning can I squeeze in before the paper is spent. I don't consider it to be the burnishing stage yet because I'm not using white to pull things together, but it is quite heavily pressed. In this example, I used Light Peach (PC 927) as the first layer. I started by pushing down a thick coat of pencil for the base. Depending on the skin tone of the subject, I'll swap out different shades to start with instead of Light Peach or mix multiple colors as needed.

It seems that there is a fairly clear trade-off between my current process and the expert's path. Applying multiple light layers, then burnishing at the very end can result in some of the most beautifully realistic portraits, but seems to be very time-consuming. I'm sure it varies, but I've heard some impressive pencil artists say, for example, just one eye and its surrounding area could take hours alone. On the other hand, utilizing heavy base layers early as I do seem to take less time; it's not uncommon for me to take a portrait from start to finish in one evening. Of course, my artwork doesn't have the level of nuance and depth of color some of the elite colored pencil artists out there achieve.

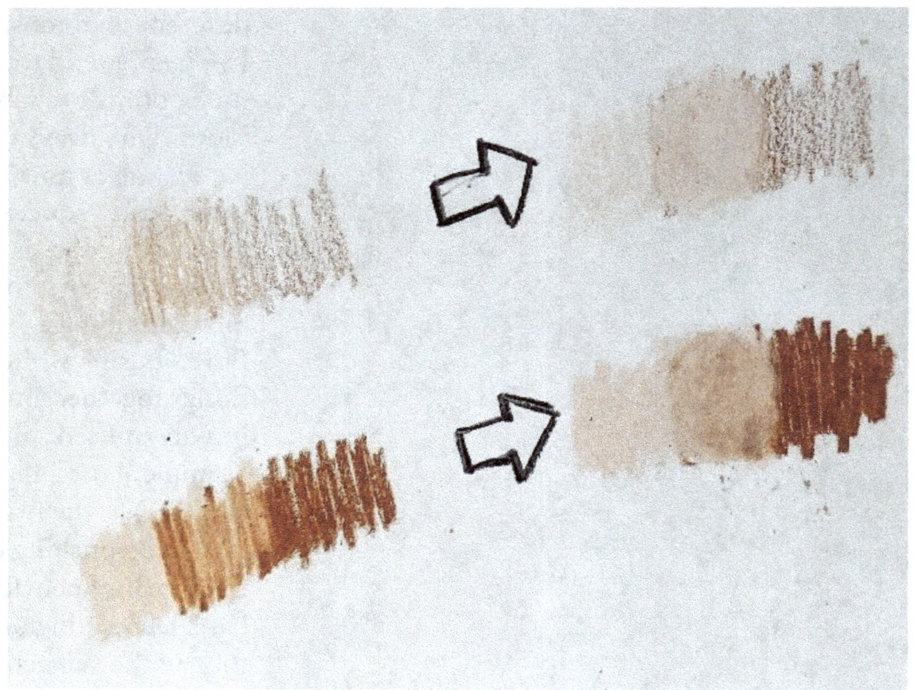

Top: Late burnish, light blend that tends to be more favored by experts. Bottom: Heavy blend, early burnish I most often use.

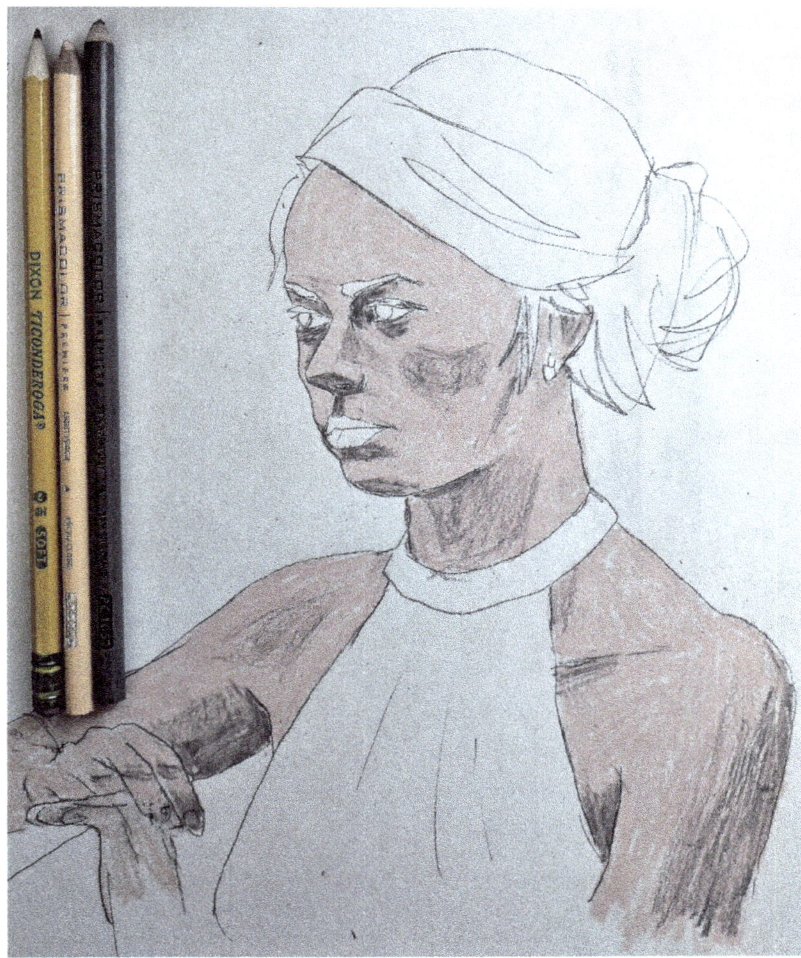

Step 3 is to fill in the shadows.

After the thick base layer(s), the next step is to start shading. The gray I use depends on the required contrast, but I often go with 30% Warm Gray (PC 1052) for this initial shading. I fill the shadows in pretty darkly because they lighten up significantly through blending in the next step. In this phase of the drawing, the subject usually starts to look like a zombie; if they look sort of ghoulish at this point, I feel like I'm on the right track. A fun distraction is to also fill in just the pupils, leaving the iris white, for some next level creepiness.

The fourth step is the big one - it's time to really start the burnishing phase. Blend everything together using White (PC 938). This step will pull all the colors together, and soften them a bit. The shadows become less harsh, and if you use multiple colors for the base skin tone layer, it will blend them together pretty smoothly. The subject will finally start to look a bit more like a normal human instead of the zombie from the previous step. At this point, the paper material is approaching critical mass in terms of how much more pencil wax it can accommodate. The hope in this phase is that I haven't overdone it, because it's definitely not complete.

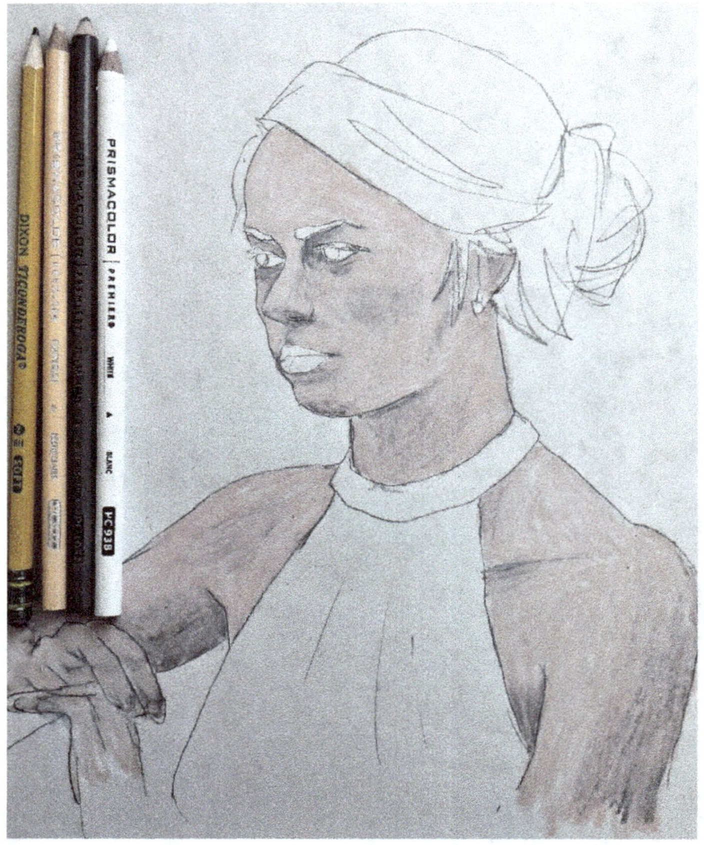

Step 4 is blend everything together using white.

It's important to point out here that the direction of your pencil strokes during burnishing is critical. Moving the White pencil in the opposite direction of your base layers will blend better than going in the same direction. Using circular motions probably achieves the most natural and realistic look for skin, but hair might look better burnished unidirectionally. In other words, the overall look and texture you achieve will be strongly influenced by burnishing directionality. Your signature style as an artist may even be influenced by yo ur burnishing tendencies.

The next step is to add some definition using darker colors. Typically, I use 70% Warm Gray (PC 1056) and 90% Warm Gray (PC 1058) for highlights here. Now I'll fill in the pupils, darker eye shading, nostrils, the underside of the nose, ears, and anything else that has deeper shadows. At this point, the drawing will probably start to come into focus and you can probably see a final product peeking back at you from around the corner.

This is almost just more of the previous step, but next, I start incorporating pink tones for the mouth and anywhere else needed. This always applies for lips, but most subjects also need more pinkish color in their cheeks and other areas of the face. In this example, I'l used Blush Pink (PC 928) and Peach (PC 939) on the lips, cheek, and side of the nose. If necessary, sometimes I also need to go back in with 50% Warm Gray (PC 1054) and more White blending to touch up.

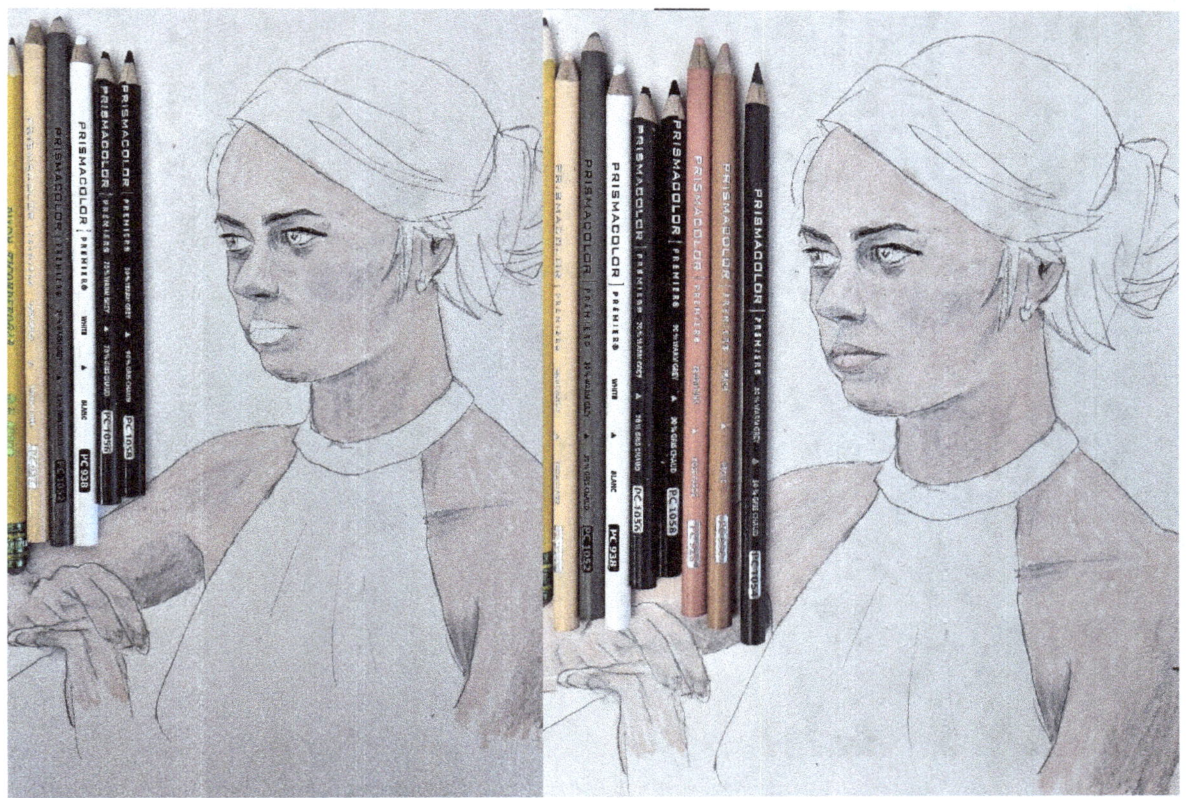

Step 5 involves detailing with darker grays, Step 6 is adding pink tones.

Next, in this example, I started working on the hair. To achieve a muted brown, I usually go with French Gray. In this case, I've used 30% French Gray (PC 1070), 50% French Gray (PC 1072), and 90% French Gray (PC 1076) to bring out the right variants. Just as with the skin, I applied these colors very heavily. Although you could blend, layer, and achieve color variation through pressure, I typically use multiple variants of French Gray so I can heavily pencil in all hair colors. For areas not reflecting light, I blended with a Colorless (PC 962) pencil. For areas with light reflection, I used white.

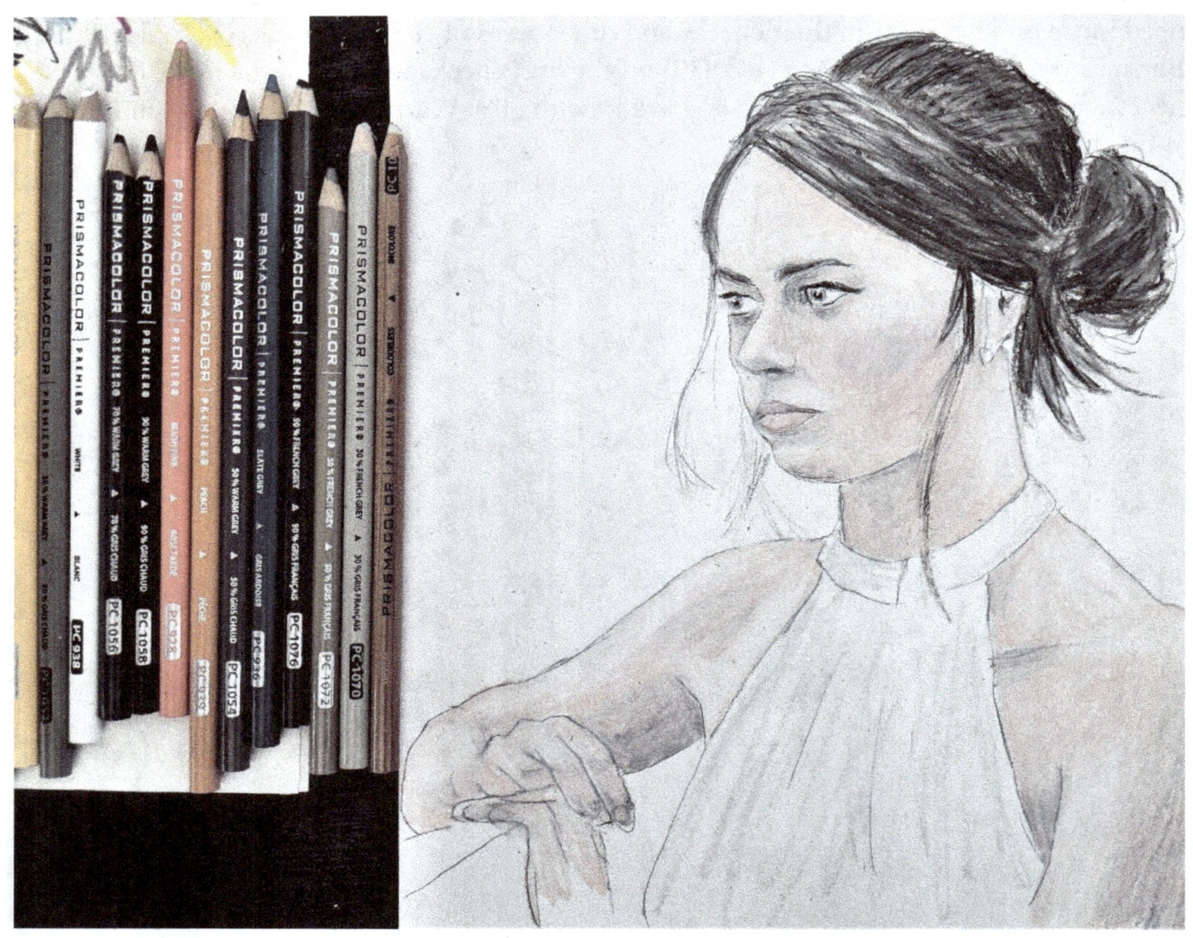

End result after adding French Grays and touch up with graphite.

The last step is sometimes not necessary. If anything needs a bit more definition, I'll return to the graphite pencil. For this example, there were some areas that didn't appear sharp enough, so I did some touch-up. I think this step might also be an "experts don't do this" example, because an argument can be made that defined lines make art look more cartoonish. But I feel like it sometimes helps if features turned out too soft.

That's sort of a lot to unpack, so here's a bulleted list for a summary:

- Expensive pencils blend more effortlessly and smoothly. You really do get what you pay for with colored pencils.
- Outline in graphite first. It doesn't matter if it's not perfect, it's probably the least important part of a colored pencil portrait.
- Burnishing (blending colors heavily) eliminates your paper's tooth (surface).
- Burnishing could be boiled down to this: Slower and better, or quicker and worse (my usual path). To be quick like an amateur Amdall, apply base layers heavily right away and burnish early. To be more realistic, go with *many* light layers.
- Burnish with White (PC 938) or a Colorless Blender.
- Directionality is important – the most natural burnishing for skin is usually circular, against the direction of your layers. This can also impact your general artistic style.

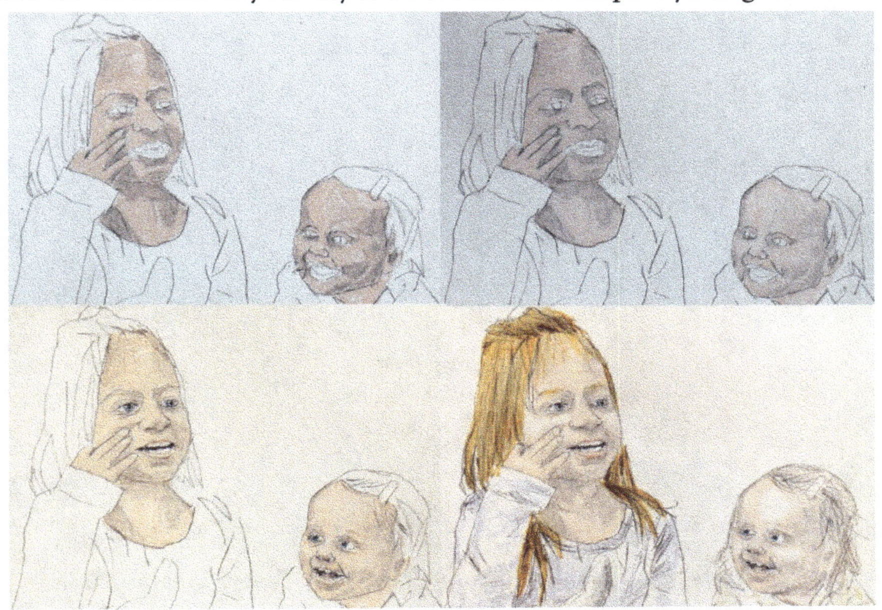

Now that we've discussed the method itself, how does this colored pencil painting style impact artwork versus a lighter penciling technique? This seems like a perfect time to provide an example demonstrating how the two styles look side-by-side. As luck would have it, I happen to have a drawing I completely redrew about a year after the original.

The original artwork was done early in my learning experience with color when I still utilized a relatively soft coloring approach. Months later, I actually ruined that sketch trying to change it too much. I regretted that for quite a while until I attempted the complete redraw. This is another scene inspired by the Dark Tower series by Stephen King featuring two of the main characters from the first sketch I shared earlier in the book.

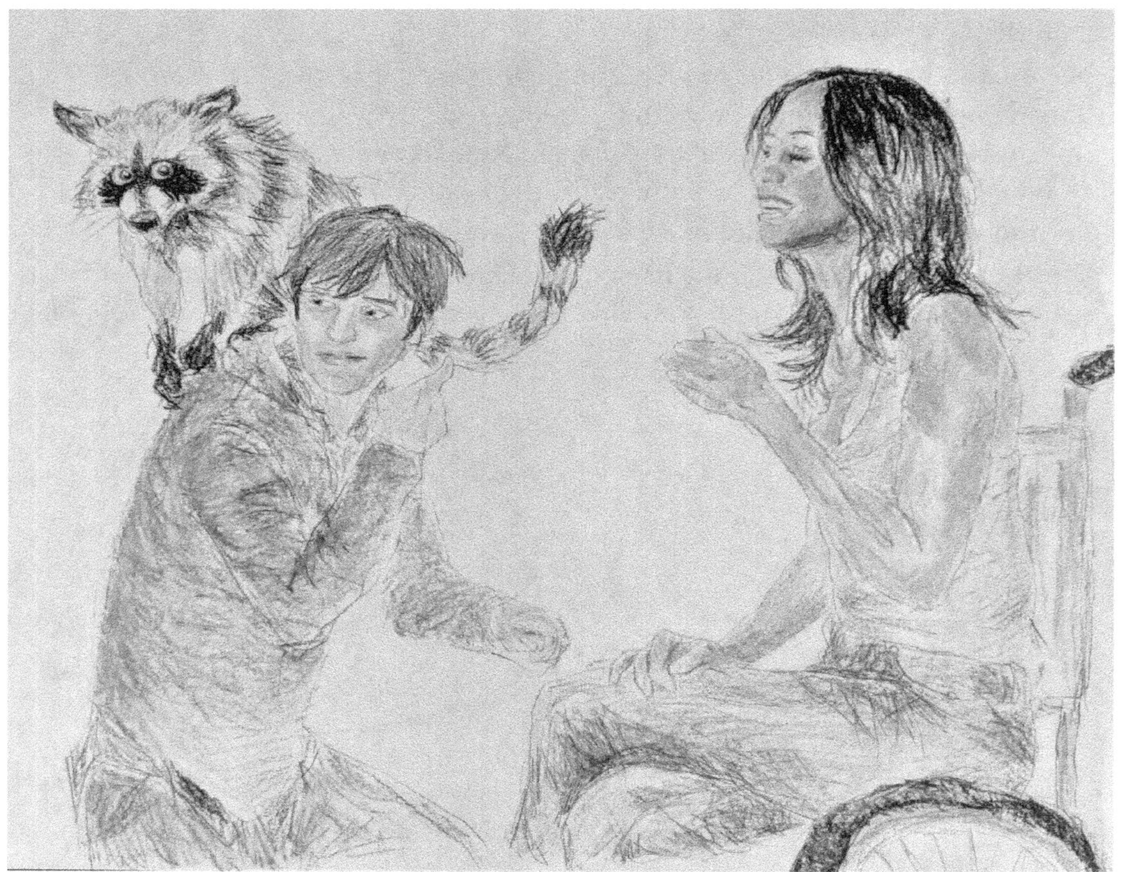

Original sketch of Susannah, Jake, and Oy from the Dark Tower, January 2018.

This time, I was much more satisfied with the detail achieved for Susannah and Jake, and I was even able to get a representation of Oy the Billybumbler I am happy with. Prior to the redraw, I knew I had improved a bit over time, but I hadn't considered how substantial the change might be in a redrawn piece. I was pleasantly surprised by the smaller touches, such as more natural looking facial features.

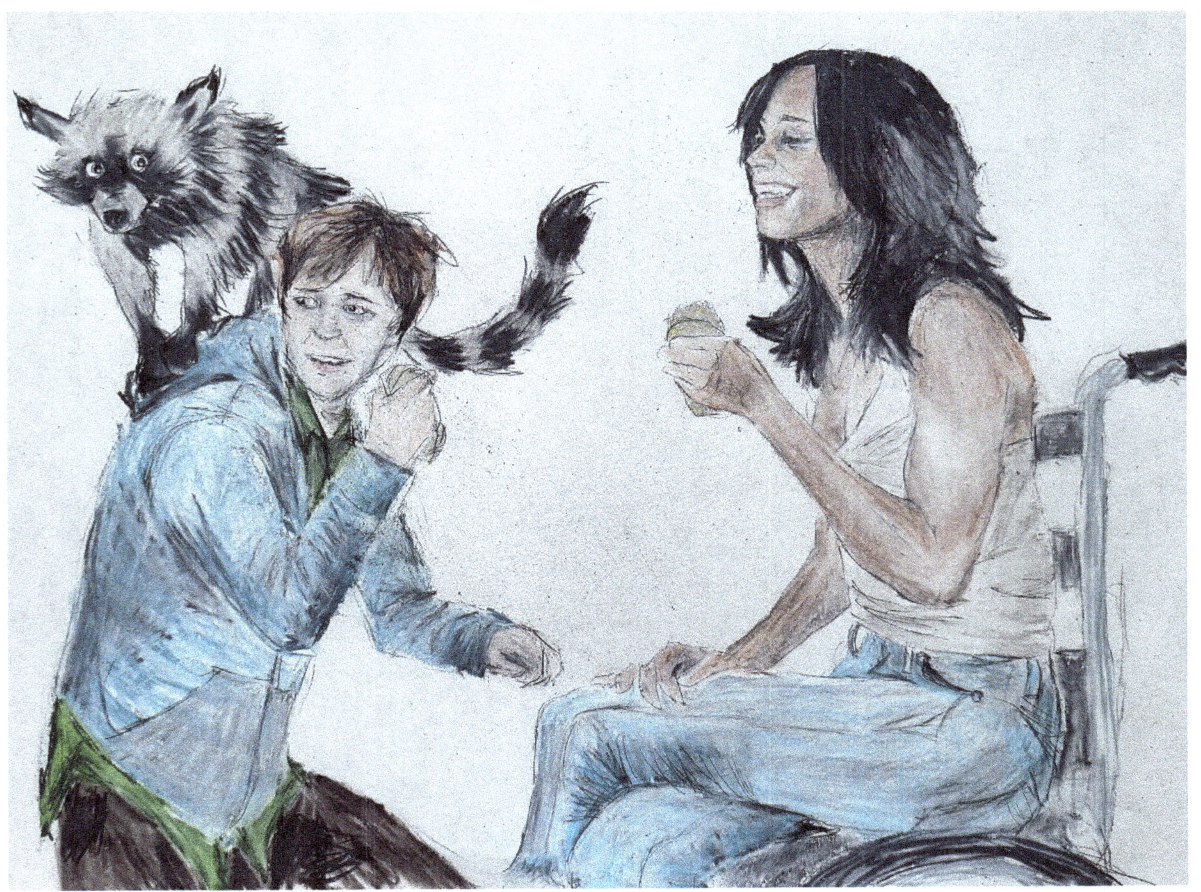

Second attempt at the same Dark Tower-inspired scene, February 2019.

Leaving aside the incremental natural improvements, you can see that the stylistic differences are fairly significant. Despite using the same color palette, the heavy pencil painting in the newer artwork is much more vibrant and visually compelling. The older image contains identical greens and blues that seem washed out and grayed in comparison. These photos were taken in identical conditions separated only by time (at my desk, same camera phone, room lights on, night time), so the difference is not simply an anomaly of photography.

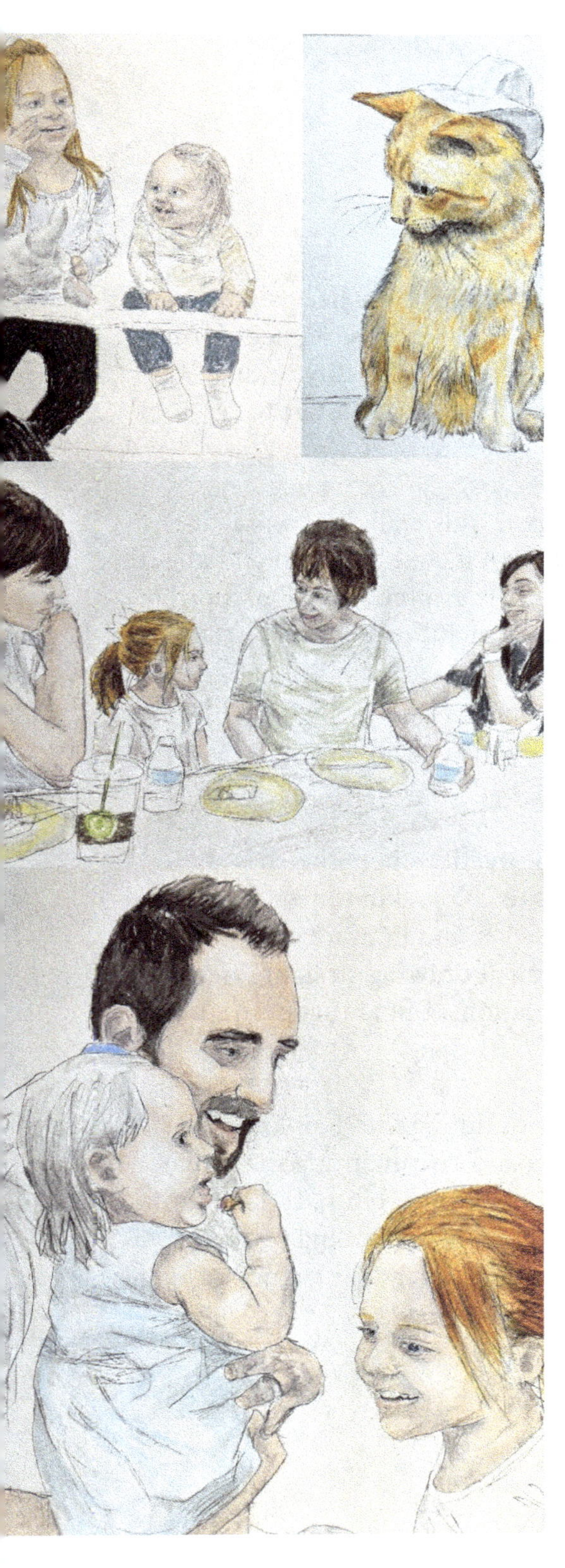

Phase 4 – Practice & Blending Improvement

MARCH 2018

Moving forward from here, you'll see portraits increasingly emphasizing heavy layering and pencil painting. The techniques outlined in the last chapter become more refined through practice, and some of the later drawings approach improved levels of fidelity to their subjects. It's the second to last "phase" in this book, so the portraits really start to resemble the current look of my artwork.

Although there are only a handful of drawings in this chapter, this really was a practice-heavy phase in which I churned out a ton of artwork. Much of it couldn't be included in this book though due to copyright reasons. I created a lot of fan art around this time, mostly related to movies and television shows. I would have liked to include them, but certainly not without permission to publish for commercial use.

KIDS IN A SHOPPING CART

From August 2017 until now, after about seven months of practice, these sketches started to look more confident. This is especially true when it comes to color; skin tones seem more realistic than they did early on, and color lay-down was thicker and in more complete layers. I still had quite a few critiques, such as a relatively weak skill at drawing straight lines, laziness on backgrounds, and somewhat unimaginative creations. But at that point, I was encouraged to see progress.

At this point, I shared my first process post on the website outlining the steps and techniques I used. This was my first attempt at formalizing and documenting the actual steps I developed over time, and what the shading process had evolved into. It did continue to change, but the post was a good step towards gaining some understanding of what I was actually doing. Sometimes, writing helps work out the details of a person's vaguer thoughts.

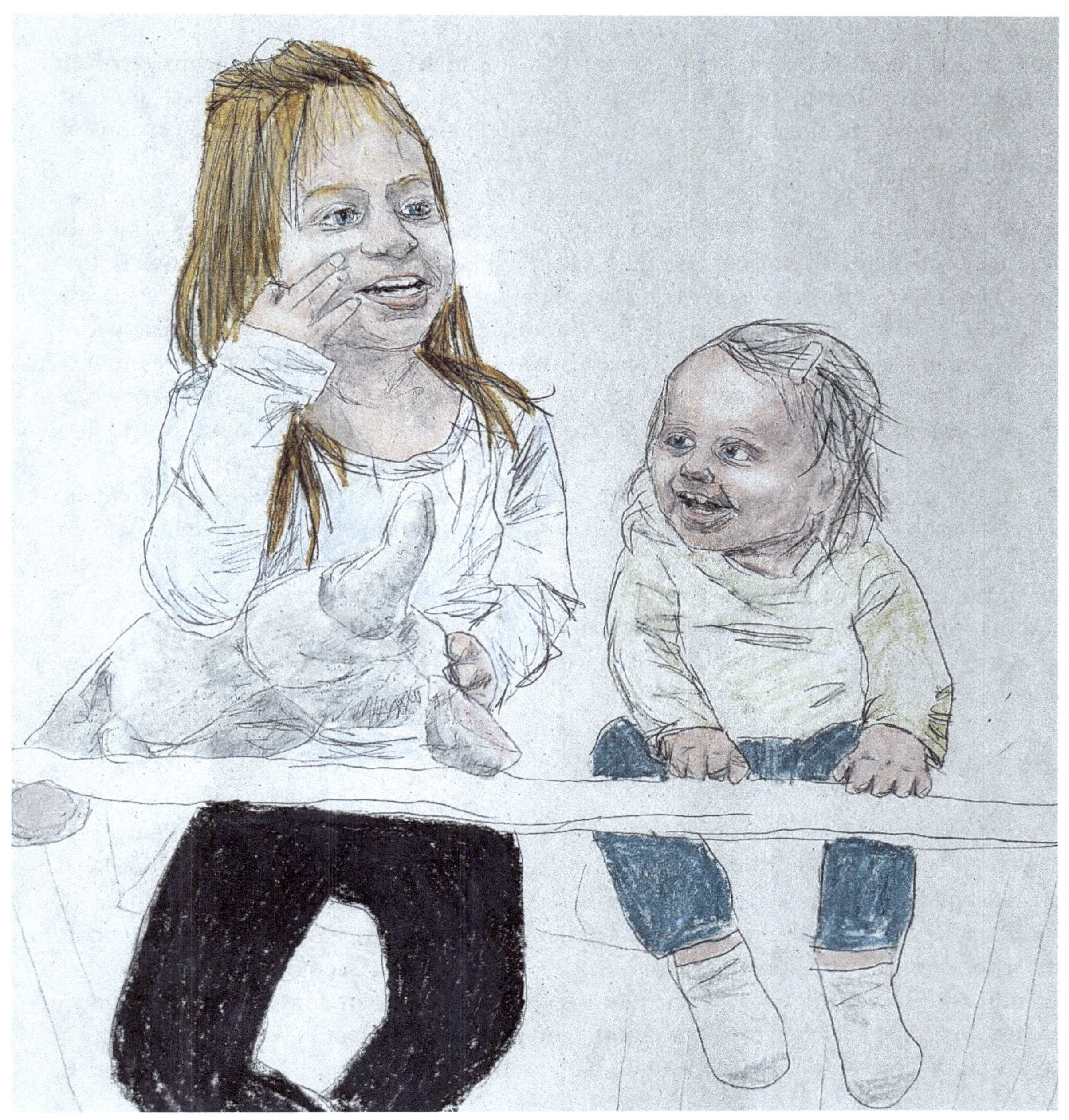

Our kids in a shopping cart (this is a theme for them).

In this case, I used a portrait of my daughters in a shopping cart to illustrate progression. I didn't know it at the time but, as with many things, the "kids in a shopping cart" portrait would become a theme for future sketches. I included some smaller, cropped versions of this drawing a few pages ago, but here I'll show the full piece.

At this stage, I had seen artists in action who were vastly more skilled using the same tools. But as an amateur still working out the kinks, I felt pretty good about where I was in the grand scheme of things. One of the biggest differences between me and the experts, aside from them having professional-caliber eyes for color, is that they use a wider variety for shading than I did. For example, where I used grays to indicate shadows, experts often seem to use browns, reds, and yellows to shade, and it looks more natural. I wasn't there yet, and to some extent, I'm still not, but I hope it is an area of improvement as I continue to grow.

As for this drawing of my daughters specifically, there were some areas for improvement. The little one's eyes were a bit wonky, and our oldest's mouth wasn't quite right. Also, in a call-back to my comment about straight lines, that shopping cart handle isn't even close to even. I'm not sure why I didn't just use a ruler or something. On the positive side of things, I did manage to include our oldest daughter's best friend in the world, Mr. Bunny. He still goes everywhere with her, and actually started out as a white rabbit…he's more of a grayish color now though.

DRAWING TWO SCENES AT ONCE

During this time frame, I wrote about being in an unusual place with this art hobby. I could see tangible improvement in my results, which made me excited to draw more. But I was still struggling to come up with subject matter and found myself running out of ideas. I'll discuss idea generation in much more detail in the next chapter. For now, though, a natural direction for my brainstorming went like this: "Which family member or friend combinations have I not drawn yet?" At this point, I had featured my immediate family in many, and I had sketched my sister, mom, and granny. But I hadn't drawn most of my wife's family, or very surprisingly, I also had not done one with just me and the two girls.

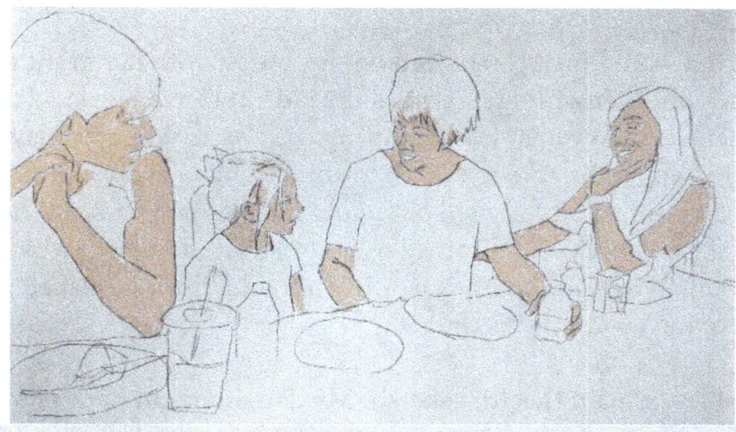

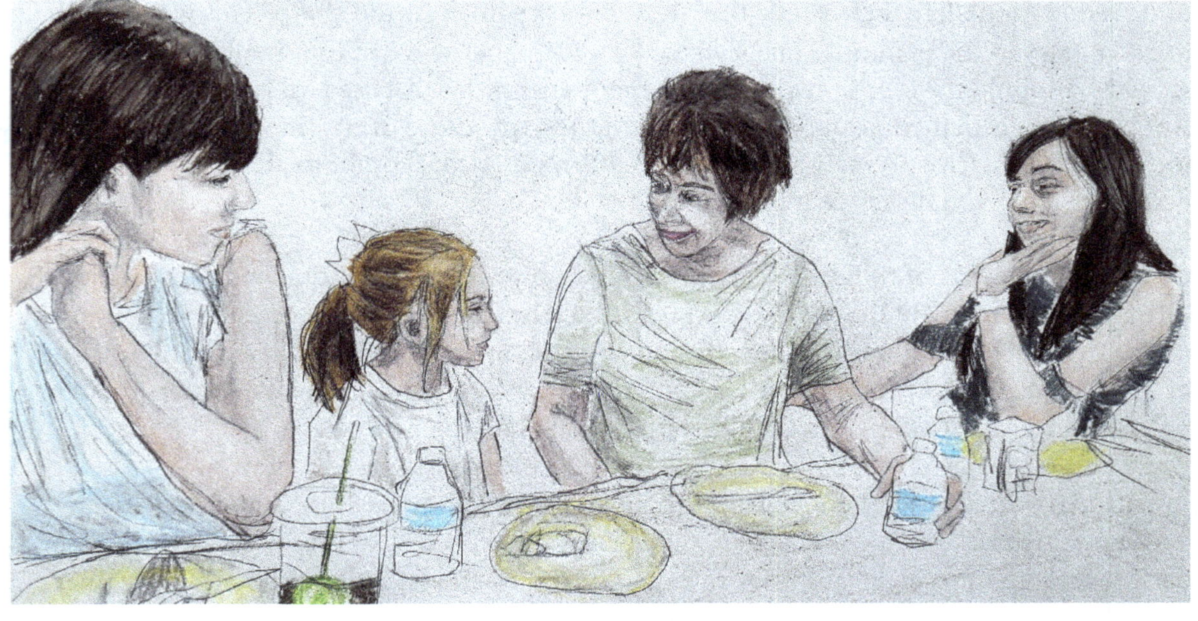

So, in the absence of a creative tidal wave of ideas, I decided to cover a couple of those combinations. Due to my excitement, I also made the interesting choice to work on two at once. Immediately after finishing, I commented on that perhaps being a bad idea, because it presented some challenges. But it wouldn't be the last time I worked on multiple at once. Occasionally, it's actually nice to switch to a different drawing for something fresh.

The two scenes I selected were a group centered on our oldest with her grandma, her aunt, and her mom, and then another with just me and the kids. It started fine as I did the outlines in graphite pencil, and even at the beginning with basic skin color layers. And as I mentioned, it was refreshing to be able to switch to something new periodically. But, as I continued on, I started getting a bit fatigued or feeling like perhaps I bit off more than I could chew. I didn't take any breaks and forced myself to move forward, which was probably not wise. I wanted to see what they would both look like as finished products, so there would be no stepping away on this one.

There are a number of issues with this first sketch. My daughter and her grandma in the middle don't look like themselves; their features are somehow too sharp. This was probably my own fault in the planning; I believe the 9″ x 12″ paper was just too small for four subjects. I should have either worked on larger paper or just focused on two people. Another issue is that you can pretty clearly see the byproducts of rushing in the objects on the table, which are extremely sloppy and malformed. Also, I forgot to add color to my daughter's bow and never went back to fix it.

On the positive side of things, it's still better than some of my older drawings. It's still less satisfying than many of the more recent color sketches, but I can still see aspects of progress. At the time, I was disappointed how this one turned out, and looking back it's still not one of my favorites. But I think for the learning process, it is important to take ownership of both the good and bad and try to take some lessons into the next one.

In part two of this series, I ended up with one of my favorite drawings. As I was switching back and forth and started layering, I could pretty quickly see that this one was working out better. Because the facial features were larger, it was much easier to capture accurate finer points. Although I didn't like my self-imposed and sort of neurotic need to rush, which increased the further along I got, I think this one really came together well.

What do I think went right specifically? Well, the skin shading was solid, and the blending in everyone's hair turned out well. In fact, I think it's the best depiction I've done on my oldest daughter's bright red-orange hair. Facial features and resemblances were also pretty much on target; this definitely looks like all three of us. I don't see any features or areas that have significant mistakes or problems. I'm even pleased I was able to get the detail of my youngest munching on a piece of cake…although it does almost look more like a pizza roll or something. I like this portrait so much that I actually turned it into a logo and used it on some business cards.

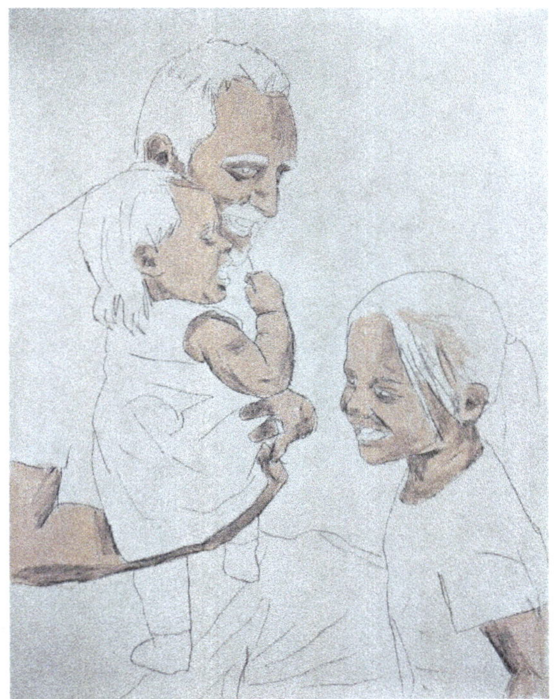 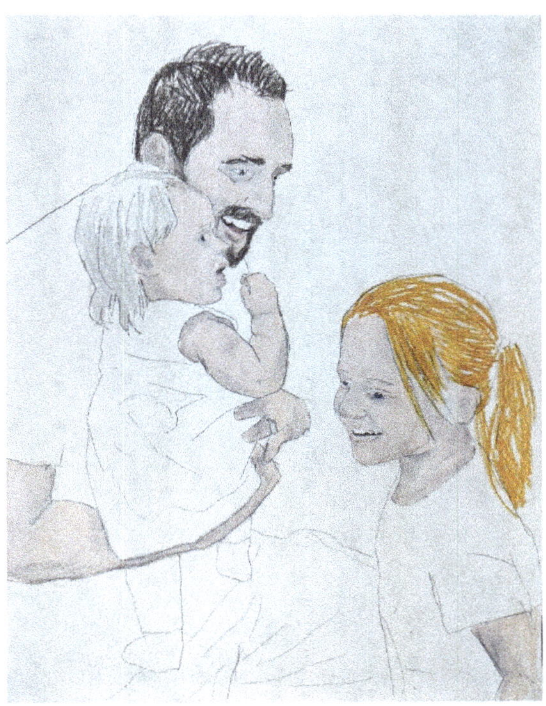

One of my favorite portraits of me and the girls. Earlier progressions above, finished portrait on the next page.

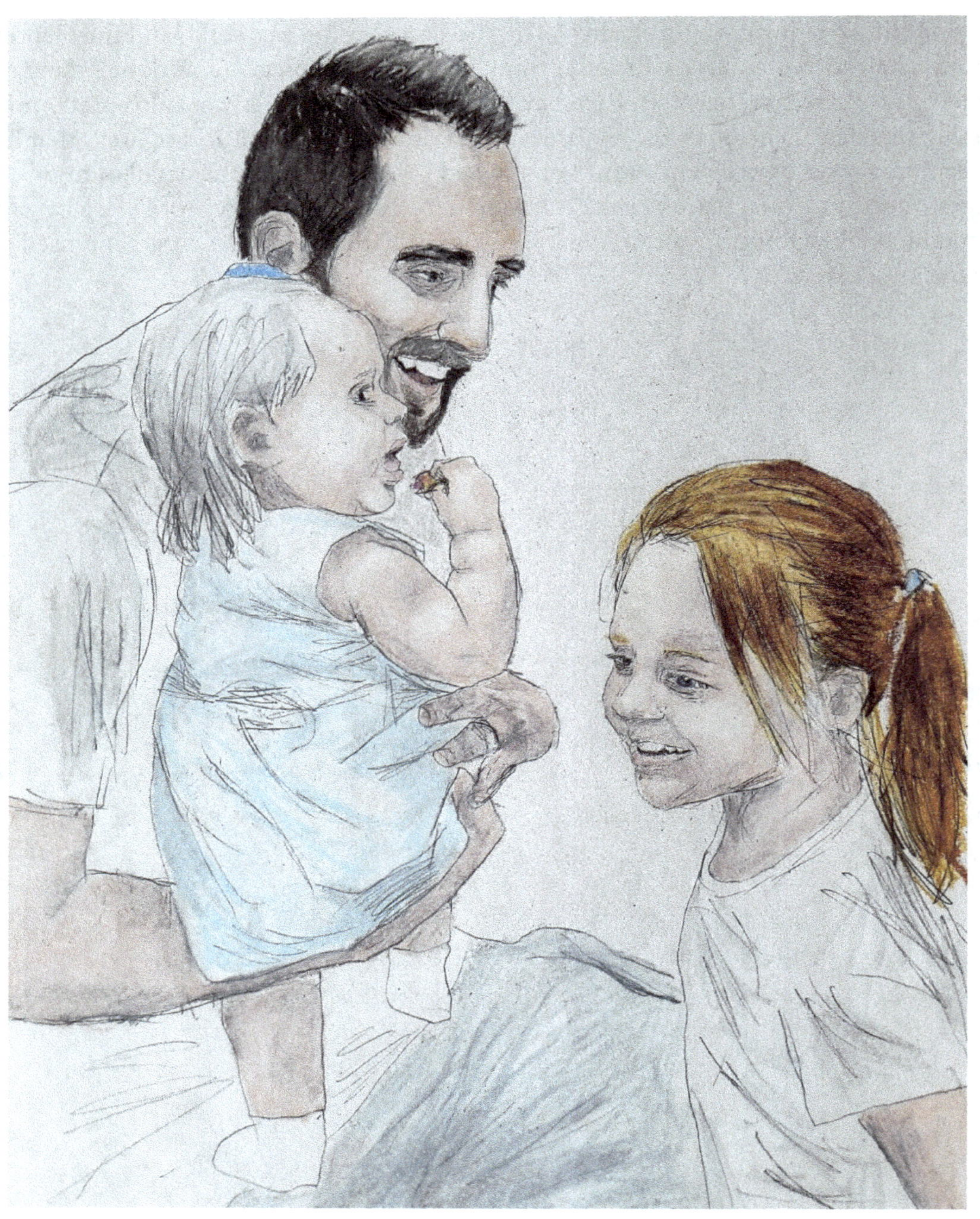

Even though I think a lot went well, there is always room for critique in my view. As usual, you can see some laziness shining through, particularly when it comes to my shirt; I never wear white t-shirts, because I'm virtually guaranteed to spill a drink or food. It would have been much more realistic to make that shirt navy or black. And, I was able to fix it in this drawing, but I need to work on my pupil positioning. In early versions of this sketch, my oldest daughter had some major googly eyes happening. Pupil positioning can be really challenging, especially when you're trying to make a subject look at something specific.

After this "two drawings at once" series, I went on a fairly long streak of drawing fictional characters and sports stars. By my count, I created 12 in a row that featured movie characters, musicians, or athletes. It was a fun change of pace to draw characters from media that I enjoy, and once I got on a roll, I didn't detour from it for quite a while. Fortunately, these drawings continued to build from the progress I had made, and I was able to capture some entertaining scenes. Of course, the downside as I mentioned at the start of this chapter, is that I can't include any of them in this book.

TRYING A NON-HUMAN SUBJECT

When we were visiting family one Mother's Day weekend, I was talking to my sister about something related to drawing. I asked her if there was anything she was interested in me drawing, and she mentioned her cat Biscuit. She may have been somewhat joking, but as I am always hungry for more art ideas, anything that sounds like a request becomes one.

Biscuit the Cat is a cool little guy. My sister and her husband have three pets, including another cat and a German Shepherd. Of all of this crew, Biscuit was the first, and he runs the pack. According to my sister, Biscuit essentially walks around their house like he bought the place. He is apparently very smart too and can open doors and problem-solve at impressive levels.

Despite the fact that I don't have much experience drawing animals, this turned out surprisingly well. I wasn't sure how successfully I could handle fur, as I've drawn a few animals. By this time, I was fairly comfortable depicting human skin, but smoothly blended tones are a totally different ballgame from millions of fine hairs. In this case, I think I adapted to simulating some furriness well on Biscuit's head and upper body but settled for too many solid lines on his legs.

Hair, in general, can be tough to represent, and in many cases, I've settled too much on blocks of outlined head shapes. Displaying the general shape of hair from an outline doesn't look very natural. It's problematic when drawing human hair, but even worse when trying to capture the look of a furry animal. Although this cat portrait was mostly a success, I can see significant room for improvement.

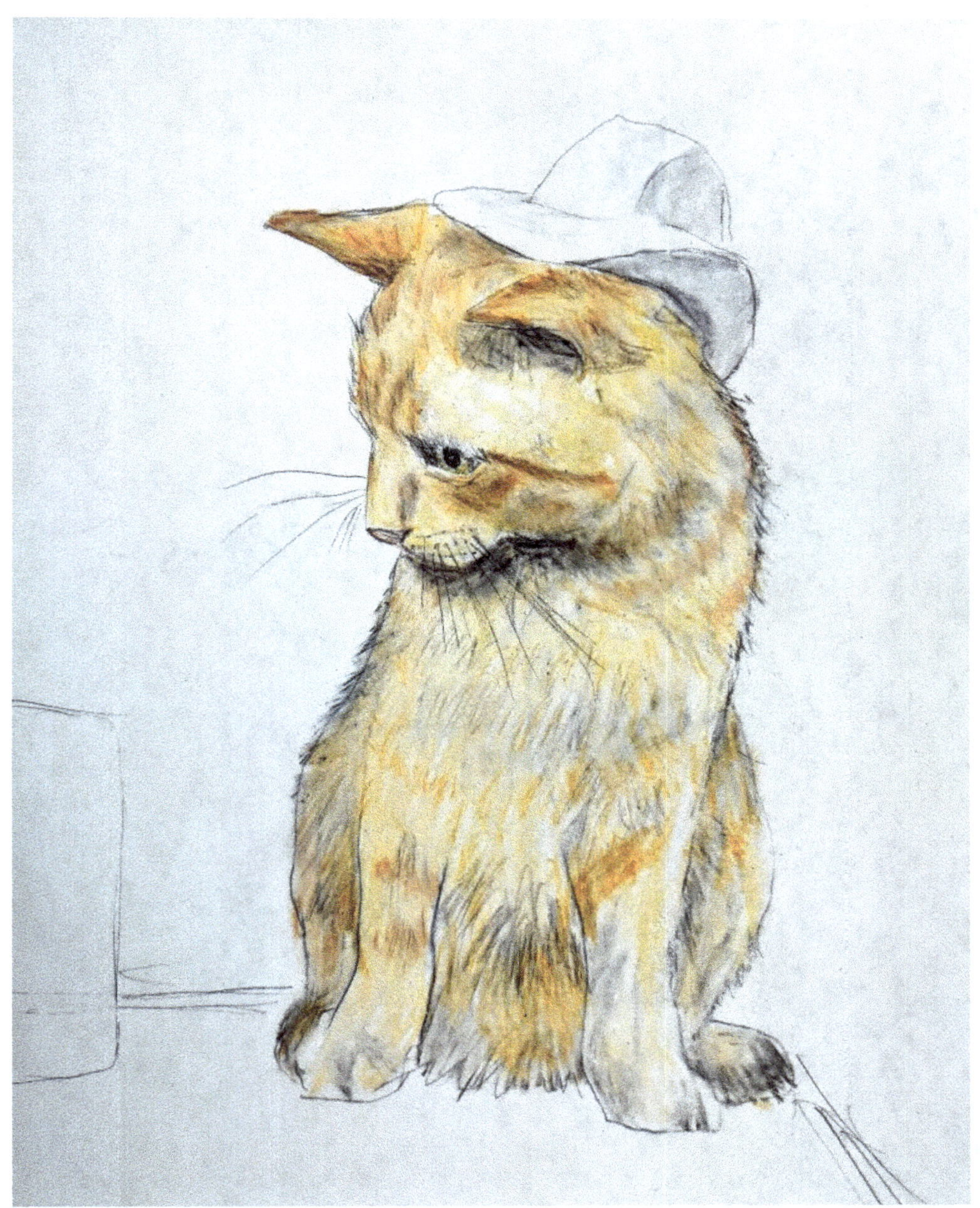

My sister's cat, very fashionable in his cowboy hat.

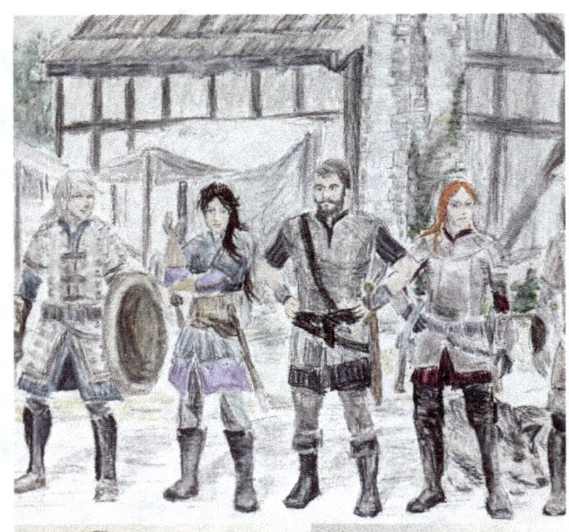

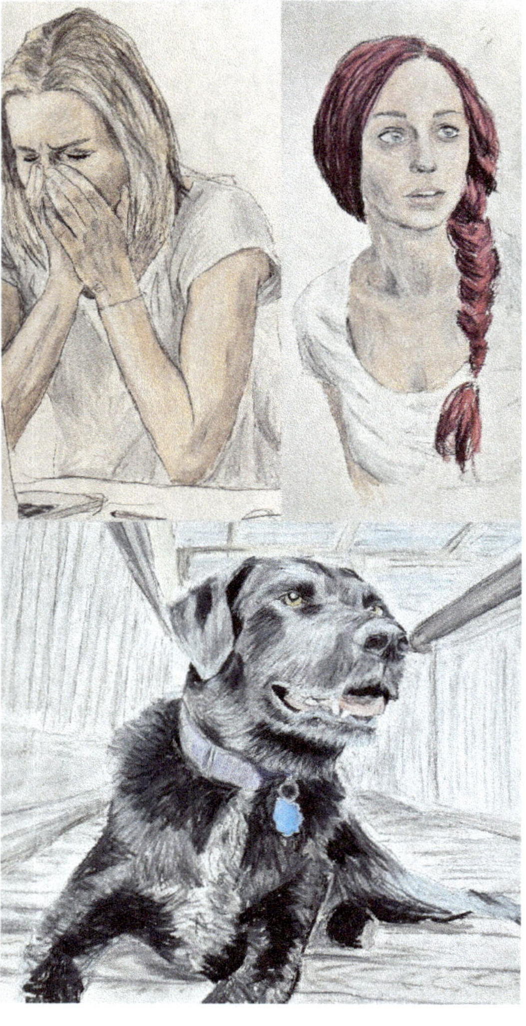

Process Notes –
Sources of
Inspiration

Although there is only one more chapter of artistic progression left to discuss, we're going to take a break from that topic for a moment. Similar to the pause to detail colored pencil painting, in this chapter, we'll take a closer look at some sources of subjects, ideas, and inspiration. This fits the overall artistic chronology as well because I really began to seek new sources in that April-May 2018 timeframe.

A broad spectrum of sources will be covered here, including things like stock images, memes, hosted giveaways, and others. I'll describe the benefits and drawbacks from my experience, and include examples where I can. Some of these ideas have either uncertain or unlikely-to-be-granted use permission rights; even in some cases where I have experience, there were examples that I simply couldn't share here.

STOCK IMAGES

The first resource we'll discuss is stock images. There was an education process for me when it came to stock images because I really didn't know much about them at first. They came onto my radar from two directions at practically the same time; social media and advertisements. Inspired by my wife's interesting finds on Pinterest, I started browsing the app to check out some of the artwork on there. Aside from some pretty incredible sketches and paintings, I discovered a massive amount of art prompts. These prompts basically consist of users sharing a variety of poses specifically for artist use. The basic idea behind Pinterest is that if you tried a pin, you post your attempt under the original. In theory, it fosters a collaborative creative environment with the originator. In practice, I think people mostly just scroll through the images without interacting much. I attached my artwork but didn't see any other activity on any other art prompt pins.

In completely unrelated social media browsing, I also stumbled across some fascinating "historical photo" sharing accounts on Twitter, which provided even more inspiration. The photographs accounts like this share are interesting and often quite varied, ranging from actual historical images containing world leaders to somewhat obscure pictures of actors or musicians. Eventually, as I researched these accounts further, I found quite a few articles criticizing them. Among the critiques I read, most serious were using images without crediting the photographer and misrepresenting or providing outright false information about the subjects or situation depicted. I've noticed some are much better now about providing credit; I suppose those critical articles had an impact after all.

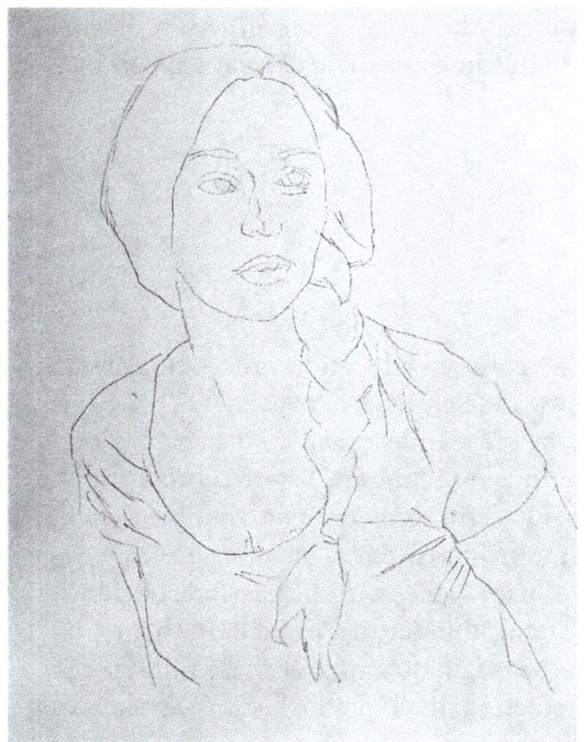
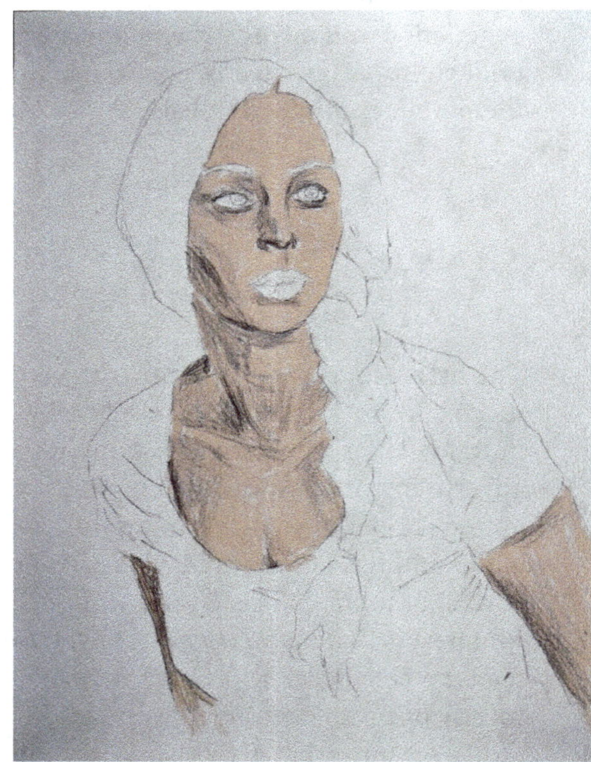

Artwork derived from photo by Jessica Truscott (Faestock) on Shutterstock. Progression sketches above, finished portrait on the next page.

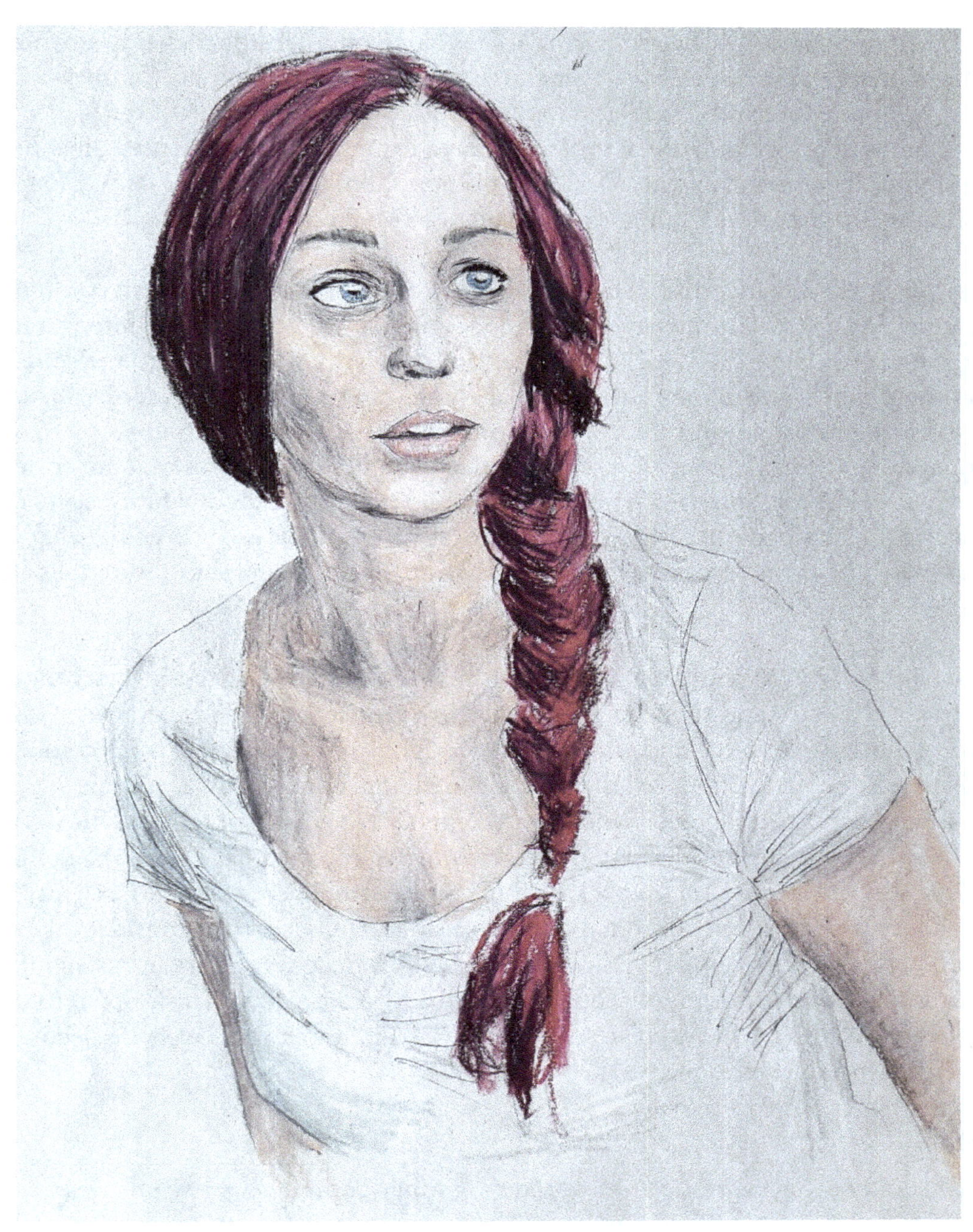

Around the same time, I started practicing scenes based on interesting advertisements. I started with a mailer I received advertising for a dentist's office, some ads for the Gap clothing, and material from an article about workplace illness etiquette. I find advertisements hilarious because of the exaggerated expressions so often used, like the absurd smiles, aggressive laughter, and awkward poses. I'm not sure if they make for interesting art for the viewer, but it is pretty fun practice for an artist.

Pinterest, Twitter, and advertisements - what do all of these resources have in common? Well, interesting artwork using new and unique subjects, yes. But the more important answer is that they all utilized stock photographs. If you're not familiar with the concept, stock photography is the monetization of images that can be used commercially. Usually, they are designated as "royalty-free" when purchased, which means a company or individual can pay for the rights to use them once, then not have to worry about royalties with every use. For example, in a book like this one, paying once for any future sales rather than paying the photographer for every one sold. It's a useful industry, because what business would have the resources to go take high-quality photographs of waterfalls and sunsets?

I set out with an artist's mind, just drawing whatever was interesting to me. Later though, I had to take a step back and reassess my mindset. I really needed to figure out where exactly these images originated from and who owns their rights, rather than just where I found them. And if I wanted to either sell them or use them in a book, I had to pay up. Fortunately, for most social media and advertisement derived artwork, I was able to track down the stock image owner through direct website and reverse image searches. For all that I could identify, it could be traced back to either Shutterstock, Getty Images, or Unsplash. I had to choose which I could afford to obtain licensing to publish, then consider the rest as non-commercial practice or "art studies." Because stock images can vary pretty significantly in price, unfortunately some of my choices of which to license didn't come down to the quality of the resulting artwork. Instead, the cost was a huge factor, as well as selecting samples from multiple example types.

Overall:

Positives: Interesting expressions, poses, and lighting. Completely new subjects.
Negatives: Can be expensive to purchase licensing rights.

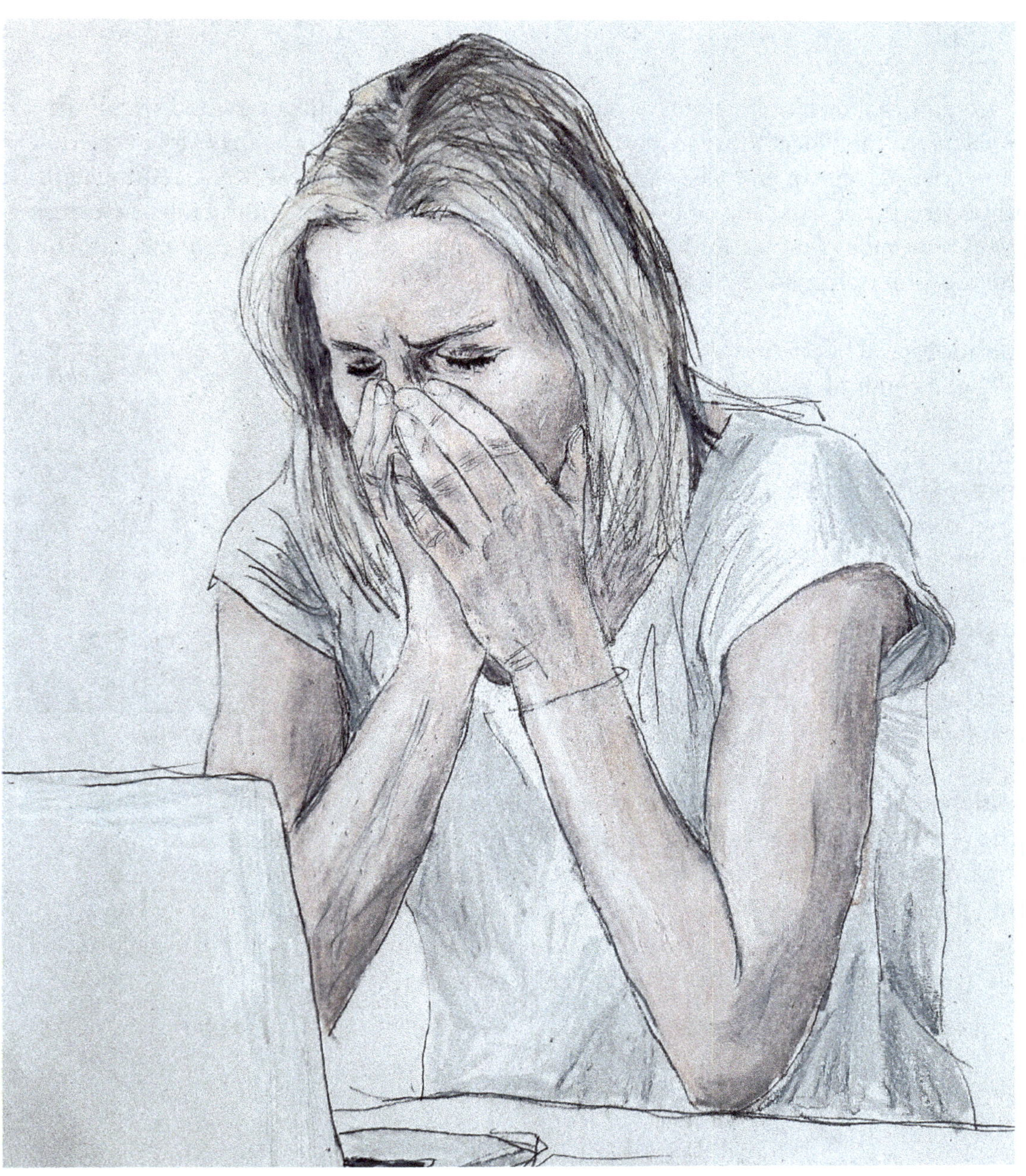

A lady sneezing (or crying). Derived from photo by Fizkes on Shutterstock.

VIDEO GAMES

I love video games. I don't play them as often as I used to, but I still get excited when I find one that falls into my wheelhouse. Although on a basic level, I enjoy a fairly large variety of genres, my favorite type of game has always been Role Playing Games (RPGs). Along with my fondness for pizza, cats, and drawing, my affinity for RPGs is one of my longest-running traits. I still remember how excited I was to finally own the original Final Fantasy game on the Nintendo Entertainment System (NES).

For some additional background on what an RPG is, essentially you can look back to the older pen and paper tabletop games like Dungeons and Dragons. Concepts like Hit Points (a character's health), attributes determining performance (i.e. Strength dictating how much damage they cause to enemies), and the high fantasy environment are common in video game RPGs and their tabletop predecessors alike. I've always found the concept of managing and equipping gear, examining how character attributes change, then seeing the results in action to be very engaging. I think it appeals to the same parts of my brain that love data and spreadsheets so much.

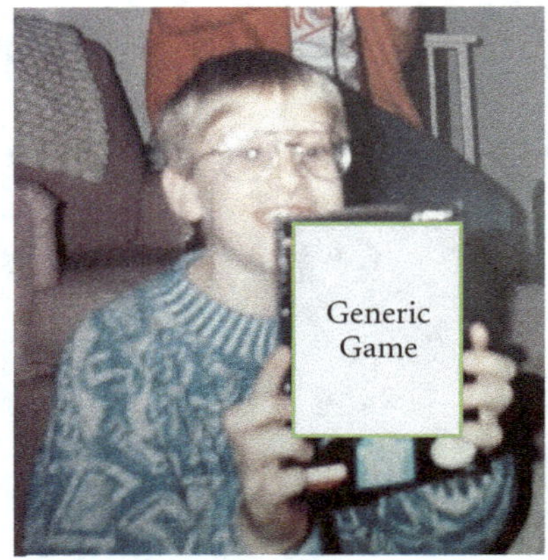

Excitement levels were at maximum for this mystery game.

As I mentioned in the first chapter of this book when I was a kid much of my sketching was directly inspired by video games. When I wasn't playing them, my imagination was often running wild with scenes related to games. It's not surprising that this could be another well to draw water from now. Although I've only attempted material inspired by video games a handful of times as an adult, it's still another enjoyable avenue for adding some variety to subject matter.

I've had a few favorites over the last decade or so, including titles like Elder Scrolls Skyrim, Dark Souls, and the especially noteworthy Dragon's Dogma. Dragon's Dogma was originally released in 2012 by Capcom and was the first RPG directed by Hideaki Itsuno. Itsuno was best known for stylish action games like the Devil May Cry series and utilized some of that well-designed combat expertise when making Dragon's Dogma. Although in every other respect it conforms to common RPGs trappings, the game's action-oriented combat really sets it apart. In classic RPG games, combat is turned based and magic is a simple target-and-wait system. Dragon's Dogma actually manages to create an engaging magic system that fits seamlessly alongside the real-time sword, dagger, and bow action.

I actually did a couple of drawings inspired by Dragon's Dogma that I was pretty satisfied with. Unfortunately, Capcom would not give me permission to include them. It was a very fun exercise though, using my imagination to build a collection of generic adventurers. It reminded me so much of drawing when I was a kid. In imagination-heavy situations like video game-inspired art, I think the detail and overall quality are lower than my traditional portraits. Sometimes artwork should be about the fun factor!

Fortunately for me, the developers of another RPG series from my favorites list was kind enough to let me publish some artwork. More recently, I did some fun sketches inspired by a series called Pillars of Eternity, made by Obsidian Entertainment. This series pulls even more from the classic tabletop games and goes absolutely wild with the detailed character attributes and combat statistics. There have been two Pillars of Eternity games so far, and both are highly placed in my "most all-time hours played" list.

While it still allows for some engaging action-based combat, this series focuses more on strategic decisions and managing actions based on strengths and weaknesses. The story relies heavily on complicated plans of the gods and their interference with mortals, but I tend to get so lost in the side quests and detours that the main storyline falls to the wayside for me. Every aspect of the game has incredible depth, but it's flexible enough to allow you to play to your comfort level in terms of complexity. Not many games feature that sort of adaptability to individual play styles.

A common theme for me when playing open/customizable games like this is that I'm boring. I think many people create imaginative characters to play or try something that they aren't. I almost always create myself as the main character and plug my family/friends in as my allies. Even in fantasy worlds with elves and dwarfs, I play as a regular human with my wife, kids, and possibly some friends as combat companions.

When I started messing around sketching a scene inspired by the Pillars of Eternity series, I went in that same direction. I put together a set of adventurers in an imagine generic village based on my family (plus a friend). Of course, since my kids are actually small children, I did some guesswork as to how they might vaguely look as adults. This was another very enjoyable call-back experience to my youth, sketching game-inspired scenes.

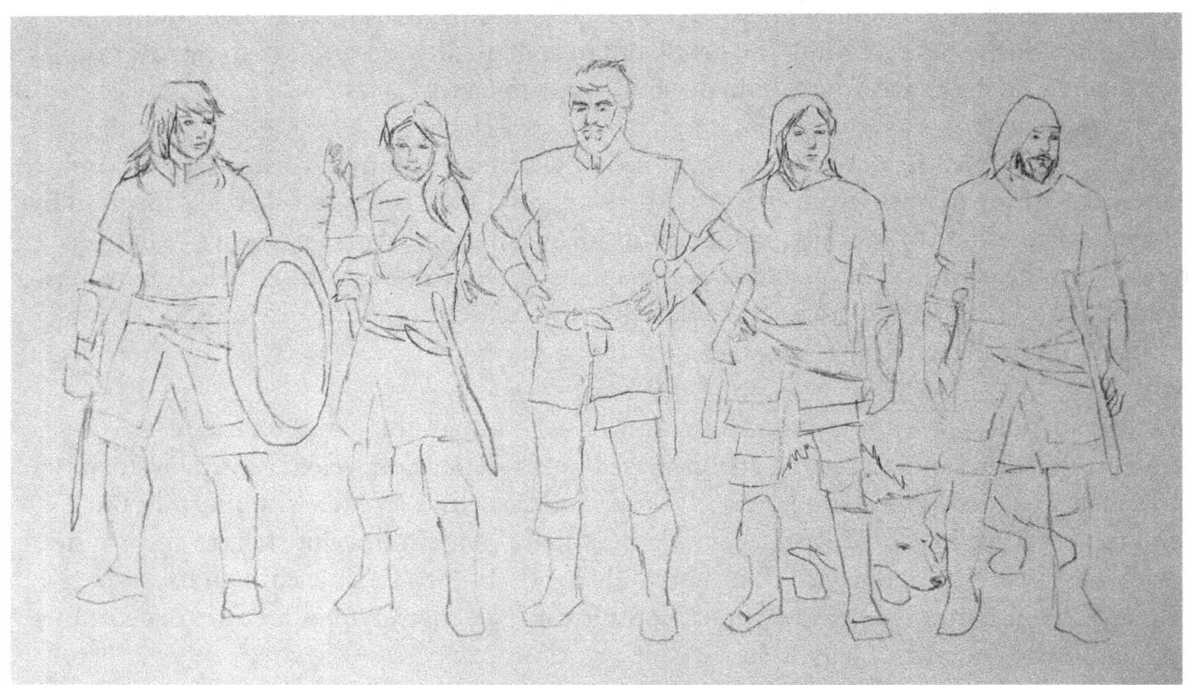

A rough outline of my generic adventuring crew. This group was loosely based on me, my wife, imaginary grown-up versions of my kids, and a friend from previous sketches.

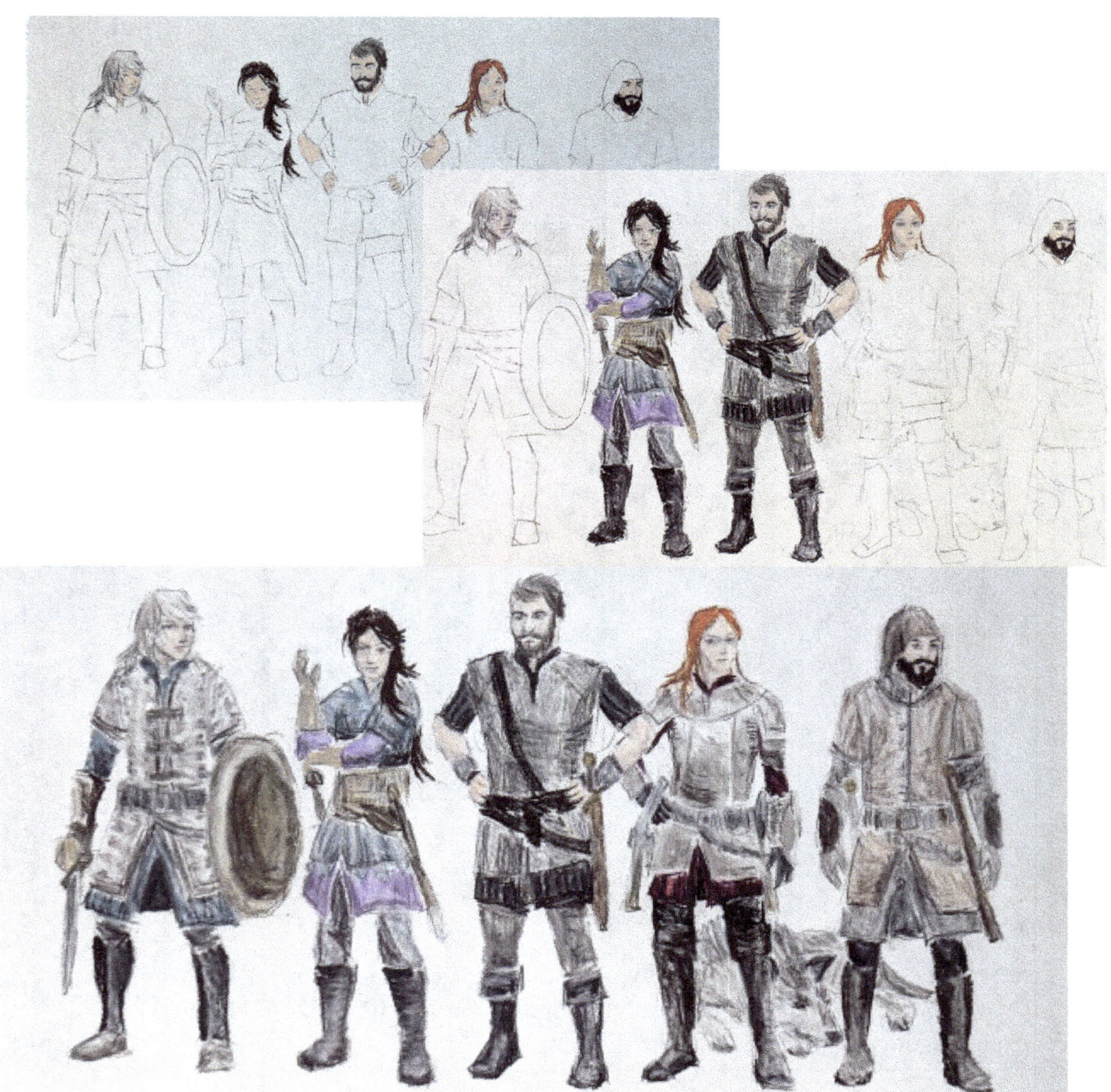

Earlier versions of the crew of adventurers. This was before I decided to be adventurous in real life by adding scenery/background to the sketch.

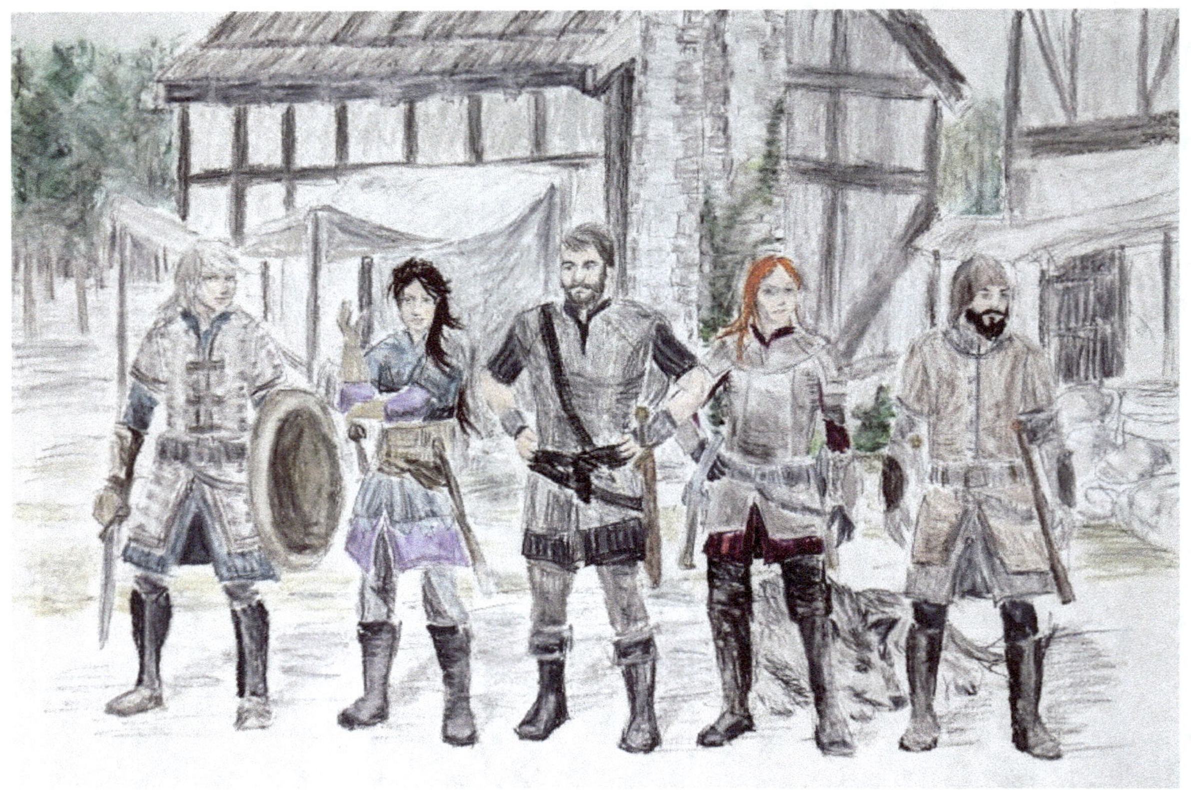

The same crew of adventurers hanging out in a generic town, which was as close as I could get to a version of me, my wife, the kids, and a friend of mine. Inspired by the Pillars of Eternity series.

Summary:

Positives: Opportunity to be imaginative. Nostalgia for childhood art (at least for me).
Negatives: Have to be careful not to use trademarked characters. Still likely need to receive permission to publish from the developer.

ARTWORK GIVEAWAYS AND RAFFLES

Another surprisingly good source for artwork ideas came to my attention just through tinkering with my website. As I was considering methods to increase traffic, I read about the concept of hosting giveaways to bring people in to see content. I was glad to learn there are free solutions to automate the entry and winner selection process and decided to attempt one myself. The first raffle I hosted ran for about 30 days, and I offered the winner their choice of prizes: $20 via PayPal, $20 worth of art supplies, or a portrait of their choice. The giveaway had a surprising amount of participation, especially considering how low the prize value was.

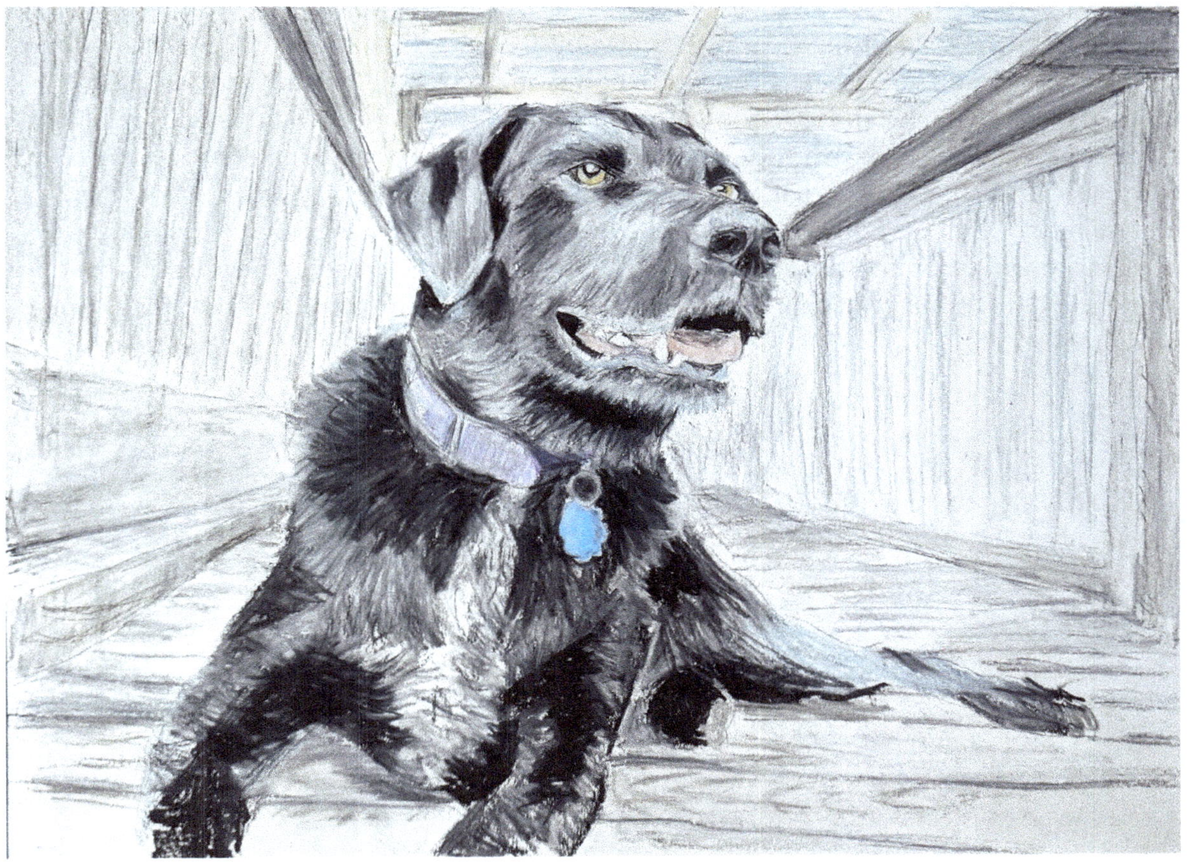

The most recent giveaway winner requested a portrait of her very cool dog.

The winner selected cash, which I expected. But it the gears in my head started turning after I realized I was a bit disappointed they didn't select the portrait. Why not host another giveaway, but this time only offer a portrait or artwork of the winner's choice? So, I did just that, and amazingly the participation was roughly the same. I've done several art-only giveaways now, and each time has actually been quite a positive experience. The winners have seemed to enjoy the portraits, and I had the benefit of drawing some entirely new faces.

There are some elements of risk here, though. The first, which I was admittedly quite nervous about, is the fear that a stranger may not like my artwork. It's actually similar to my fear with publishing this book; although I know some people do like my portraits, the thought of receiving harsh feedback makes me a bit unsettled. I know criticism is a fact of life, but hey - I can admit that those feelings lurk around my psyche sometimes. But I have worried with each giveaway that the winner will see the result and say, "you know what, that's alright… I don't want it." It hasn't happened yet, but I regard that as a risk. Also, another possible looming issue is my ability to draw someone I've only seen from one photograph. It's gone fine so far, but I wonder if I'll come upon a face or scene that I just can't handle.

Summary:

Positives: Can drive traffic to a website while simultaneously getting a hand-delivered new idea for a portrait.
Negatives: Feedback from the winner could be a wildcard.

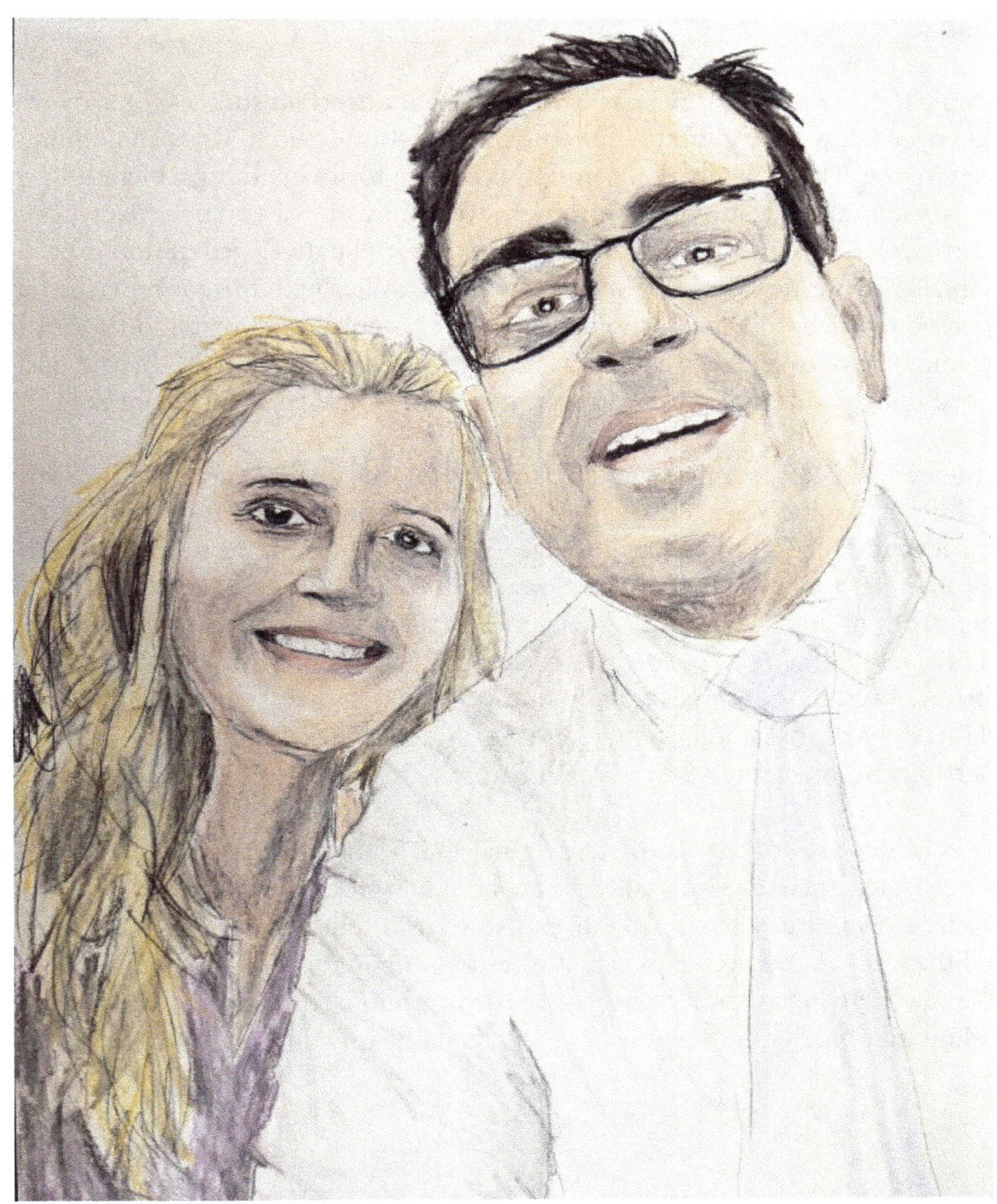

First portrait giveaway result. The winner wanted a portrait with her husband.

MEMES AND UNCERTAIN SOURCES

The last topic for this section is primarily to talk about uncertain sources for artwork ideas. My initial voyage down this rabbit hole came from a whim I had to draw something from an Internet meme. The Millennial generation is known for many things, including craft beer, skinny jeans, and "destroying" seemingly every industry (if you believe cynical clickbait articles). One development from the first "digital native" generation is particularly entertaining: The Internet Meme. If you aren't very familiar with the concept, the term was originally used by Richard Dawkins to describe the way cultural information spreads. Internet memes have overtaken his original definition, and now "meme" usually just refers to captioned images, obscure sub-culture reference, or nonsensical inside jokes.

Because memes are created quickly and by any person, the quality varies wildly; some are hilarious, but just as many are terrible. Most sites use a voting system, so users determine what is funny and makes it to the "front page." The concept is interesting because the content is always fresh and often reflects news or cultural topics of the day. Meme-creators pull images from millions of sources (social media, news, ads, etc.), slap captions on them, and then proliferate them across the Internet using fake screen names. Once a meme has passed through untold thousands of anonymous people, how do you determine where it started? How do you give an originator (likely a photographer) credit? This is a deceptively tricky question and one I hadn't considered before I attempted to draw one.

Unfortunately, I could not determine an original source for the drawing I attempted, which perfectly illustrates the issue. Some memes are based on stock photography, which is easy enough to figure out. But when it isn't, even using a time-filtered reverse image search may not help if the image is obscure enough. Without an original source, naturally, it's impossible to obtain permission or license to use in a book. And without either, it would be a tremendous gamble that I hope most people would be unwilling to take.

Another interesting, but potentially uncertain, source I've come across is Internet forums. I have found several major forums that feature "draw me" threads. In these threads, users post a photograph of themselves, then other participants draw or paint portraits and share the results within the thread. They're interesting threads just for general browsing purposes because it's nice to see the variety of art styles and results that appear. From my perspective, I also considered participating for yet another source of portrait ideas. A similar concern exists here though; who actually took the photograph, and do you have permission to do anything with it? My thought was that you could request commercial use permission from the original poster, but those threads usually move so fast, I'm not sure if that would be effective.

Summary:

Positives: Interesting ideas. Results might be funny and/or popular online.
Negatives: Obtaining permission or licensing might be impossible in some cases.

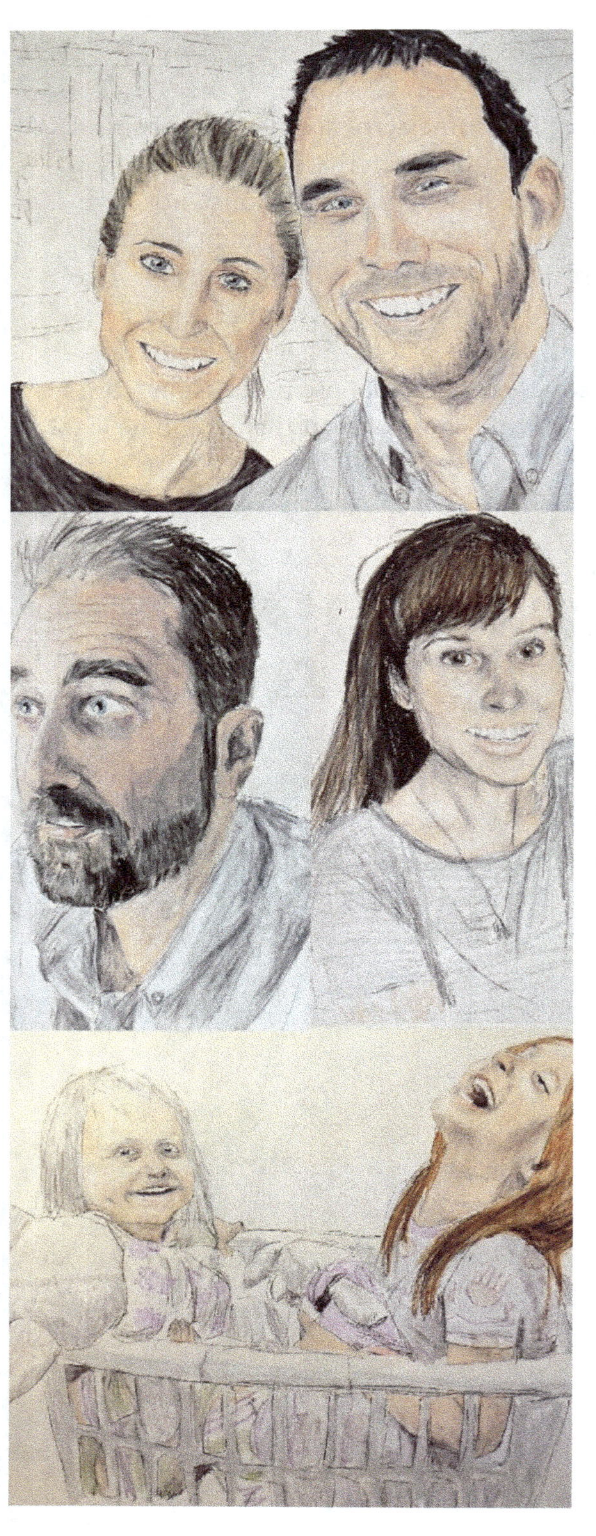

Phase 5 – Refinement & Realism

JUNE 2018

In this book, I've frequently been referring to "phases" of art. I feel like it's important to point out that in this context, a phase is very much an artificial construct. I'm using it in this context only to facilitate splitting content into something organized and readable. But progress has really been a fluid and sometimes uneven thing, and I believe that's probably true for most artists. Some projects just work, others might be a step backward; the point is that I don't want to give the impression of a strictly linear progression.

With that being said, this chapter will cover my most recent art phase. I think at this point, the artwork shows how my heavy layering and blending comfort level has grown. I still make mistakes, and surely always will, but the mistakes seem to less often derail what I was trying to accomplish. Progress is slow, but practice definitely shows dividends. Just comparing pieces from this section of the book to the earlier chapters, it's gratifying to see growth.

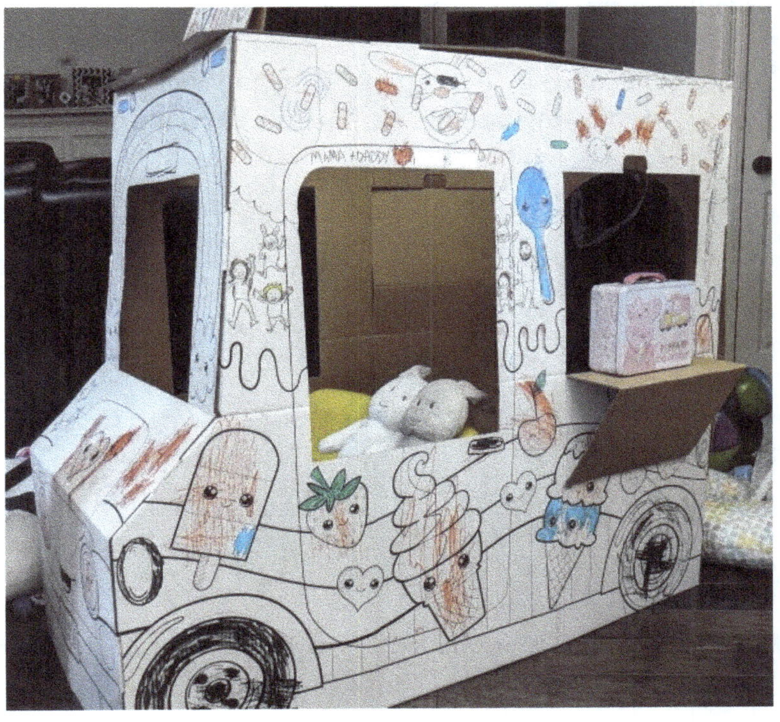

A cardboard ice cream truck that we all decorated together with markers.

BACK TO BASICS

In June 2018, I made my first clumsy attempt at digital art. And over the previous few months, I had been almost exclusively drawing fictional characters from movies, athletes, and performers. That was a significant change from earlier in the artwork, when I pretty much always sketched my family. At a point, I felt I needed to diversify my subjects, and I was able to accomplish that.

Although I resolved to continue mixing things up, I thought this was a good time to get back to the basics (well, my basics anyway). And it felt especially appropriate after those rough digital sketch attempts. To me, my family always represents a safe and comfortable drawing experience. I just know their faces so well and have drawn them so many times, it's usually a fairly smooth process.

Although it ended up being pretty close in perspective, the drawing I put together was based on the kids hanging out in a cardboard ice cream truck.

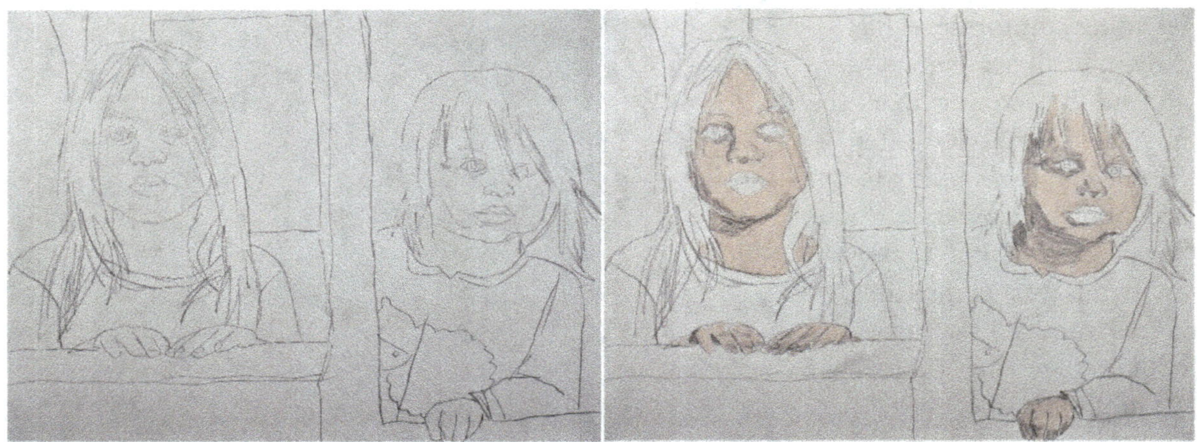

Portrait of the girls playing in their cardboard ice cream truck. Progression sketches above.

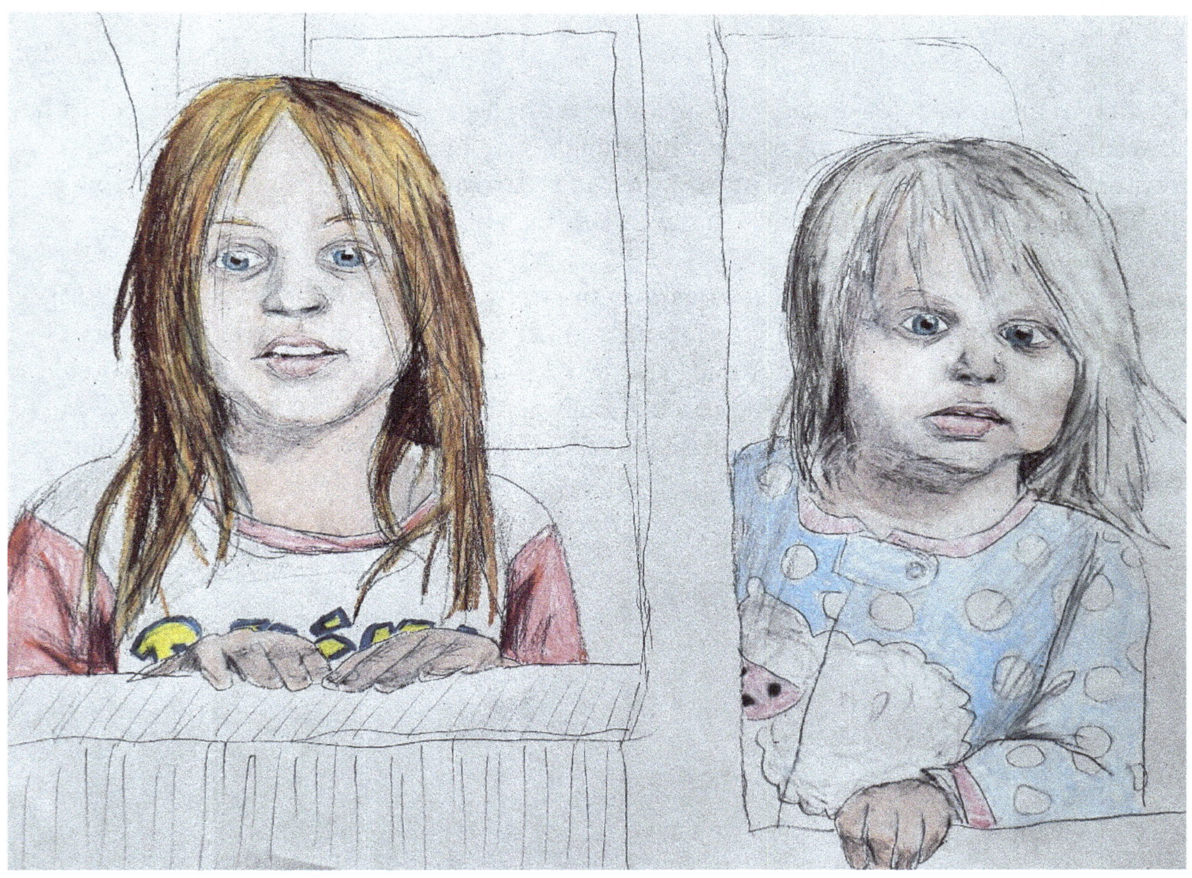

Final version of the girls in their ice cream truck.

The girls were depicted accurately here I think, and you can certainly tell it's them. I even represented some of their favorite pajamas in the scene. I think I did a good job capturing their mouths and noses, and more or less got the hair colors right. Of course, none of my artwork is perfect and this is no exception. I did a somewhat poor job on our youngest's left eye (left from her perspective) and her face seems like it might be lopsided. One of her eyes is bigger than the other in the sketch, and I drew her a bit cross-eyed. So, it's not the most accurate depiction of her. To sum this up, getting back to drawing the kiddos was like riding a bike. I jumped right into it easily enough, but I did make some mistakes.

GIFT SKETCHES

I've drawn my mom a few times, but for some reason have struggled somewhat to depict her accurately. I'm usually able to get a decent enough near-likeness, but with some slight feature appearing off. I think one of the aspects I've struggled with is her smile; there's a slight upturn at the edges that I haven't been able to capture.

For her birthday in 2018, I decided a birthday present project was in order. I decided to try two different scenes, one including my mom and her two grandkids, and the other was a scene of my mom as a kid with her dad. This was another instance of working on two drawings at the same time, but I'll start by discussing the throwback to her childhood. I used an old photograph of my mom and her dad riding horses. The photo was extremely blurry, and sort of far off, so it was pretty difficult to get the details right. I've drawn her dad (my sister and I called him Paw Paw) before, but never as a younger man.

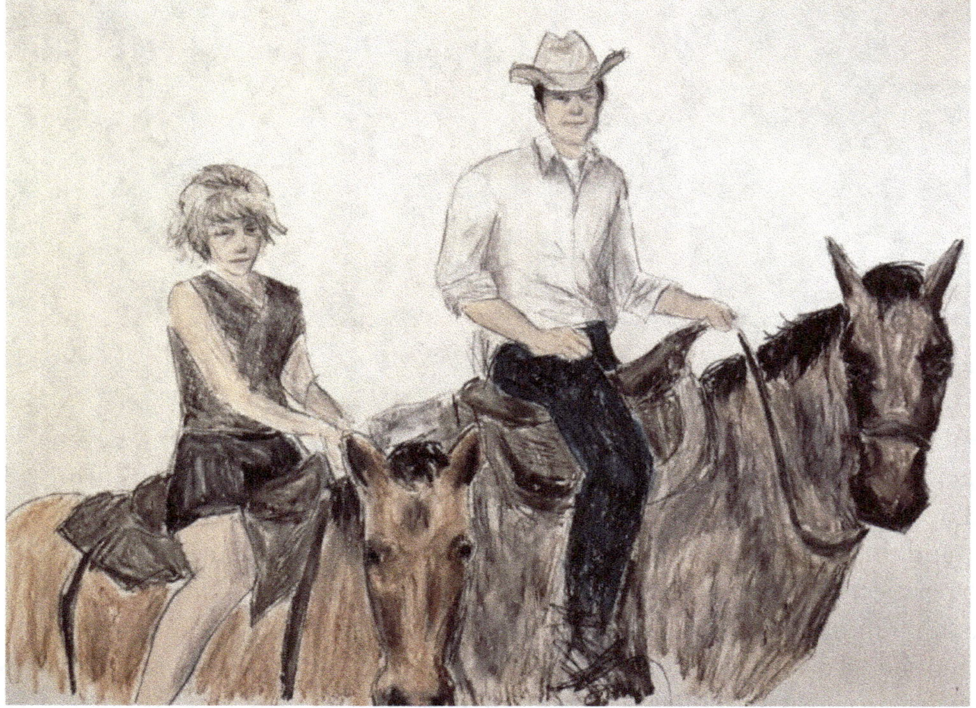

My mom and her dad (we called him Paw Paw) riding their trusty steeds.

It's certainly no masterpiece; it was a challenge to imagine features on younger versions of them that I never knew. But for something that only had a basic guide from a blurry photograph, it's not a bad effort. I gave myself bonus points for the fact that I don't think I'd ever drawn a horse before. The horses aren't amazing, but at least they do look like horses. And I think I captured a decent general representation of my mom and her dad. It sort of looks like them. This particular viewpoint is also not a strong point for me; I've mentioned before, I'm at my best in close up views of faces. This is panned sort of far out, which took me out of my comfort zone.

The next drawing was a recent scene of my mom and the kids. I got a chance to work some perspective on this one, with my youngest in the foreground, oldest in the middle, and my mom behind them. It was good to be closer than I was in the horse sketch, but I still think I would have been more comfortable zooming in a bit more.

I really did well on my youngest daughter. This isn't much of a surprise though, because she was the largest figure and I could get after the finer details easily. The weakest part of the drawing might be my oldest daughter; I think I went over the areas of her face too much. I ended up with so many layers of pencil, I couldn't impact her features with a pencil anymore. This is a good example of the downside of the way I approach pencil painting; if I judge shading or feature details incorrectly early, sometimes it's not fixable later. In terms of my mom, finally captured a fairly accurate version of her smile.

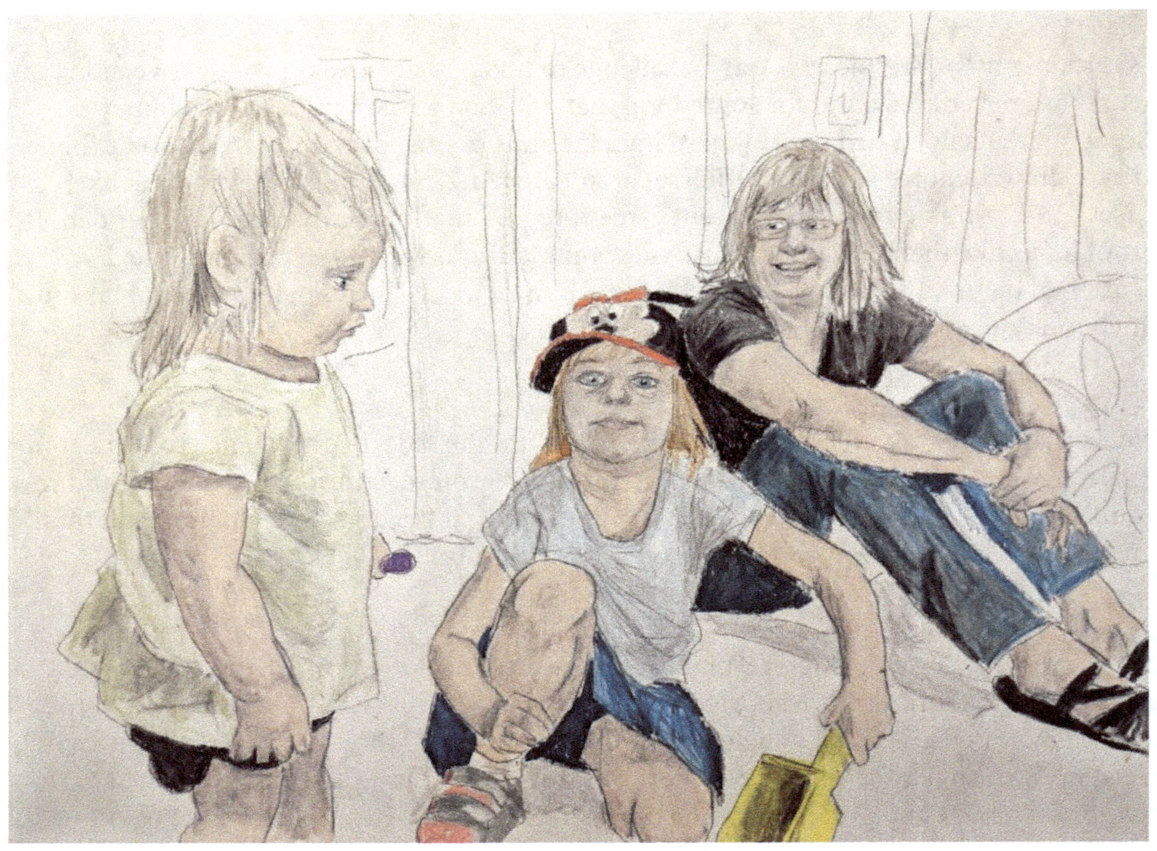

My mom and the girls playing.

When I started, it seemed like only the drawing with my mom and kids was going to be decent enough to actually give to her. But, after fine-tuning, I ended up giving both drawings to her. I am a terrible judge of my own art, and can never actually tell what people would like, but she seemed happy with them.

A FAMILY PORTRAIT FROM NEW ORLEANS

Artwork, like most hobbies, seems to ebb and flow. Sometimes, I'll average almost 10 drawings a month, then other months I might only get one finished. Peaks tend to coincide with periods when we don't have much going on and the weekends are somewhat unclaimed. Valleys certainly align with times when we're on the go, typically during weeks or months with a lot of travel. During one of those busy travel times during the summer, I had to travel to New Orleans for work. When it's possible, I like to bring my wife and kids with me so we can turn it into a working semi-vacation. This New Orleans trip, we all headed down to the French Quarter for a major dining upgrade.

I decided to commemorate the trip with some artwork. The scene I decided on was me, my wife, and kids at Cafe Du Monde. All these places we visited were great on that trip; I always enjoy getting my hands on some authentic shrimp and grits, etouffee, or a roast beef po-boy. But a must-visit every time we're in New Orleans is Cafe Du Monde for some beignets. In hindsight on this drawing, it's a shame I didn't include any scenery. This place has a very distinctive green and white awning, so it would have been a nice touch. Since I typically complete the coloring of people right away, my concern is always ruining a finished portrait by adding scenery. If I were to work on the background at the same time, perhaps this would become less of a concern.

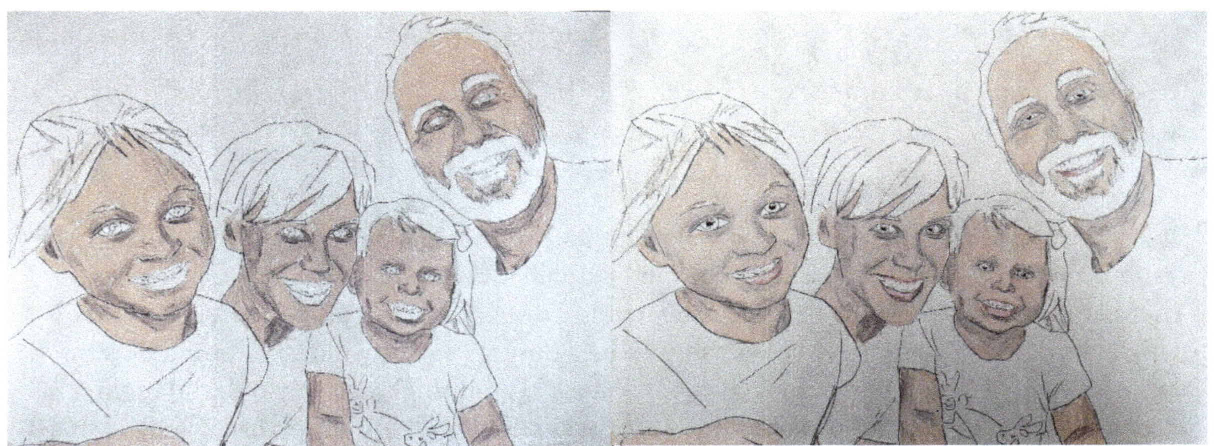

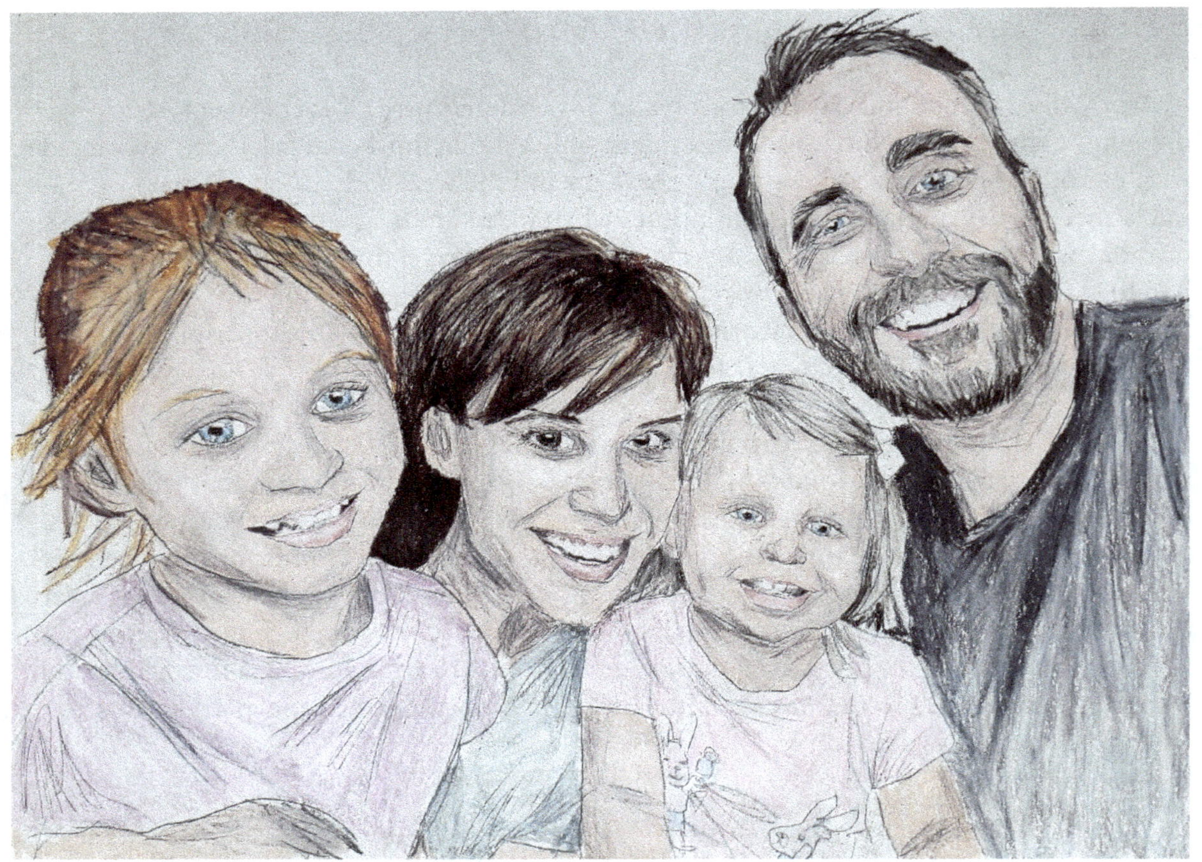

A family portrait from a trip to New Orleans. We were at our favorite beignet place (Café Du Monde)...wouldn't it have been nice if I had drawn that too?

This portrait worked out better than I expected. I can't say it's perfect, but I like the end result quite a bit. For the most part, I think I actually captured everyone's look accurately. There are a few small things that probably could have gone better such as the eye colors, which aren't really accurate. My eyes should be a darker blue, my oldest's should be a bit darker too. And I actually applied layers of color a bit too thickly on my oldest daughter's face, which prevented me from adding more detail. Also, it doesn't look like I got the shape of my wife's face quite right; it's very close, but something does seem slightly off. It's sort of rare for me to include so many subjects and actually get all of them mostly right.

BIG KID AND HER APPLE

After the New Orleans drawing, I had a somewhat extended break. Certainly not on the level of that 15-year break from the start of the book, but it was a bit more than a month between drawings. I've felt it's important to continue drawing occasionally to keep myself in the habit because I really don't want months to turn into years again. Drifting into another long period without art seems like a good thing to avoid. And a good way to bust out of a slump is to head to a comfort zone, back to subjects or styles that are familiar. For me, that is, of course, my family.

My oldest daughter started school in 2018, which was pretty exciting. She struggled a bit at the beginning because she wasn't used to being away from us. We were fortunate to not have to put either kid into daycare prior to them being school-aged. But the downside to that is the adjustment period is rough. But my oldest is a very social child, so once she got used to the concept, she absolutely loved it. She's learning a ton in her Montessori school, and I love when she comes home and tells us all about what she learned. At the time of this drawing, she was totally preoccupied with the planets and our solar system, and with the parts of an apple. She colored an apple booklet that she's very proud of, and got to play with some plastic apples in class.

After over a month off from drawing, I expected some rust, but surprisingly I didn't find any. I jumped right into it and it felt like I'd just drawn yesterday. This definitely looks like her and I believe I did a solid job of capturing the right perspective. It's sort of a downward view, and that looks right at a glance. I think I could have done a better job on the shading/shadows on her shirt and jeans though. I'm not sure what happened there, but the shadows particularly in her shirt don't look natural and probably needed a different color than the gray I used. That is actually an area I need to work on even now; I rely on grays too much for shadows, and I need to learn to incorporate darker versions of similar colors.

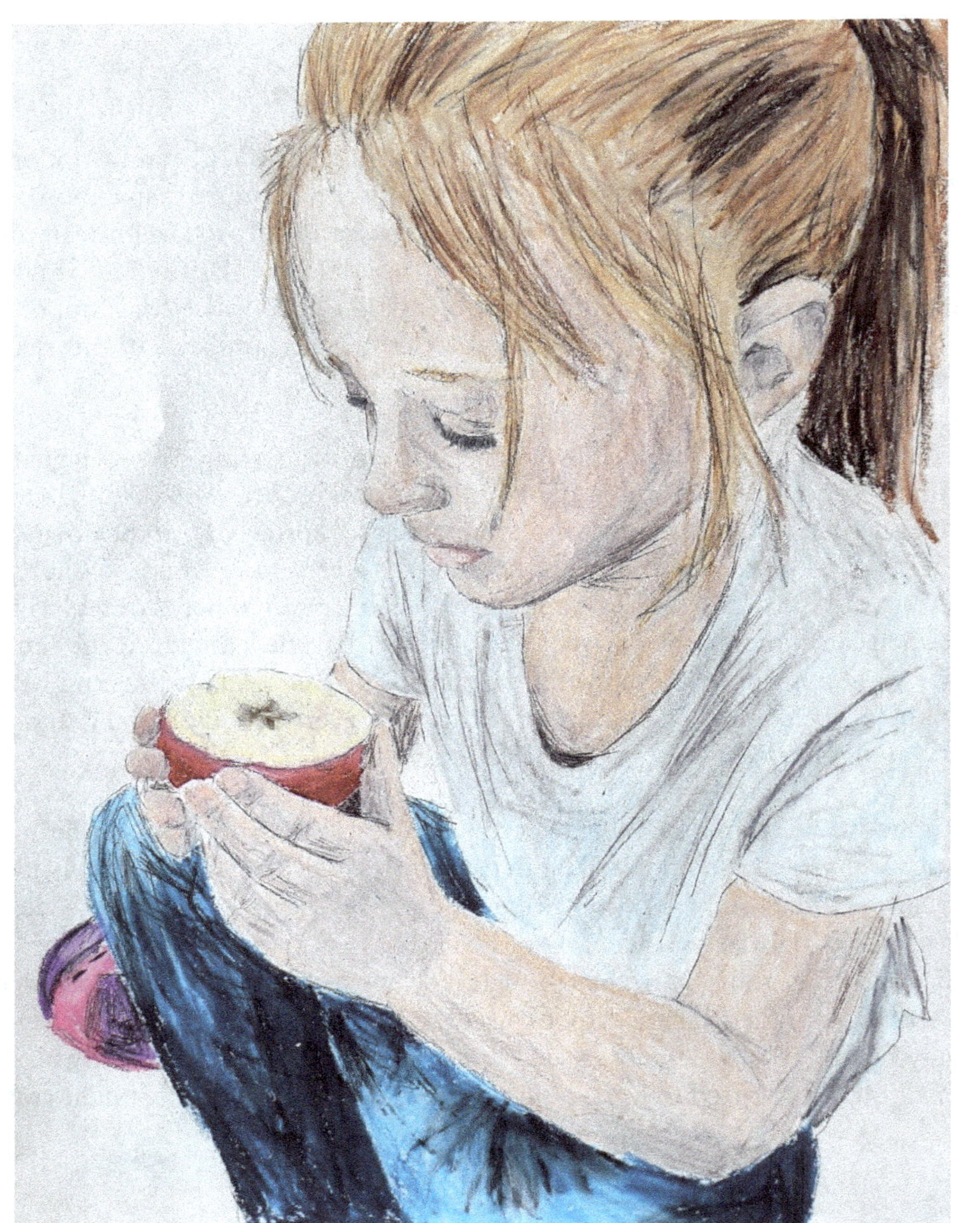

Our big kid and her very weird looking apple.

Also, that apple looks pretty weird, definitely not very natural looking. Part of the issue is she was actually holding a plastic apple, and I tried to make it look like a real one. I placed a curve at the top as if the stem would be there, but then put a core running perpendicular. And there's no inward curve at the bottom. It's definitely not like any apple I've ever seen. Once I realized this, it's sort of hard to unsee Schrodinger's apple that exists in two states of being at once.

THE LAUNDRY BASKET GIRLS

After my apple drawing, I went on another somewhat extended run of movie, television, and other subjects that I couldn't publish. I went on a major artwork tear again, which lasted about a month. Eventually, I came back to my favorite portrait subjects as usual. At this point, I had been drawing again for well over a year and started thinking about what I've made. I hadn't done a full accounting of people or types of artwork I'd done, but felt pretty confident my wife and kids were the most frequently drawn people. This felt like a spreadsheet begging to be made, which is an idea I returned to later. But for now, I felt like working on another portrait featuring the kids.

I decided to go with a scene from when the girls were playing in a laundry basket. Of course, a laundry basket is just what boring adults call it; in reality, it's either an incredible space ship and a boat (the situation seemed to change every couple of minutes). And when our kitchen became the depths of space (or a vast ocean), was pretty hard to make dinner. I'm consistently amazed at their imaginations. I know most kids play similarly, but I love watching as the act out such funny situations.

As large as they both were at the time, they both somehow managed to fold themselves up fit in one laundry basket. It was a pretty funny site – despite how cramped it looked, they had so much fun. It seemed like a perfect scene to draw. I don't even know exactly what they were laughing about; they may have just been in a feedback loop, laughing more because they were laughing. This was one of those sketches that started off roughly, and I wasn't sure if it was going to work. I realized during the graphite and early shading steps that the facial expressions I was trying to depict were more challenging than I initially realized. It seems like that happens often because I'm not very good at looking ahead on these.

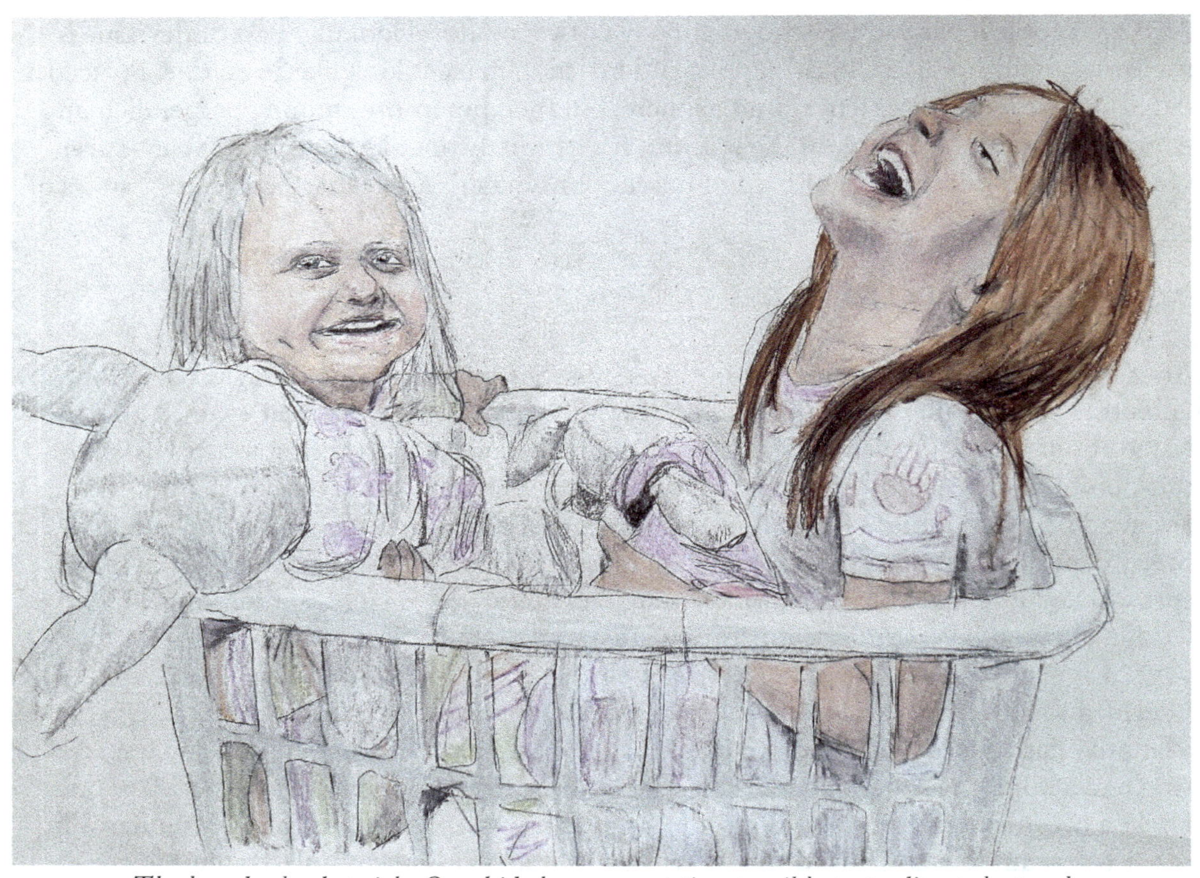

The laundry basket girls. Our kids have a great time possibly pretending to be towels.

The look I tried to convey is pure joy and happiness, but I didn't get all the way there. My youngest daughter looks more sleepy than happy; although she is smiling here, she was supposed to be cracking up. This looks more like a slight smile, which isn't what I was trying to do. I did a better job on my oldest daughter's expression, which is surprising because I thought the open-mouth laugh at that angle would be more difficult. Another issue I had was the basket; my lines were very uneven. I was probably trying to go too quickly.

SELF PORTRAIT – SHADOW AND CONTRAST STRUGGLES

I came across an article towards the end of 2018 called *How to Be an Artist – 33 Rules to Take you from Clueless Amateur to Generational Talent (or at Least Help you Live Life a Little More Creatively)*. It's a long title, but the article had detailed advice for artists from a professional art critic. As I've said, I am an untrained hobbyist still trying to learn. Because of my lack of formal art instruction, I may not have enough experience to fully relate to everything in the article. But some of the advice seemed very useful, like the author's encouragement not to be embarrassed, and some insightful ideas on brainstorming and idea generation. Even though I don't anticipate ever becoming a professional artist, it's always nice to find useful, practical advice.

The article put me in a mood of self-reflection about my artwork. My drawings are generally pretty informal, and many are fictional characters or performers of some sort. The sketches of movie characters, for example, are essentially fan art. In other words, they may not be real "art" in the way a professional critic might consider. I'm okay with that because it's fun and that is mostly what this hobby is about. But it did get me thinking about what a fellow like myself could do that was more along those "professional" lines. A self-portrait seemed like something even famous artists have done, so I decided to try a more detailed study of my own face. I thought I could push for greater depth of shadow and contrast, which is something I sometimes struggle with.

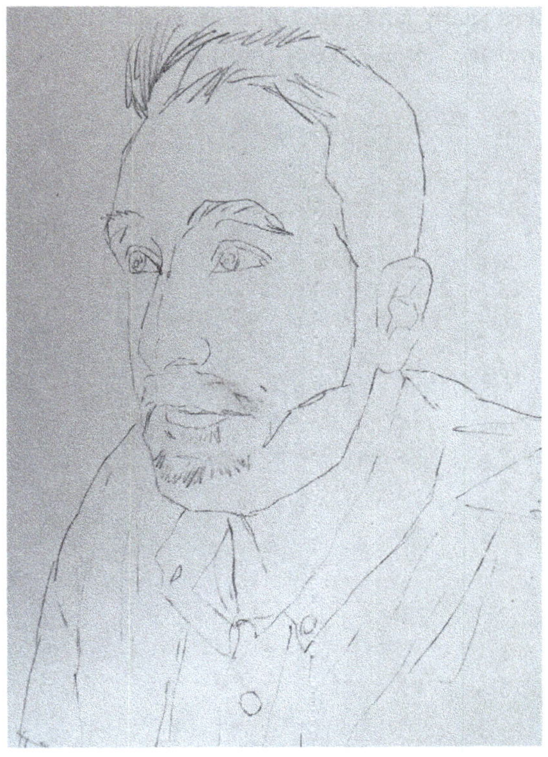

Self-portrait attempt emphasize shadows and more realistic skin tones. Progressions on this page and next, followed by the final version.

Usually, when I draw myself, my wife and kids are also in the sketch, and I'm much more focused on making sure I do a good job on them. So, often there are details that I flub on myself, like a botched nose shape, weird beard, or other facial feature oddities. This time though, I think I put together a relatively accurate version of myself. I captured my large beak, long face, and deep-set eyes, and small mouth pretty much in the right proportions. I think I got the hair and beard color right too, which hasn't always happened.

I'm honestly a little afraid sometimes to venture out of my comfort zone. I've overcome a few big hurdles, like trying color and then applying color thickly. But one of those lingering hesitations is depicting deep shadows and bright light. I'm just not great at it, and even now I feel like it's something I need to become a better artist. With this self-portrait, I really tried to force higher contrast, which I came closer to doing, but not as far as I'd have liked. If this was really accurate to life, I would have had much deeper shadows on the right side of the picture (eyes, side of the nose, etc.).

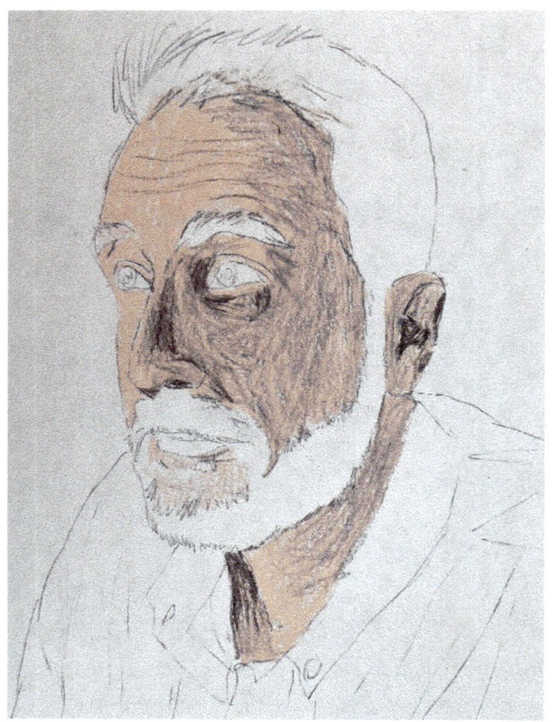 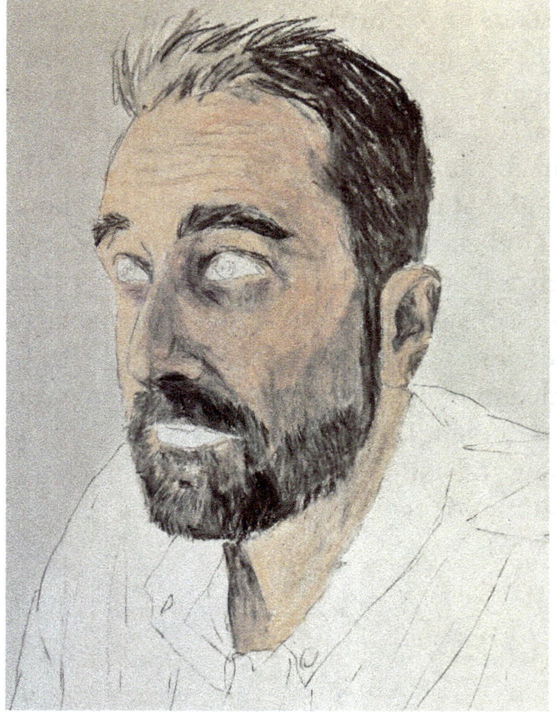

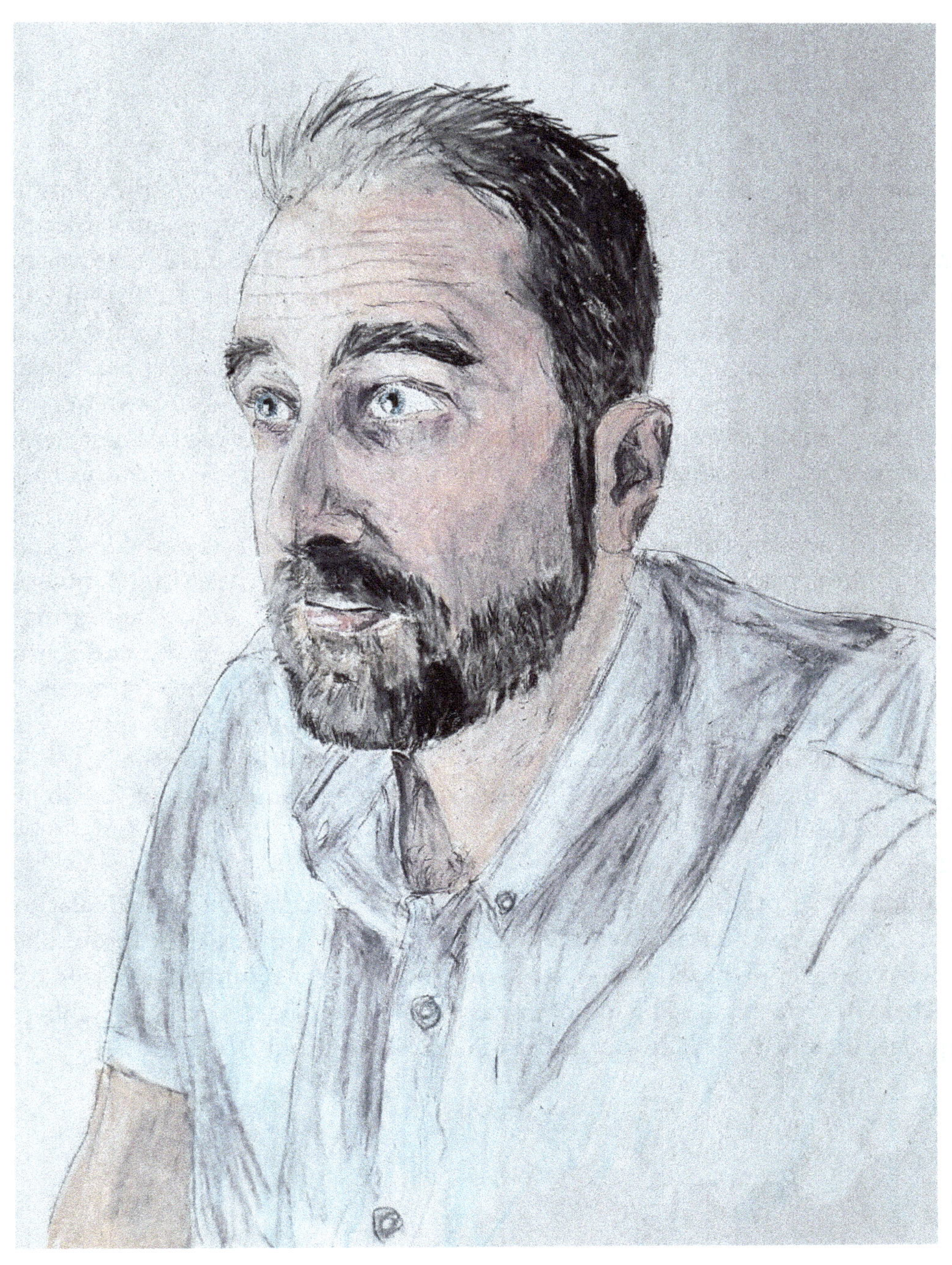

SUBJECT COUNTS AND WIFE PORTRAITS

Since getting back into drawing in 2017, I've generally been under the impression that most of my artwork has been of my family. I also had a feeling the most frequent subject was either my wife or our kids. Because data analysis is always fun, I decided there was no point in just assuming or guessing – better to crunch the numbers and find out for sure. I utilized some website data exports and the magic of functions and pivot tables to generate an up-to-date spreadsheet. The basic idea was to see a tally of each time someone appears in artwork, whether as part of a group or individually. Then I broke those down into two tiers of additional categories. For example, the initial tally would be for a specific character or actor, then categorized as a particular show, and finally more broadly as an actor category.

The results were actually sort of surprising. When looking at subjects individually, my oldest daughter was the top subject appearing in 20 drawings, with her little sister coming in second at 16. The big surprise was that my wife wasn't even third – I was, appearing in 13 sketches. My wife came in fourth with 12. No other individual subject was close (my mom was actually next, appearing in only four drawings). When grouped into categories, naturally our immediate family (me, my wife, and the kids) completely outpaced everything else. I also tried grouping the smaller-numbered subjects, while keeping the larger tallies (like my wife and the kids) as individual counts. It's sort of an inconsistent way to look at it, but I found the counts interesting

I was legitimately surprised by how many actors I'd drawn. Only one individual actor had more than one (Patrick Stewart), but the total number was far more than I would have guessed. Another fact I realized is that, aside from the marriage proposal drawing of her I mentioned a few chapters ago, I had not drawn my wife by herself. Since everything I had done typically included our kids too, as her total increased, so did theirs.

Gallery Subjects	#	%
The Amdalls	61	35.5%
Actors	26	15.1%
Video Game Characters	13	7.6%
Extended Family	13	7.6%
Unknown People	12	7.0%
Friends	11	6.4%
Dark Tower Characters	9	5.2%
Athletes	9	5.2%
Musicians	6	3.5%
Radio Hosts	3	1.7%
Various Old Sketches	3	1.7%
Animals	3	1.7%
Contest Winners	2	1.2%
Scientists	1	0.6%
Grand Total	**172**	**100.0%**

Gallery Subjects 2	#	%
Actors	26	15.4%
Oldest Daughter	20	11.8%
Youngest Daughter	16	9.5%
Video Game Characters	13	7.7%
Me	13	7.7%
Unknown People	12	7.1%
Wife	12	7.1%
Friends	11	6.5%
Dark Tower Characters	9	5.3%
Athletes	9	5.3%
Musicians	6	3.6%
Mom	4	2.4%
Animals	3	1.8%
Radio Hosts	3	1.8%
Grandfather	2	1.2%
Contest Winners	2	1.2%
Sister in Law	2	1.2%
Sister	2	1.2%
Mother in Law	1	0.6%
Scientists	1	0.6%
Granny	1	0.6%
Brother in Law	1	0.6%
Grand Total	**169**	**100.0%**

Amdall Gallery subject counts. Left: All categories grouped. Right: Family listed as individuals, all other categories grouped.

It's true what they say – data speaks, and in this case, it suggested quite clearly what my next set of portraits should be. This seemed like a great opportunity to do a couple of individual sketches of my wife without the kids or a husband. I wanted to get some slightly different poses of her as well and decided to start with a straight-on view with a fairly standard pose.

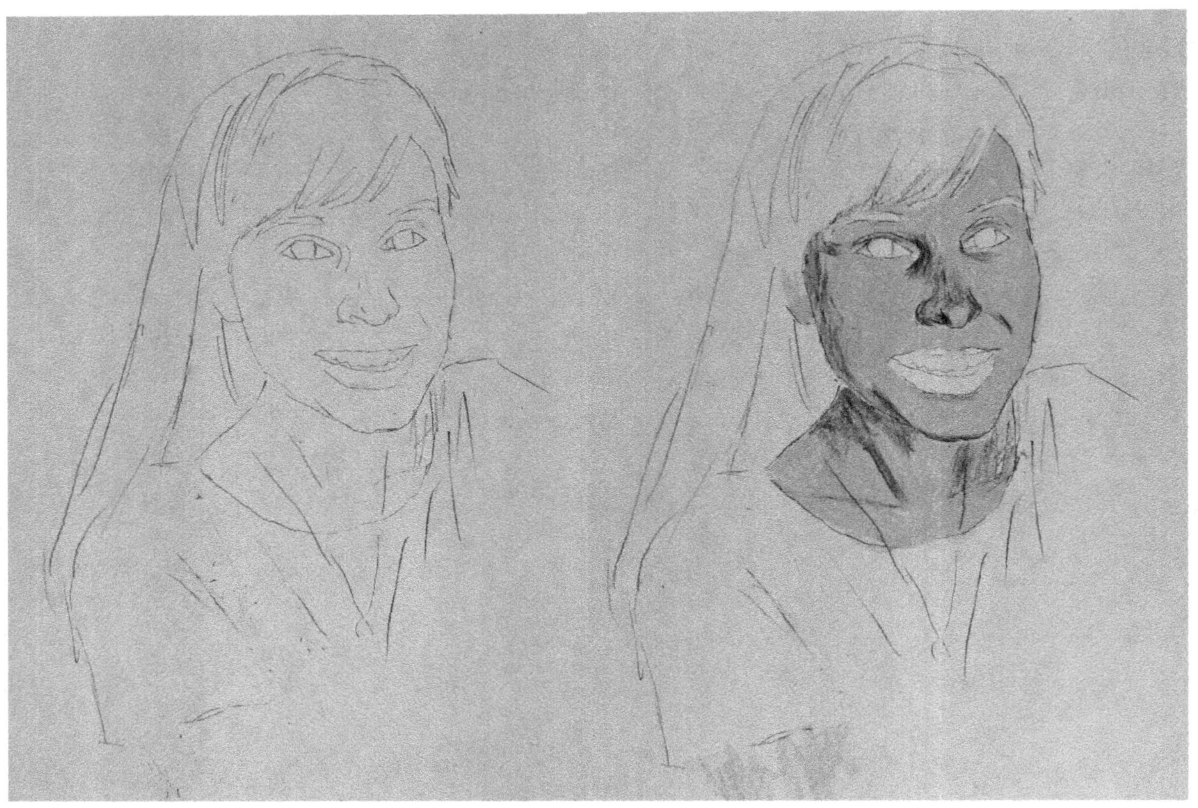

Portrait of my wife. This one might be the most accurate I've done of her to date. Progression images above, followed by final portrait on the next page.

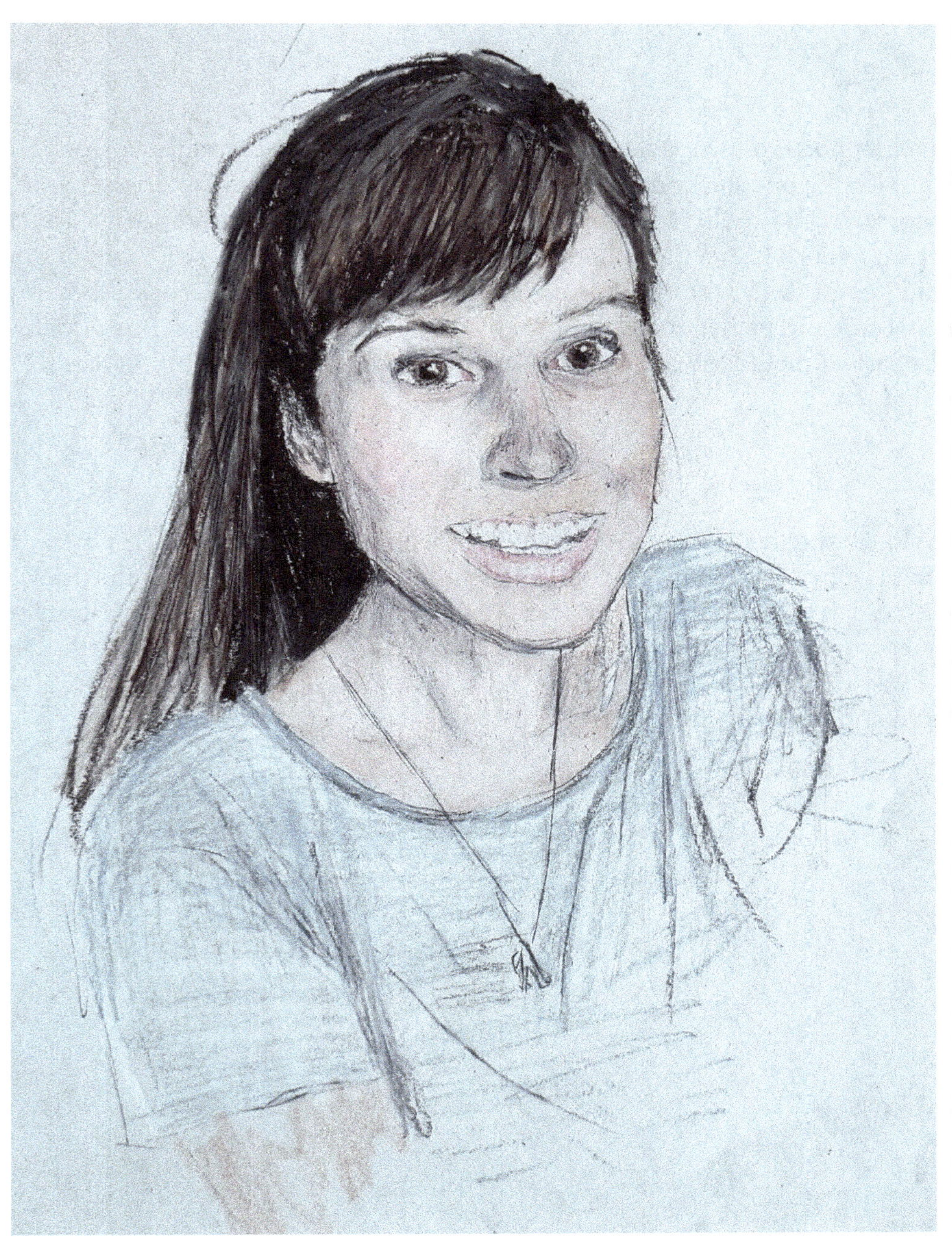

I think the first portrait turned out the best of the two I did concurrently. It looks the most like her and it's the one she said she liked the most. The features all look right to me and fit together correctly. Naturally, I see my wife all the time, so it's important that a sketch of her passes the "at a quick glance" test. In other words, if I briefly looked at it without examining closely, did I come away with the impression that it looks right? I can always closely examine my own artwork and pick it apart, finding any number of smaller flaws. But a quick glance test can be a good method to almost see it as a casual observer would. In this case, I believe it passes that test.

I was able to capture her nose and eye shapes. I even managed to accurately portray her lips here, which I'm not always able to do. I felt as good about this one during the drawing process as I did at the end. When I look at the sketch, I feel like I am looking at my wife. If any area needs improvement from a technical standpoint, it's probably the teeth. They look fine, but I was afraid to try for more detail for fear of messing it up. I already felt good about the rest of it and didn't want to get into a messy erasing cycle.

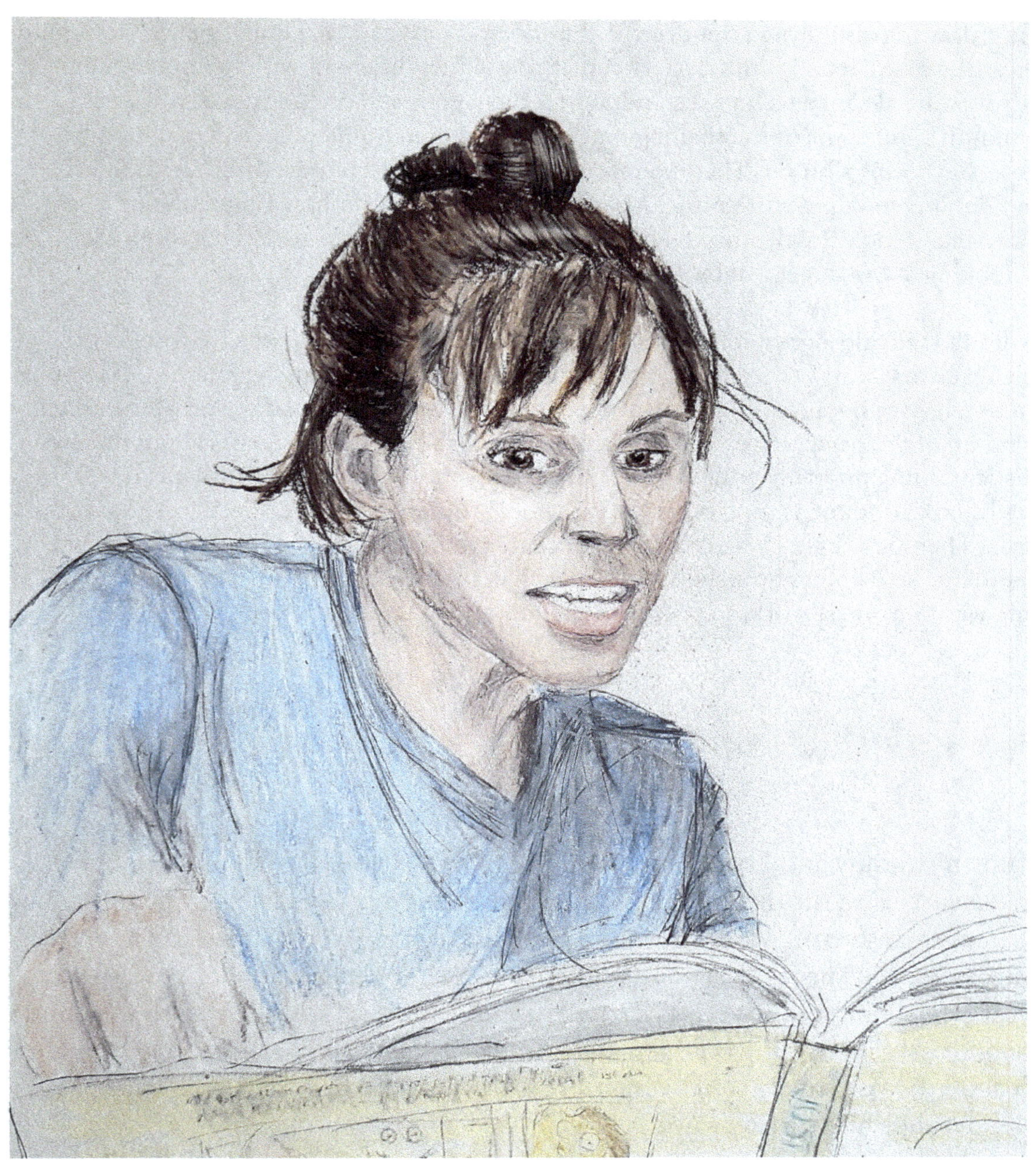

The next drawing also turned out decently but doesn't pass the "at a quick glance" test quite as well as the first. Here, I wanted to try something a little different, with her not looking directly forward. From a technical standpoint, I did a good job on the basic shapes (eyes, nose, mouth). But some of the shading and coloration aren't quite where they should be – it's close, but seems a bit off. There were some deep shadows from overhead lights in this scene, I don't believe I captured that. Also, I'm not certain about how I placed the pupils…when I look closely, they seem fine, but a browsing glance makes me think they aren't looking at the same spot by a hair.

I also didn't really do a great job on the book or her shirt. I wish I could have a do-over, especially for that shirt because I didn't select a good color or shading technique. Her hands were a tough issue because I didn't want them to draw attention from the rest of the sketch. But because of the perspective, the book and her hands would have been focal points. Lack of artistic training probably got me here. I'm also not sure about the facial shape; it's definitely close, but not as spot-on as the first one. From my wife's perspective, she says this one makes her look tired. I wasn't aiming for that, and I don't get that impression when I look at it, but who knows how she looks better than the lady herself? I did mention the shading wasn't my best work, so possibly I did too much under her eyes.

ART ON A SHOPPING CART

Any time my family and I take a trip to the store, we try to grab one of those bulky shopping carts with the dual kid seats. You know the type; usually brightly-colored, sometimes with steering wheels for the kids, but they're always giant-sized monstrosities. I'm sure they are annoying to other shoppers because of how much space they take up, but those carts sure are useful with two kids. We're also to a point where both kids love riding on them and specifically ask to go to the store so they can climb aboard. We actually select which stores to visit for major shopping trips based on whether they have these or not.

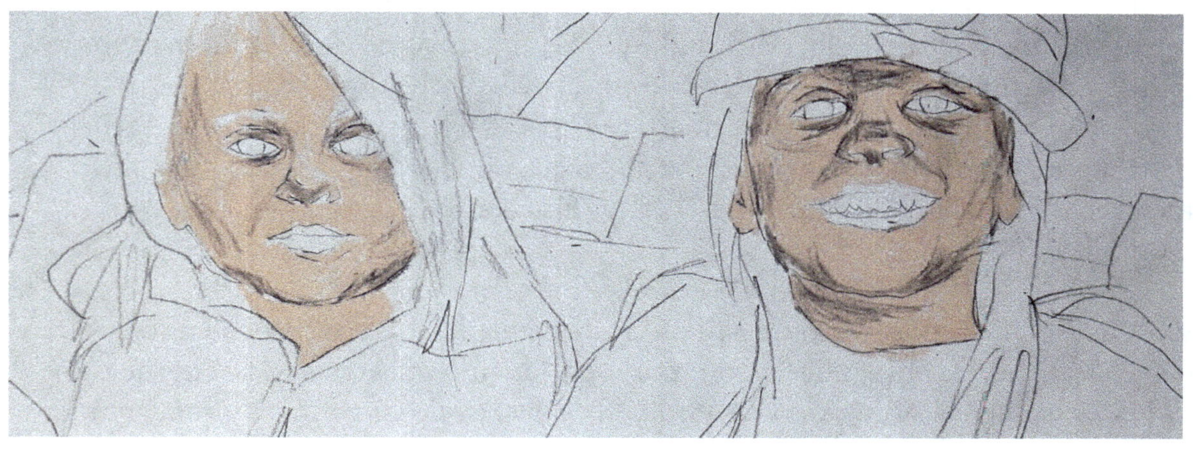

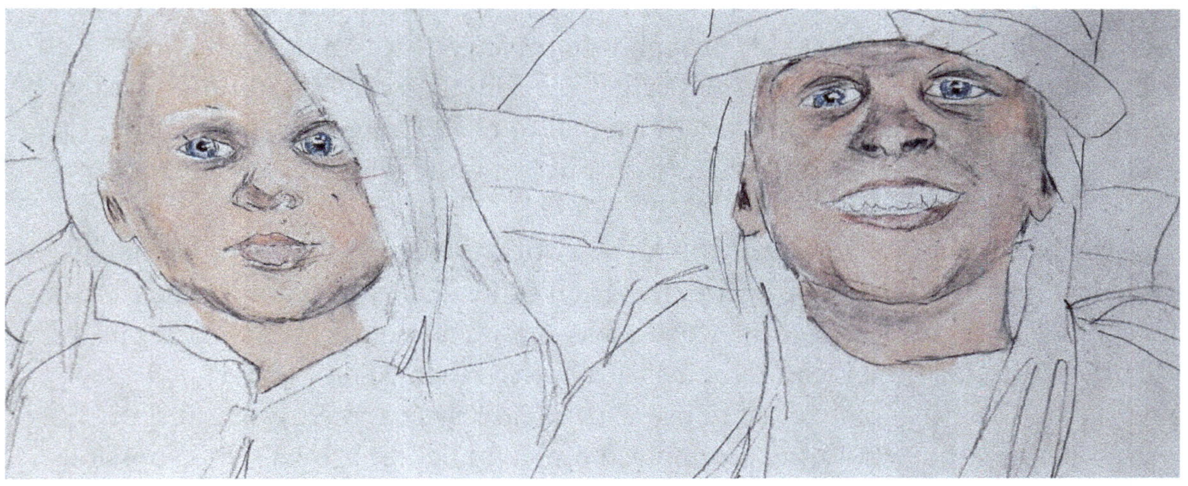

Two early progressions depicting shading on the kids' faces. First the base layers and initial definition, then some pink hues with white burnishing.

As I mentioned in a previous chapter, shopping carts are also an artwork theme for me. One day, I was pondering what to draw next and thought to do yet another one featuring the girls in a shopping cart. I like continuing that theme because they grow so quickly. Even within as few as a few months, particularly for my youngest daughter, they look a bit different. I'm not exactly covering new ground with this subject matter. But I enjoy it, and maybe I'll have an interesting series of them after some time. Variety is good sometimes, but it's also comforting to draw what you know well.

My youngest daughter at the time had officially entered her "terrible two" phase with a vengeance. She has always been a bit more serious-minded at times, but in the last couple weeks, she had thrown some absolutely cataclysmic tantrums. I mean, getting so angry that my wife and I just looked at each other like, "*what in the world is happening here?!*" But then other times, she's just as happy and bubbly as can be. I remember this with our oldest a couple of years ago, but in the interim, I think I had allowed myself to forget. Most kids probably go through this – in fact, when my oldest was two years old, we sometimes called her "bipolar baby" due to her rapidly shifting mood at the time. So, an aspect I wanted to reflect here is: Is the child about to smile, or is she about to yell? A tricky one, but I'm quite familiar with the look.

Getting back to the artwork, I really think I've gotten the hang of drawing these kids. Obviously, I have had a ton of practice, but I can somewhat easily capture their looks with accuracy now. Some previous efforts haven't always been as accurate for one kid or the other, but this time I was on point with both of them. The perspective I used also worked well, and I was excited to use what I had learned recently about skin pigment blending: Incorporating more blush pink and lighter browns when possible, instead of always using warm grays.

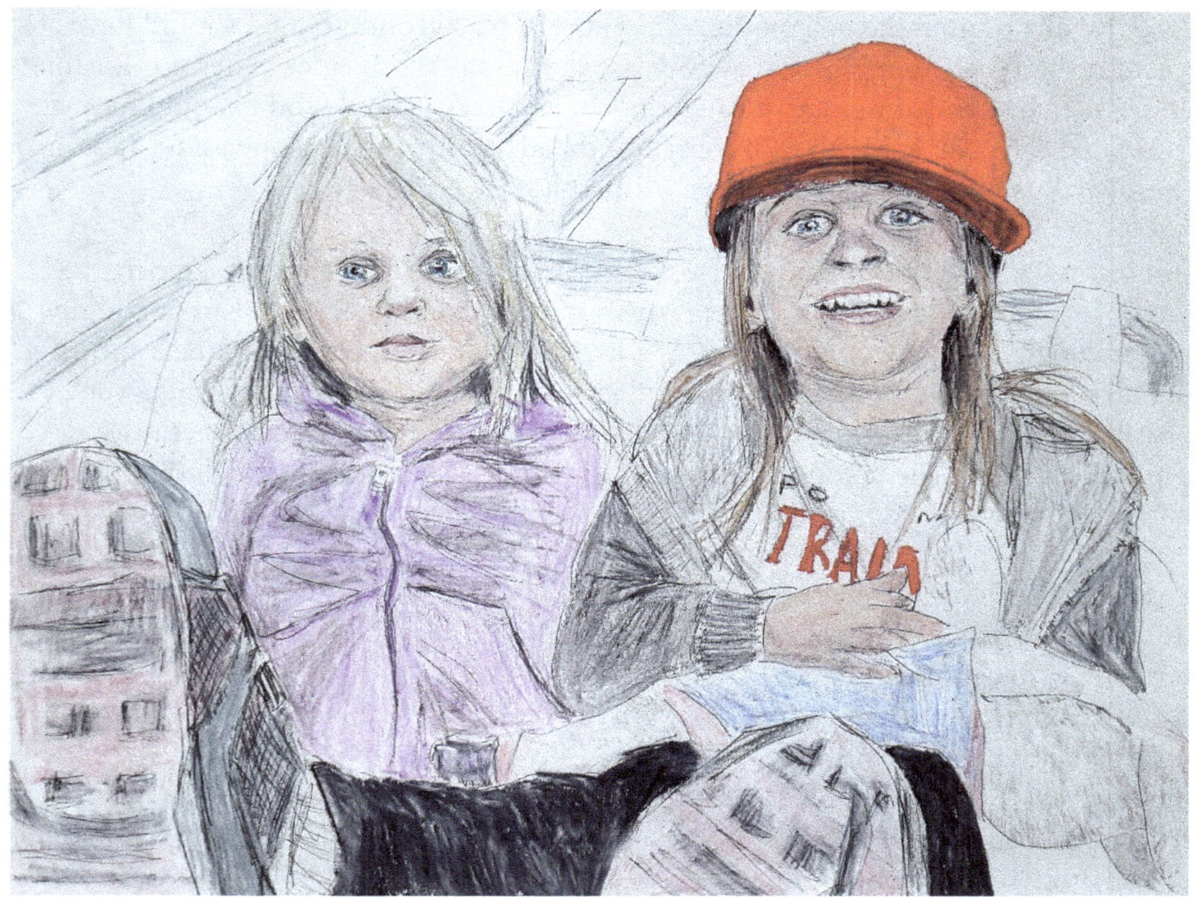

The kids riding in a shopping cart, which happens to be one of their favorite activities.

In terms of areas for improvement, I really needed to focus on a lighter graphite sketch at the beginning, particularly for mouths. There are not necessarily real lines around lips, and if there are, they shouldn't be as heavy as I often show. Lips should more seamlessly blend into the rest of the face. Also, I showed here that I still need to work on my depictions of teeth, particularly where they blend into gums. After this portrait, I actually considered just drawing a huge mouth for practice.

Also, I really punted the ball on doing any sort of background here; I should have at least finished the shopping cart. Wasn't the shopping cart the idea generator for this entire sketch? I ended up with a roughly sketched background, and I should have at least tried to go farther with it. But my mind had already put this one aside, and once that switch is flipped, I typically have a difficult time going back.

Interestingly, with this portrait, I had to get a bit creative after the fact. During the long process of seeking publishing permission for various artwork, I had hoped my oldest daughter's hat would make it. She loves a certain game that features capturing digital monsters and prefers to wear clothes featuring those characters whenever possible. The hat was originally in a similar color pattern to the game's creature-capturing device. The company informed me they did not want me including that hat, which they consider one of their logos.

So, I ended up completely re-drawing just the hat and coloring it plain red. Then, I used some software craftsmanship to digitally add the new hat to the old portrait. This is probably a fairly common trick, but I was proud of myself for overcoming the hurdle. I really like this sketch of the girls, it would have been a shame to have to exclude it completely.

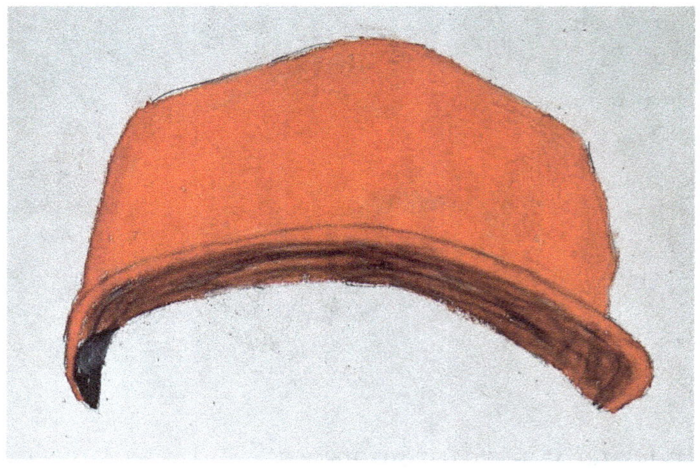

A lonely red hat with no logos.

LONG TERM GOALS AND SKETCH IMPULSIVITY

As has been mentioned with other sketches, my artwork's immediate direction is often impulsively determined. I get the urge to draw, some internal spark occurs, and I take action. I often neglect planned or topical pieces in favor of any recent spontaneous inspiration. If that random internal spark to work on a sketch doesn't happen, it's a real possibility that drawing might collect dust. I do some vague long-term planning, but it's usually just broad aspirational topics, such as "I should draw my mom again".

I had wanted to work on a portrait of my sister and her husband for quite some time. She had been in a few larger family scenes with mixed results, and the one time I tried depicting my brother-in-law, it really didn't look like him at all. So, that was one of these broad long-term goals - to get a more accurate portrait featuring the two of them. I'm really not sure what made me suddenly decide to accomplish that goal, because I hadn't thought about it for a while, but suddenly it was front and center in my brain. Who am I to ignore The Random Spark™?

My original thought was to do something featuring my sister, brother-in-law, and all of their animals (two cats and a dog). Considering I didn't really have an accurate, satisfactory sketch of both humans, I decided adding critters might be too ambitious this time. I also wanted a closer, zoomed-in view more in my comfort zone, and that's not really conducive to little animals. I figured if I could successfully capture them in my favorite head-and-shoulders style, then maybe I could try to be more adventurous with the pets another time.

Because this was a comfort zone piece, somewhat predictably, the result was right along the same lines as similar drawings. This one has decent fidelity to the real subjects – not perfect, but people who know them should be able to tell it's them. Relying less on grays to shade once again worked well here and seemed to be a good trend.

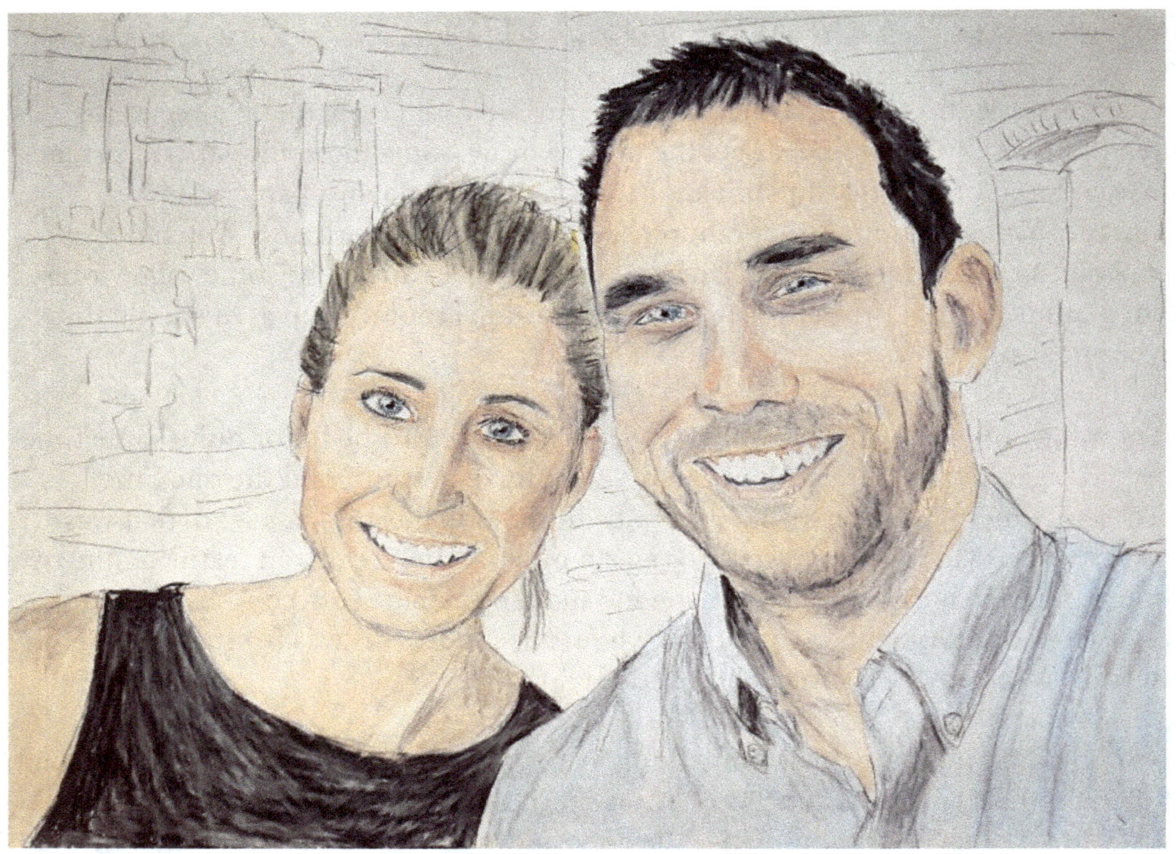

My sister and brother-in-law in a vague, generic restaurant setting.

I did have some basic shape issues, though. Although I got in the ballpark, something doesn't seem quite right about the shape of my sister's face, especially towards her chin. Also, this was another good illustration of my need to try new color combinations for clothing. Shading that light blue shirt with grays did not result in a natural look at all. I think there are lessons I could learn for clothing from my more recent skin pigment blending. I added some rough generic restaurant background stuff…I considered trying to flesh that out more but ultimately decided against it. I wanted to send them this drawing and didn't want to jeopardize the entire piece.

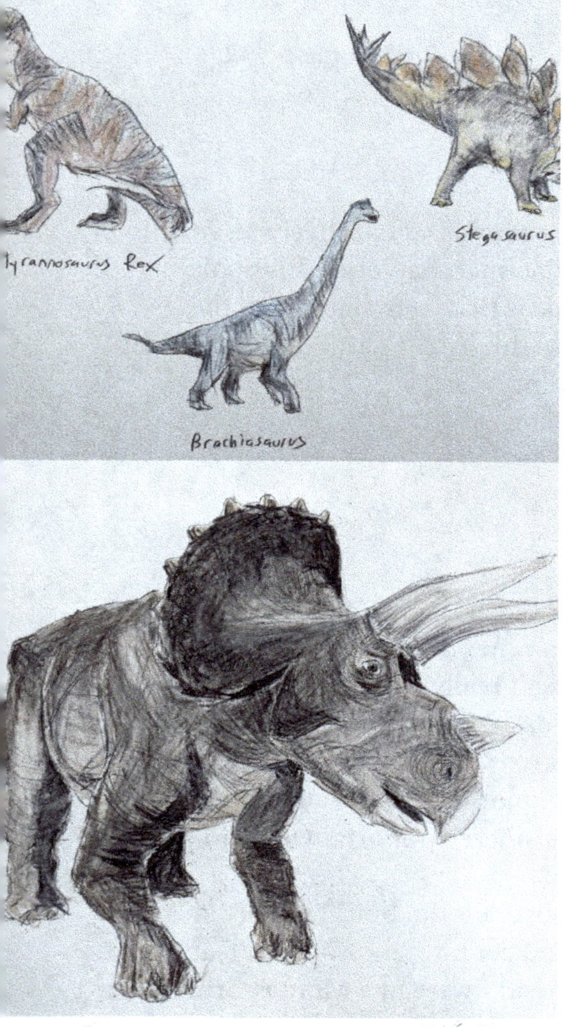

Process Notes – Experiments & the Future

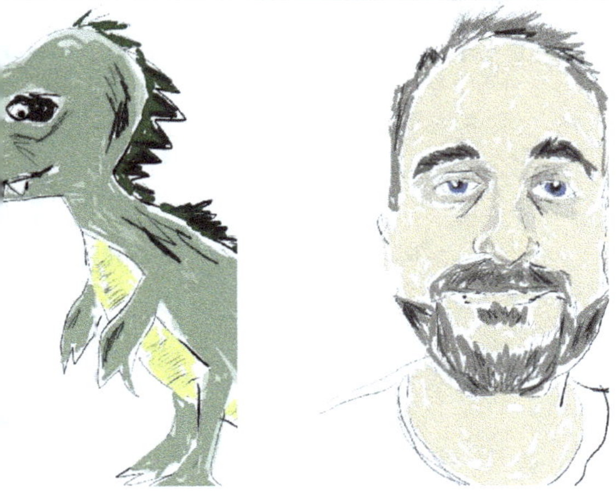

JULY 2018

Although the previous chapter contains the most recent artwork and effectively represents my current phase of portrait drawing, it's obviously not the final chapter of this book. Before we close this discussion, I wanted to cover some ideas that were slightly off the beaten path for me. I'm certain that many people try these things as a natural outgrowth of their artistic curiosity, but I felt they were worth mentioning.

LOST DINOSAUR TIMELINE

I think artists are largely built from their experiences. Those who create pieces of thoughtful art worth pondering (i.e. not life-emulating portraits like mine) have stories to tell through what they paint or draw. Although art from children doesn't really pull from vast experience, it's still fascinating in its own way. Because kids aren't polished stones, worn at the edges by the working world, they have unique perspectives that are sometimes captured via art. Those fresh, unshaped expressions can be worth exploring. And as an adult, it can be positive to returning to some of those topics you once considered important as a child.

When I was little, I absolutely loved dinosaurs. I know most kids do, but I was sort of obsessed with them. I was all about any book or toy I could get my hands on that featured dinosaurs. During our early elementary grades, my sister and I were in a Montessori school. If you aren't familiar, the Montessori model basically lets students learn in an open classroom, working on projects, learning tasks, and assignments on their own or in small groups.

Very early on, probably in Kindergarten or First Grade, I started drawing dinosaurs. My memory is a little cloudy going back that far, but somehow, I got it in my head to draw every species in one book. Then, I decided to draw every species in all the books in our classroom. I taped the pages together, and eventually, I had to start rolling it up. I called it my "dinosaur timeline," even though it wasn't actually in any chronological order; I basically drew them in the order I found each species. The early ones were common fellows like Tyrannosaurus Rex and Pterodactyl, but later things got much more obscure.

Later on, I branched out to every dinosaur book I could find. Library books, books I had at home, anything that had a new type of dinosaur. I am not sure how many I drew, but it must have been hundreds because the roll was four or five inches in diameter. I typically included three or four dinosaurs per sheet of paper, and a sheet looked something like this mock-up I made (below).

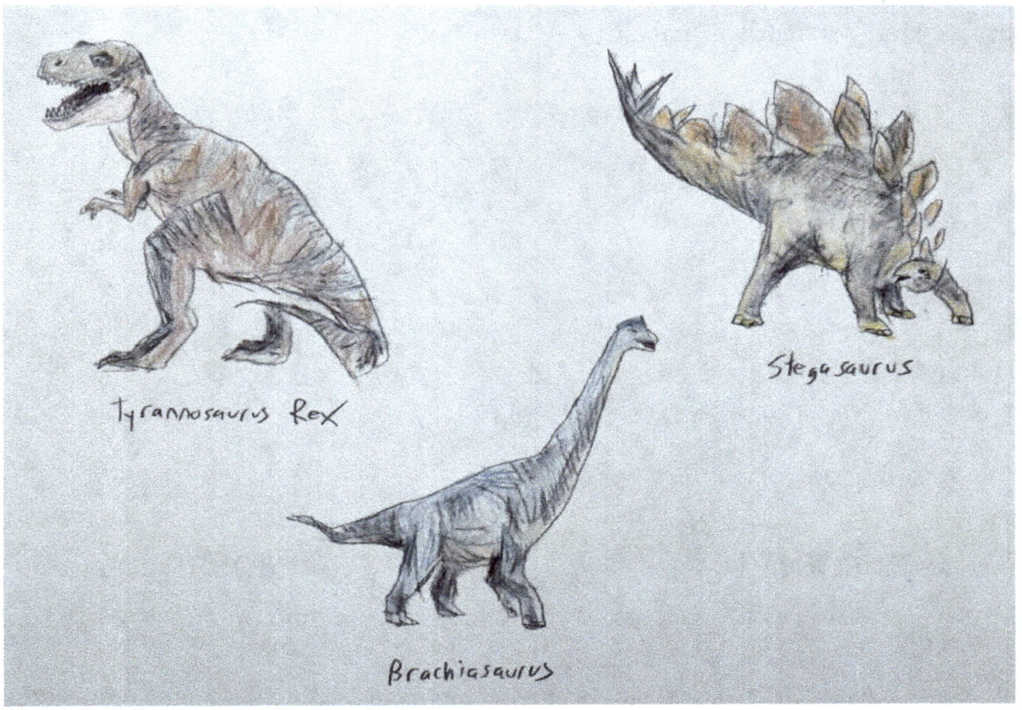

A mock-up of how pages in my Dinosaur Timeline looked. One page often consisted of three or four dinosaurs, with a sketch and name below each.

You might be wondering, why share a mock-up of a Dinosaur Timeline page? Why not post something from the actual Timeline? Unfortunately, I managed to lose it at some point. I had actually found it at one point, wrapped in plastic and packed away in a box. Because it's so long, I wasn't able to unroll it in the house, so the timeline sat on my desk for a couple of months. Then I had the bright idea to put it away somewhere "safe" so it wouldn't get damaged. I turned the house upside down trying to find it again, but I apparently hid it somewhere so safe that it's protected from me even looking at it.

Even though I can't share the Timeline, I decided that wouldn't prevent me from re-exploring this significant part of my childhood. I created a basic sketch to simulate the old dinosaur timeline, and also thought I might do a larger sketch. My two childhood favorites were the Triceratops and the Brontosaurus. Interestingly enough, some scientists do not believe either dinosaur is actually its own genus or species! Some say the Triceratops is a juvenile form of the Torosaurus, while the Brontosaurus could be the juvenile form of the Apatosaurus. Here's a handy visual aid:

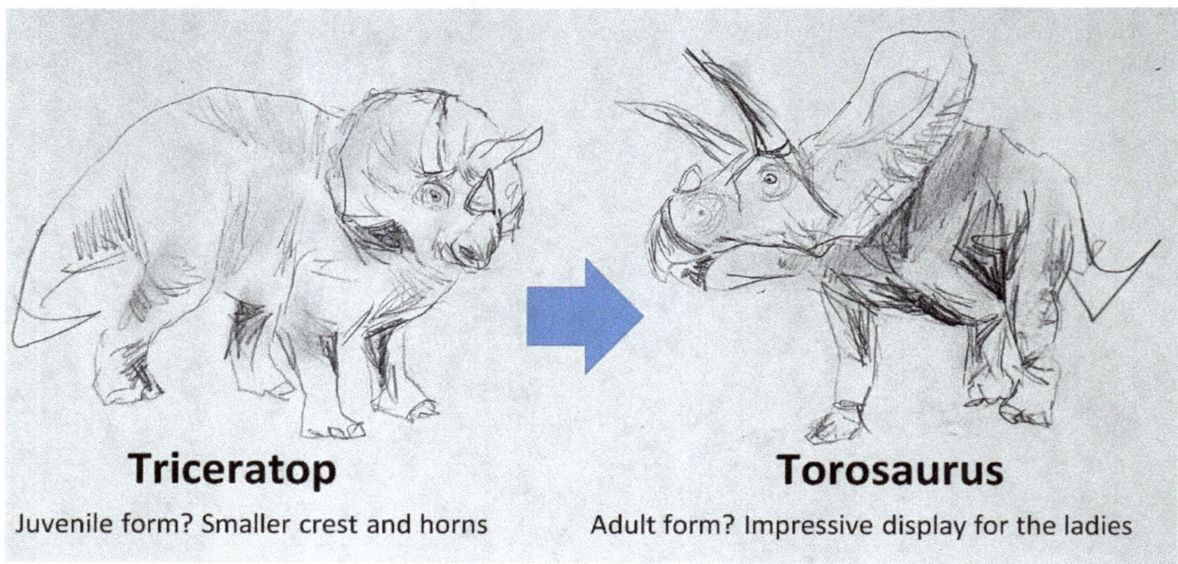

Rough Triceratops vs. Torosaurus sketch (yes I know this one is bad). Is the smaller armament on Triceratops indicative of a juvenile? It could be sort of like deer/antelope horn growth. This is a matter of debate though, because some scientists still think they are separate species/genus.

Based on my armchair paleontology internet research, it seems like scientists are still arguing about the status and classification of both Triceratops and Brontosaurus. It's really hard to know definitively about creatures that lived millions of years ago. Either way, they are awesome and I was a big fan as a kid. I decided to work on a more detailed Triceratops drawing, modeled after a couple of things. I leaned heavily on how rhinoceroses look, especially for the body and legs. Elephant tusks and rhino horns were good models for Triceratops' horns. I also referenced models and exhibits from Natural History Museums (Chicago, Los Angeles, and Hong Kong's Museums). The skin was sort of difficult to figure out because most representations show it as being tough and scaly. I didn't quite capture that, but at least it doesn't exactly look smooth.

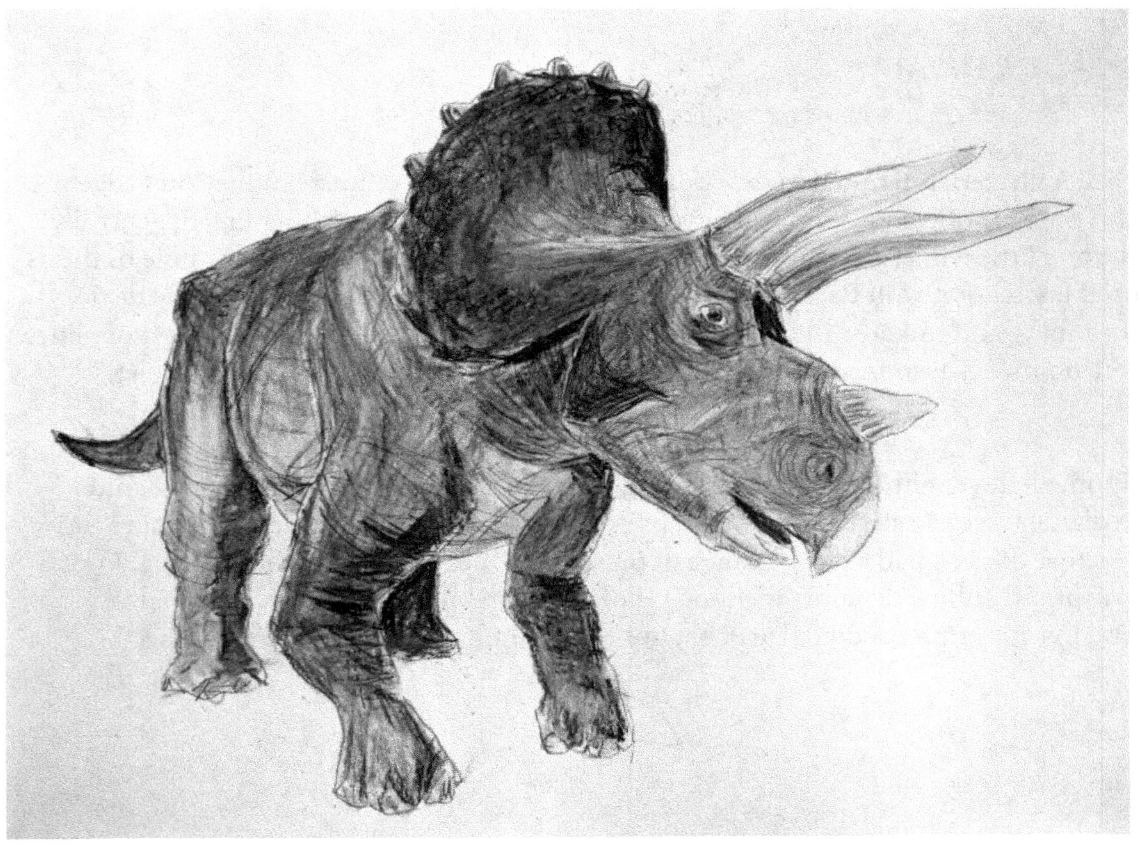

A Triceratops or juvenile Torosaurus, depending on which scientists you believe.

Going full circle back to the first paragraph of this section, I wouldn't say I gained any great philosophical insight from my childhood self or anything like that. But it was nice to reminisce about something that motivated me and made me happy as a child. It was especially compelling because my oldest daughter is approaching that same age, and it made me wonder what will energize her in a similar way. It was an enjoyable dose of nostalgia, and something I may return to someday.

DIGITAL DRAWING

I am generally very interested in tech-related things, and love to waste money on gadgets. I am also the type of person who will have a wild idea based on something I read, get really into it for a little while, then abandon it forever after a few weeks. A great example of this is my brief fascination with Raspberry Pi mini-computers. I put together one of the devices, got it running and tinkered for a few weeks, and haven't touched it again. Along those lines, at some point, I determined I would learn to create digital art using a drawing tablet.

I had some leftover gift card money burning a hole in my pocket, so I picked up a mid-range digital tablet. I selected one with a pretty good-sized drawing space, made sure from reviews that the pen had a strong range of pressures. Once I started experimenting, I was a little surprised at how dynamic the touch is of the digital pen. I'm sure part of that is because I've never used a digital art pen, but I could immediately see the potential.

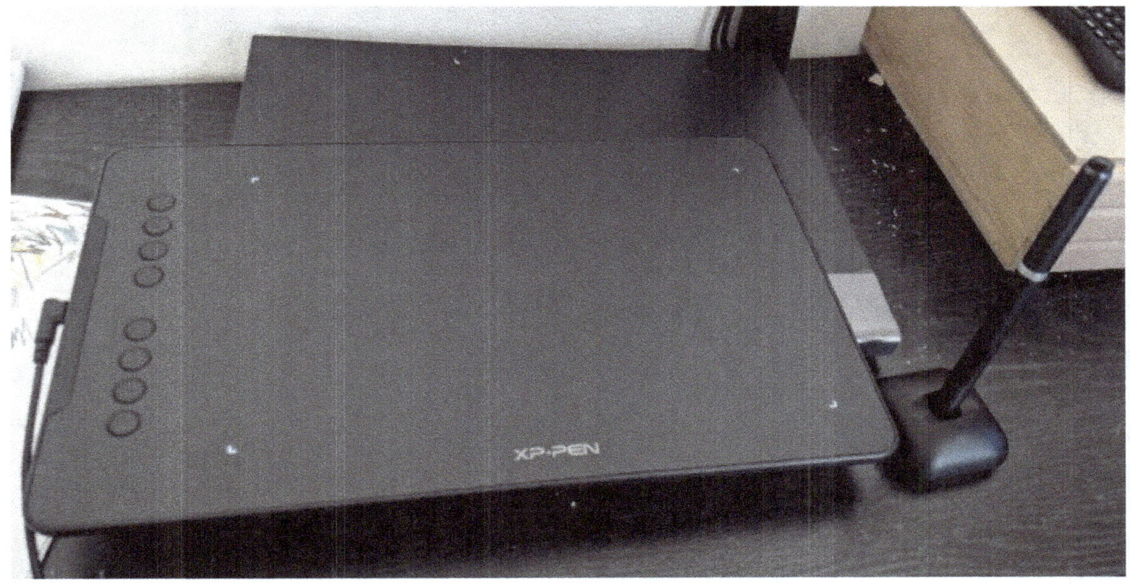

The drawing tablet and digital pen setup I used.

So, with the tablet in hand, I was ready to start drawing right? Well, not quite…to actually use it, I needed to find and select a program to use it in. There are a ton of choices out there, some of which cost money. Fortunately, there are some great free options too. Based on my research, some of the most popular free digital artwork programs seem to be Krita, GIMP, MyPaint, Paint.net, and Artweaver. After reading a few sources saying positive things about Krita, I made that my choice.

So, with Krita installed and my new tablet plugged in, I dove in head-first. First, I did some random scribbling to figure out how the pen works. Eventually, I tried to do some basic sloppy people sketches; the results were not good. I erased all of those doodles, and said, "okay, let's try a dinosaur." Dinosaurs are pretty easy, so I figured that was a good place to start. This is when I realized just how steep the learning curve would be.

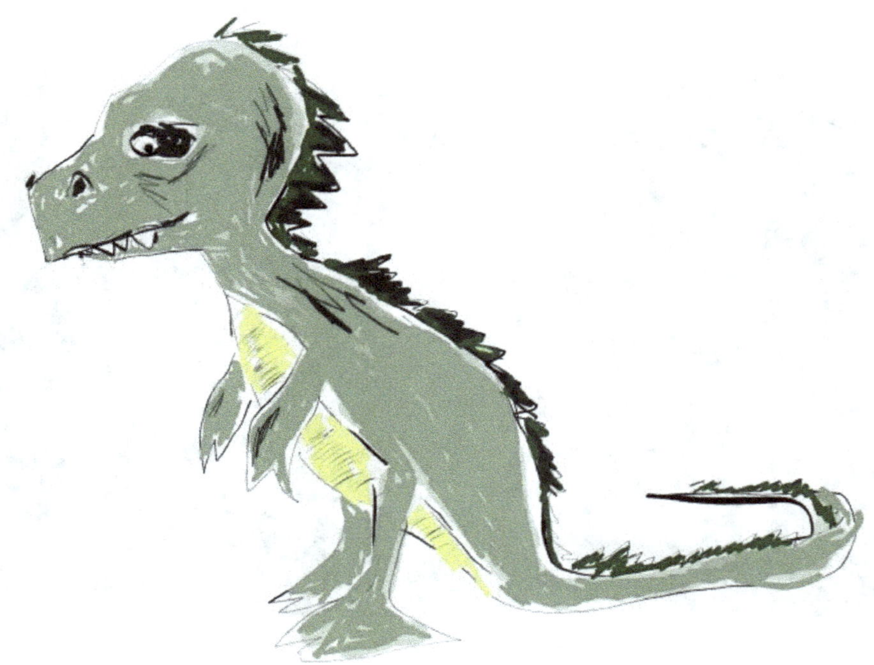

Look at this digital dinosaur, he is disappointed in himself.

As clumsy as the digital sketch looks, it took a surprising amount of time and concentration. If I had done that using colored pencils, it would have taken five minutes and looked much better. The next digital drawing was an attempt at a self-portrait. This one was a slight improvement, and does resemble me, but was still very challenging. One of the most difficult things about this was drawing a straight line. I'm honestly not great with them even using a pencil on regular paper, but a digital pen-on-tablet straight line was almost impossible for me. I'm not sure if this is a common difficulty for people who are new to this, but tight control of lines felt so much harder. And really, line control is everything – that's a simple way to define pencil drawing.

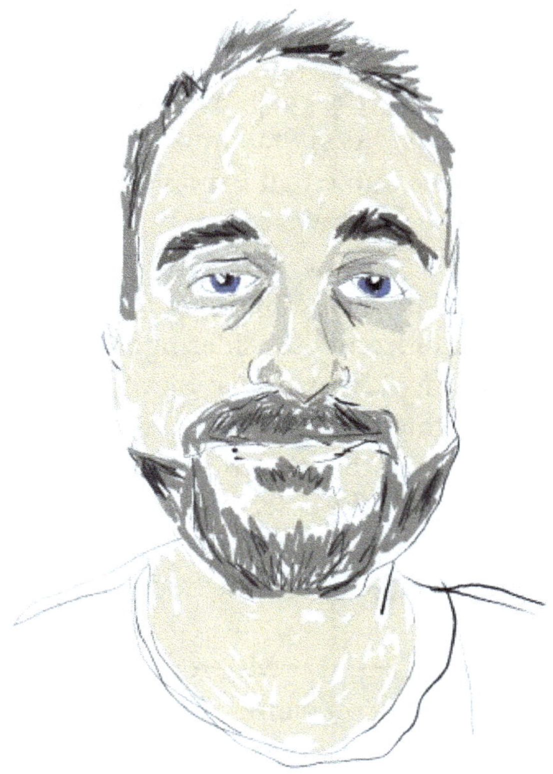

Hey that's me, except I forgot how to draw lines and make normal shapes.
My attempt at a self-portrait using a tablet and digital pen.

I'm sure most aspects would get easier over time, especially once you're familiar with the interface. I was slow selecting colors and figuring out program tools, and I'm sure that becomes faster with practice. But the shaky lines seemed like a large a barrier for me. It's a fun tool, but could it become a practical substitute for real paper? It was an interesting experiment, but I have yet to try it again. The learning curve was much steeper than I thought it would be, although in hindsight I have no idea why I thought it would be easier. It would take an investment of time and effort similar to my colored pencil journey.

WHERE TO FROM HERE?

With this being the final artwork-specific chapter, a fair question to ask now is; what's next for this artist? Assuming I don't fall into another long break from artwork, I think it's reasonable to assume that I should continue to learn and develop. But, can I predict to any extent what form that growth might take?

One possibility I have considered is whether it might be time to rely less on the heavy pencil painting style. That's sort of ironic, considering that most of this book has been about colored pencil painting. But an evolution of the technique I've used might be the use of additional lighter layers of varied shades. I see other artists approach their artwork this way, and that may be because they're well trained or more experienced than I am. If that's the case, this may be a natural progression from what I do now. I can see how you might be able to achieve more realistic colors, shadows, and contrast with a more deliberate method.

For quite some time, I've looked at painters with some degree of envy. I find the looks achievable from watercolor and oil paints very appealing for some reason. The colors seem more vibrant and real than some other mediums. I know my fondness for that look is what drew me to heavily layered colored pencil in the first place; it was my best attempt to simulate it. So, perhaps painting could be in my future? I would enjoy learning but have some roadblocks that currently allow me easy excuses (kids, workspace, supplies, and so on).

Regardless, I want to thank you, the reader, for joining me through this discussion of pencils, portraits, and process. I hope something I passed along was useful because the goal from the outset was to provide insight for someone on a similar journey. The final chapter contains some varied advice and thoughts that only tangentially relate to art - it may not be relevant if you're only here for a process-specific read. So, if that isn't for you, thank you again for reading and good luck!

Additional Thoughts & Advice

Who wouldn't want to take advice from someone who has already mentioned 100 times that he's an amateur artist? If you've come this far in the book, the answer might actually be you! Most of this book has been about my learning experience specifically related to drawing processes. But there are some other things I've learned over the same time frame that are only tangentially related – they didn't fit in previous chapters, but I still thought they might be useful to pass along.

PHOTOGRAPHING YOUR ARTWORK

Capturing a digitized version of artwork has become quite important. From sharing via social media to simply having a high-quality archive record/backup of your work, there are many reasons to figure out an effective way to make it happen. It can actually be somewhat difficult to consistently capture artwork with high fidelity to real life. There are two primary options available (that I'm aware of, anyway); scanning or photography.

Although it's not my preferred method, some artists use a scanner to digitize. This seems like a great way to control certain variables like light and position, and likely doesn't require much effort. The biggest downside, which happens to keep me away, is that I'm told you need a higher end scanner to achieve acceptable results. If you are willing to spend the money, this is probably a good way to go.

Due to its lower barrier of entry, I prefer taking photos of my artwork. Most people just happen to carry high-end digital cameras in their pockets at all times in the form of smartphones. Although my phone's camera is more than up to the challenge, there is typically some preparation work I do to help facilitate a clean image. I'm certainly not an expert, but I have learned a few tricks over time:

- Your main goal is to avoid shadows while still having a brightly lit area. You can do this pretty effectively using a combination of natural light and/or multiple indoor light sources. Experiment with different configurations until you find a position that doesn't cast any shadows over your artwork.
- White light is better than yellow in my experience if you have multiple light bulb options available.
- Don't use a flash - it will wash out and impact the colors in your artwork. The flash will also cast additional shadows, which you are trying to avoid.
- If you're using a smartphone, open the camera app, get it in position, then lay the phone flat on the page. Steadying with both hands, slowly raise the phone. This helps keep it in a level position and prevents viewing angle distortion. Alternatively, use a camera stand or positioning arm to keep things level.
- If you're taking photos from overhead (with the paper laying flat), try to hold your body away from the shot to minimize shadows.
- If you're taking photos from the side (with the paper vertical laying against a stand), make sure the light source isn't behind you as that might cast your shadow over the artwork.
- Use your elbows to steady your hands if you don't have a camera stand. For overhead photos, use your elbows on the table surface. For side photos, steady your elbows on your knees.
- If it's available on your device, HDR or HDR+ mode is very useful. Also, utilize tap-to-focus features if your camera/smartphone has them.

ENGAGE WITH OTHERS ABOUT ART

As I started getting back into drawing, I didn't really consider interacting with other artists. Not that I was opposed to it; the thought just never crossed my mind. Fortunately, by virtue of setting up my website via WordPress, I was already connected to a relatively large community of artists through the platforms Reader.

As I tagged my WordPress posts with keywords like "drawing", "art", and "sketch," others with similar interests were able to find my art and follow my site. Artists commented on my sketches, providing advice and feedback, and I connected to their sites and did the same (as best I could anyway). Eventually, I realized I actually organically become part of an art community without even intending to!

Interacting with other artists in person may provide the most effective and direct feedback, but for many casual artists that may not always be practical. For the hobbyist, online communities can be a fantastic resource for advice and support. Especially for people like me who are still learning and could use advice. Many artists share details of their creative process through their websites, and some may even directly provide tips through your interactions online.

Although I'm certain this isn't a definitive list and there are other great options, here are some ideas and tips related to engaging with others about your art:

- Blog about your experiences and process. As I said, I use WordPress.com but there are other options available like Blogger (owned by Google), Tumblr, or a self-hosted WordPress. WordPress.com, Blogger, and Tumblr all have free options available, so you can start right away at no cost. You can interact with other similar blogs to help your learning process and grow your audience naturally through those connections.
- Don't just wait for people to check out your art. Explore other artists' sites and artwork - engage with what others creating.
- Get connected with other social media sites. Some like Facebook, Twitter, and Tumblr will even connect directly with a WordPress blog and allow you to automatically publish content. Different, unique online communities exist within each space and can provide varying types of interactions. Some sites are more heavily image-focused, like Pinterest and Instagram, while others are more geared towards conversations, like Reddit.

ENSURE YOU'RE ON FIRM LEGAL GROUND

First, let me provide a caveat: I am not an attorney, and you shouldn't consider anything I say to be legal advice. I'm just going to pass along some common-sense thoughts and opinions on potential copyright minefields. Overall, my best recommendation would be to exercise utmost caution about your use of names, likenesses, logos, and any copyrighted intellectual property. If there is any commercial purpose to what you're doing, such as selling artwork, merchandise, or a book, there is a potential risk without permission or licensing.

Here are some of my general thoughts on the matter. Since this book is the first real commercial purpose I've used my artwork for, most of this list contains things I considered when putting the book together.

- For subjects you photograph or sketch in person, obtain a signed model release/consent. There are a ton of model release form examples online, most contain variants of similar language. I've included an example below, which I have on the back of my business cards.

<table>
<tr><td colspan="2">This is an Agreement between Parties:</td></tr>
<tr><td></td><td>Artist</td></tr>
<tr><td></td><td>Model</td></tr>
<tr><td colspan="2">All photographs and images taken by the Artist remain the sole copyrighted intellectual property of the Artist. Artist may use, publish, reproduce, or distribute the images for any artistic or commercial purpose. Model agrees to release to the Artist any proprietary interest in materials that result from the session, and agrees the Artist may publish, sell, or distribute artwork derived from these photographs.</td></tr>
<tr><td>Artist Signature</td><td>Date</td></tr>
<tr><td>Model Signature</td><td>Date</td></tr>
</table>

- If you didn't obtain a model release, email the portrait subject to request permission to use their likeness. For this book, many subjects are family members so I didn't get a model release form signed. Just to make sure I was covered, I emailed each person individually asking for consent to use their likeness for a commercial purpose. In the email, I described exactly what would be in the book (how their likeness would be used).

- Be careful about using real names. I opt not to use names of regular folks (i.e. non-famous, not publicly recognizable people) as a personal preference. Just be sure it's clear to the subject ahead of time what will be used.

- An artistic interpretation of a written-word character seems like a gray area. Because I haven't found something firm enough to make me comfortable, I defaulted to requesting the author's permission (in my case, to use artwork based on novel characters). As I've said repeatedly - I think it's better to be overcautious on these matters.

- For visually-depicted fictional characters or artwork based on other copyrighted material, it's essential you obtain permission from the copyright owner to use your artwork for a commercial purpose. It can actually be tricky to figure out who owns the rights to a character and may take you through multiple entities to track down. A drawing based on a movie character (fan art) is considered a "derivative work," and many copyright holders will enforce their ownership rights to protect their intellectual property. I always consider the lack of response to be a "no." In my experience, most copyright holders will either decline or not respond at all.

- When in doubt, don't include it. If you aren't sure, it's better to be safe and omit anything you don't have written permission for or a clear use exception (e.g. a drawing done based on a Renaissance painting). If you contacted someone asking to use a likeness and they won't respond, it's safest to assume that means you don't have permission.

- If you're unsure, but don't want to default to excluding something, your best bet is to consult an attorney. Specifically, try to find someone with experience in this realm. If you're considering whether something you're doing constitutes "Fair Use," it might be wise to double-check with a lawyer.

- Requesting permissions can be a very lengthy process, both in terms of the sheer number of emails sent/calls placed/contact forms submitted and the time it takes to receive a response. For just one image, you might need separate permission from multiple entities, or you might have to hunt down rights because they've been transferred or aren't listed anywhere. My advice is to seek permission as early as possible; in my case, I began sending emails the same week I started writing.

Because I love statistics, I've also been keeping track of permissions I've received by category. I thought it was interesting, so here are some data points from my experience with this book:

- 100% of my friends and family granted permission to use their likeness (thanks everyone, this book would hardly have any content without you).
- 100% of stock image rights owners licensed the use of their photos for derivative artwork. Most of those charged money for licensing though, so I used only 25% of the images I initially considered.
- 0% of movie copyright holders granted derivative work use permission.
- 0% of television copyright holders granted derivative work use permission.
- For my artwork inspired by video games (but *not* featuring copyrighted characters), 33% of companies approved my use request.
- 100% of novel authors granted permission to use my visual interpretations of their written-word characters.

What have I learned about use permissions from writing this book? Well, naturally friends, family, and any other models personally photographed are by far the best resource. They're the lowest hassle and lowest cost. On the stock image company side, Shutterstock isn't too bad. Their website and smartphone app are both easy to use, and they have a reverse image search. Their licensing for images is relatively affordable too; I paid about $10 per image.

Getty Images was the most expensive of what I looked at – about 5-50 times more expensive than Shutterstock depending on the image. Aside from huge corporations, I am not sure who could afford some of their prices. And last but not least, there's Unsplash. Of course, I like that Unsplash's photographers provide images for commercial use at no cost…but I'm not sure I understand their business model. If images are free to use, how do the company and photographers who participate make any money?

Leverage Technology

We've already touched on some aspects related to technology with the discussions of social media and photography. But there are a few other useful things to mention:

I haven't had success with it yet, but it's exploring the world of digital drawing/art tablets. There are quite a few free programs available to use in conjunction with a tablet, such as Krita, Artweaver, Paint.net. I have not devoted the time to master digital drawing, but I can definitely see its value and convenience.

Create animated .gif images of your artwork. This is a habit I developed when I started drawing again. I take photographs of my drawings as they progress, and then roll them into an animated image to share how the art developed over time. There are many options online available - just search for "gif maker" or "gif creator." You can upload the images and customize some aspects like transition speed, then download the resulting .gif.

Digitally editing photographs of your art. There are a ton of software programs available to enhance photographs of your artwork, some of which are free. It seems like the gold standard is Adobe Photoshop, but I have had good success with Windows built-in "Photos" editor for minor tweaks. Because photographs sometimes result in a muted color palette compared to real-life viewing, it can be useful to make adjustments to brightness or contrast to some degree.

STEP OUT OF YOUR COMFORT ZONE

I know this is strange advice to hear from someone who admittedly loves his comfort zone and has difficulty breaking out of routines. But, even though it's difficult for me, I've done some of my best artwork by making the effort to try something new. Even if it's a small thing, like trying to be more aggressive with contrast or darker colors, it helps facilitate learning and artistic growth.

Sometimes, I think about what my current status would be when it comes to art if I had just stuck with what was comfortable. If I had continued to sketch using grids and graphite pencils. I may have gotten a bit better at that specific skill, but I wonder if I would have ultimately dropped the hobby because of the stagnation. Making the choice to try going gridless, then to try using colors, were both big moves that required pushing aside my natural tendencies to some extent.

My point is, it doesn't hurt to try something new. Best case scenario, you learn something new that could grow into a previously unseen new artistic direction. Worst case scenario, you don't enjoy it or it doesn't work out and you drop it. The nice thing is, though...no one ever has to know!

My goal moving forward is certainly to do exactly this. As much as I love drifting into a comfort zone, I want to continue pushing myself towards learning new skills and techniques.

Index

About the Author

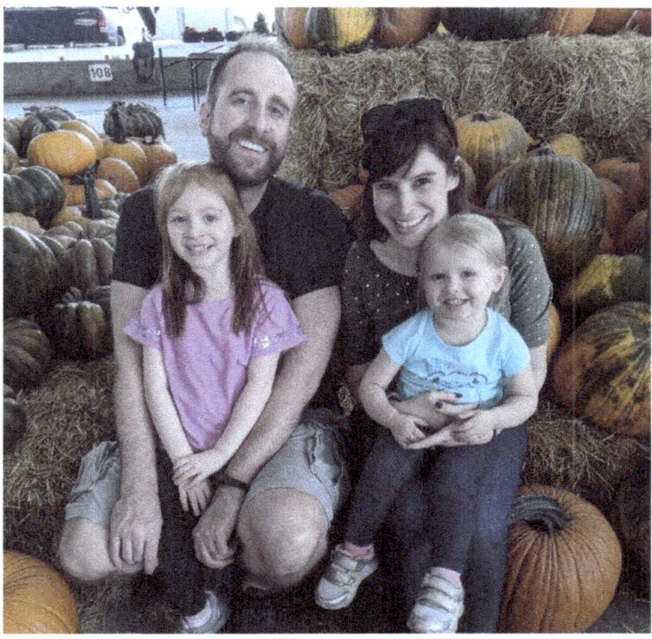

Jon Amdall is a portrait artist by hobby and data analyst by profession. He graduated from the University of North Texas Health Science Center with an M.S. in Biomedical Science and the University of Texas at Dallas with a B.A. in Biology. Jon runs the Amdall Gallery blog at jonamdall.com where he shares artwork, research projects, and tech-related interests.

Jon lives in Louisiana with his wife and children. Although his day job doesn't involve art, he creates portraits when time allows using graphite and wax-based colored pencils. Jon also has a great fondness for spreadsheets and pizza but has not yet figured out how to combine these interests.